ST ANTONY'S/MACMILLAN SERIES

General Editors: Archie Brown (1978–85), Rosemary Thorp (1985–92), and Alex Pravda (1992–), all Fellows of St Antony's College, Oxford

Recent titles include

Mark D. Alleyne
INTERNATIONAL POWER AND INTERNATIONAL
COMMUNICATION

Daniel Bell, David Brown, Kanishka Jayasuryia and David Martin Jones
TOWARDS ILLIBERAL DEMOCRACY IN PACIFIC ASIA

Judith M. Brown and Rosemary Foot (*editors*)
MIGRATION: The Asian Experience

Anne Deighton (*editor*)
BUILDING POSTWAR EUROPE: National Decision-Makers and
European Institutions, 1948–63

Simon Duke
THE NEW EUROPEAN SECURITY DISORDER

Christoph Gassenschmidt
JEWISH LIBERAL POLITICS IN TSARIST RUSSIA, 1900–14: The
Modernization of Russian Jewry

Amitzur Ilan
THE ORIGIN OF THE ARAB–ISRAELI ARMS RACE: Arms,
Embargo, Military Power and Decision in the 1948 Palestine War

Hiroshi Ishida
SOCIAL MOBILITY IN CONTEMPORARY JAPAN

Austen Ivereigh
CATHOLICISM AND POLITICS IN ARGENTINA, 1910–60

Leroy Jin
MONETARY POLICY AND THE DESIGN OF FINANCIAL INSTITU-
TIONS IN CHINA, 1978–90

Matthew Jones
BRITAIN, THE UNITED STATES AND THE MEDITERRANEAN
WAR, 1942–44

Anthony Kirk-Greene and Daniel Bach (*editors*)
STATE AND SOCIETY IN FRANCOPHONE AFRICA SINCE
INDEPENDENCE

Leslie McLoughlin
IBN SAUD: Founder of a Kingdom

Rosalind Marsh
HISTORY AND LITERATURE IN CONTEMPORARY RUSSIA

David Nicholls
THE PLURALIST STATE: The Political Ideas of J. N. Figgis and his
Contemporaries

J. L. Porket
UNEMPLOYMENT IN CAPITALIST, COMMUNIST AND
POST-COMMUNIST ECONOMIES

Charles Powell
JUAN CARLOS OF SPAIN: Self-made Monarch

H. Gordon Skilling
T. G. MASARYK: Against the Current, 1882–1914

William J. Tompson
KHRUSHCHEV: A Political Life

Christopher Tremewan
THE POLITICAL ECONOMY OF SOCIAL CONTROL IN SINGAPORE

Stephen Welch
THE CONCEPT OF POLITICAL CULTURE

Jennifer M. Welsh
EDMUND BURKE AND INTERNATIONAL RELATIONS: The
Commonwealth of Europe and the Crusade against the French Revolution

International Power and International Communication

Mark D. Alleyne

Assistant Professor and Director
National Center for Freedom of Information Studies
Department of Communication, College of Arts and Sciences
Loyola University of Chicago

in association with
ST ANTONY'S COLLEGE, OXFORD

First published 1995 by
MACMILLAN PRESS LTD
Houndmills, Basingstoke, Hampshire RG21 6XS
and London
Companies and representatives
throughout the world

ISBN 0–333–63212–5 hardcover
ISBN 0–333–64051–9 paperback

A catalogue record for this book is available
from the British Library.

10   9   8   7   6   5   4   3   2   1
04   03   02   01   00   99   98   97   96   95

Printed in Hong Kong

Dedicated to

Frederick Dacosta Alleyne (1933–1994)

and to the pupils, staff and teachers of
The Alleyne School, St Andrew, Barbados

Contents

Preface

This book represents the culmination of an eight-year odyssey that began with my arrival for graduate study at St Antony's College, University of Oxford, in the autumn of 1986 and ended with my completion of a sabbatical year as Research Fellow, The Freedom Forum Media Studies Center, Columbia University.

Along the way my intellectual enquiry underwent several transformations in exposition, and even in method, but what did remain consistent was my intrigue with the links between international political power and international communication. I would be the first to admit, perhaps in a tradition of dispassionate scholarship, that the end of my personal odyssey is not synonymous with the discovery of answers to that complex relationship. But the road towards the book and the book itself hopefully symbolise my intellectual and wider personal growth and my willingness to grow more. They should also represent what I want to be my scholarly mission. This mission is guided by a few maxims; the most important come from the admonition of Ngugi wa Thiong'o (in *Decolonising the Mind*) that writers and scholars like me should be 'relevant' and the life examples of Mandela and Biko who showed that the epitome of relevance is self-respect, courage and tenacity.

A number of institutions in various places underwrote my research over the past eight years but influenced neither my choice of subject nor my conclusions. I owe great thanks to the Rhodes Trust in Oxford and Wardens Robin Fletcher and Anthony Kenny. The Warden and staff of my college, St Antony's, also supplied invaluable support, including providing a grant for a second research trip to the US in 1988 and support to my successful application to the Webb Medley Fund for research into political economy. Gratitude is also extended to the trustees of the Cyril Foster and Norman Chester funds at Oxford. I also thank the School of Communications and Cognitive Science, Hampshire College, Massachusetts, and the School of International Service, The American University, for the various grants I won while I was a faculty member at those institutions.

Librarians in many places were invaluable and very tolerant when I got impatient due to the pressures of research. My warm thanks go to the staff of: the Bodleian; the library of the Division of Free Flow of Information at UNESCO in Paris; St Antony's Library; the Library of Congress; Hampshire College Library (Massachusetts); Bender Library, The

American University (Washington, DC); McKeldin Library, University of Maryland; the libraries of Smith and Mount Holyoke Colleges (in Massachusetts); and the Barbados Public Library. I owe a special debt of gratitude to Ms Paula Mark of the Reference Department of the University of Massachusetts who kindly handed over to me the very valuable file on the NWICO that she had maintained for a number of years, giving my research a significant boost.

It was in Anju Grover Chaudhary's journalism class at Howard University that my interest in the NWICO was sparked while I was still an undergraduate. I am grateful to her as well as to the School of Communications, Howard University, for all the encouragement it has given over the years.

I began this research as a student of the late Dr John Vincent, the man responsible for changing me from a journalistic writer to a scholar. I could think of no better tribute to his memory than to finish my project and finish it well. Andrew Hurrell, Lecturer in International Relations at Oxford, had the very difficult task of being a long-distance Supervisor most of the time, but I could not have wished for a more rigorous, encouraging colleague and friend. Professor Susan Strange has gone beyond the call of duty to encourage my work and help me survive in the world of scholarship.

All the friends who have provided intellectual and emotional support cannot be mentioned here but I would be remiss if I did not single out my intellectual cohorts in Barbados: Reudon Eversley, Hallam Hope, Angela and Gary Cole, Margaret Harris, Grace-Anne Crichlow-Brathwaite, Errol Devonish, and countless people who often meet me on the street there and engage me in inspiring conversations that I often do not get at universities in the United States and Europe. I have also been grateful for the friendship and help rendered on various occasions by James Miller, Linden Lewis, Rennos Ehaliotis, Maria Williamson, Maria Molina Lovo, Lyn Liquornik, Hilbourne Watson, and 'Dimple'.

All who have helped contributed to what is best in the work and are not responsible for its failings.

MARK D. ALLEYNE

List of Tables and Figure

List of Abbreviations

AFP – Agence France-Presse
AP – Associated Press
ASCAP – American Society of Composers, Authors, and Publishers
BBC – British Broadcasting Corporation
BMI – Broadcast Music Incorporated
CIA – Central Intelligence Agency
CTD – Center for Telecommunications Development (at the ITU)
FBI – Federal Bureau of Investigations
GATT – General Agreement on Tariffs and Trade
GSO – Geo-stationary Orbit
IMF – International Monetary Fund
INTELSAT – International Telecommunications Satellite Organisation
IOJ – International Organisation of Journalists
IPDC – International Programme for the Development of Communication
    (at UNESCO)
IPI – International Press Institute
ISBN – International Standard Book Number
ISO – International Organisation for Standardisation
ISSN – International Standard Serial Number
ITAR – Information Telegraph Agency of Russia (ITAR-TASS became
    the new name for the reorganised old news agency, TASS.)
ITU – International Telecommunication Union
NAM – Non-Aligned Movement
NIEO – New International Economic Order
NWICO – New World Information and Communication Order (also
    called: NIIO, New International Information Order and NWIO, New
    World Information Order)
PRS – Performing Rights Society
RFE – Radio Free Europe
RL – Radio Liberty
TASS – Telegraph Agency of the Soviet Union (Telegrafnoye Agentstvo
    Sovietskavo Soyuza).
UNCTAD – United Nations Conference on Trade and Development
UNESCO – United Nations Educational, Scientific and Cultural
    Organisation
UPI – United Press International
UPU – Universal Postal Union

USIA – United States Information Agency
VOA – Voice of America
WARC – World Administrative Radio Conference
WARC-ORB – World Administrative Radio Conference on the
  geo-stationary orbit
WIPO – World Intellectual Property Organisation
WPFC – World Press Freedom Committee

1 The Larger Questions: Communication in the Literature of International Relations and in International Relations Theory

The United States makes less than 10 per cent of the long films produced annually but it dominates the international trade in movies. Six companies controlled by Americans, Europeans and Japanese control the world's $20-plus billion annual pop music market. For millions around the globe the definition of what is news is being determined by a transnational television network, CNN, based in the United States and controlled by Americans. But what do these developments mean for international politics? What does the use of new international communications technologies mean for the distribution of power and influence in the world?

These basic questions about the relationship between international communication and international power animate this book. But the early warning and caveat are that the reader might end the book still without having answers to the questions. The book puts in one place a collection of information that assists the curious in gaining a better understanding of what might be the possible answers to the questions. This information puts the debates about international communication into historical context, it explains the structure of international communication, the institutions that manage and regulate international communication, the philosophical ideas that have guided the postures of states to international communication, and the book explains why efforts in the past and the present to reform the structure of international communication have been at best difficult. This will be done over the course of seven chapters.

To some an opus that traverses such a vast terrain might seem to be a daunting, over-extended work. But such is the nature of the subject matter. There used to be a time when scholars of communication and scholars of international politics laboured in separate cubicles. But, with

1

2   *International Power and International Communication*

the transnationalisation of communications, such a separation is now imprudent and short-sighted. Can we really fully understand the transformation of political culture and the collapse of national governments without looking at the influence of global communications media that serve to undermine national autonomy? Similarly, there once seemed to be little connecting the analysis of telecommunications (telephones, telex, etc.) to the study of mass communications (newspapers, television, etc.), and there was apparently little direct connection between mass communications and computing. But now communications technologies have converged, making it necessary to consider them together. In the rich countries especially, television service is being supplied over telephone lines; computers have graduated from being mere tools of computation to being 'multimedia' instruments, supplying sounds, pictures and words; and televisions, through videotex, are relaying the information that used to be gained mainly from the newspaper. New social reality therefore requires new, less narrow ways of speculating about the present and the future.

We will be paying especial attention to the implications these new technological developments have for the smaller, poorer, non-white states of the so-called 'global South'. Not only because this writer is from the South, but also because since the 1970s many of these countries realized the high stakes involved and collectively attempted to raise the status of international communication on the agenda of international politics.

DEFINING COMMUNICATION/DEFINING POWER

Because the consideration of communication has been marked by much conceptual fuzziness it is necessary to explain at the outset what we do and do not mean when we use the term *communication*.

The word communication is often used in close association with the word information. It is understandable that discussion of the two concepts represented by the two words often involves the idea that communication and information embody valuable potentialities because such goodly features are intrinsic to the Latin roots of both words.

It is significant that 'communication' and 'community' both share the Latin root *communis*, meaning common. From this root we got the other Latin word *communicare* meaning 'to make common to many, share, impart, divide'.[1] Therefore, intrinsic to the definition of communication is the idea of sharing. Indeed, communication (when it is used as a verb) – '[t]he imparting, conveying, or exchange of ideas, knowledge, information, etc. (whether by speech, writing, or signs)' – cannot occur unless something is shared. And the logical consequence of sharing is that two or more persons would have something in common. Therefore, one of the definitions of community is 'common character; quality in common; commonness, agreement, identity'. What this all means is that communication is essential for the creation of something known as a *community* at both the domestic and international levels. Implanted in the assertion that there is such a thing as an 'international community' must be the assumption that the members are communicating. Communication is vital to sustaining that community because it is only through communication that values, for example, can be shared and made common to the group.[2] We simply cannot have a world community unless the members of that community, be they states, organizations or individuals, are communicating. This fundamental point explains why it is so important to understand the role of communications in international relations.

Although *communication* can and is used as a noun to refer to that which is communicated, it is often used today as a noun to describe the *process* of communication. This process involves systems and means of communication (such as telephones, satellites, books, etc.). It is assumed that the 'raw matter' processed in this way is *information*.[3] Mowlana notes that information is also associated with noble features. Its Latin origins

had the sense of image, instruction, and formation [,] while in classic French the word *information* was used in singular term *une information* to mean processing and collecting facts in legal investigation. In its common and everyday usage, information is associated with a human situation, with a communication medium, with something that can be added and accumulated, with something factual, valuable, useful, useless, or with knowledge. Thus it is said that information is good, and more information is better, that information is power, information is lost; that a book, a letter, a newspaper, or a conference contains information.[4]

While communication and information are related concepts, it is necessary for analytical purposes to make clear the distinction between the two. For the purpose of this book, therefore, communication is conceived of as a process, involving set arrangements and media that must be in place for any relay of information to occur. Seen in this way, a study of communication is not necessarily a study of information. For example, liberal-democratic political theory and liberal trade theory discussed later in the book are concerned more with the social and economic value of communication than with the social and economic value of various types of information. In other words, the value of my being able to watch three television channels from three different countries at breakfast is different from the worth of the information carried by those channels. The fact that mere access to three channels can be considered valuable in and of itself is separate from whether the programmes carried on Channel A are more valuable to me, because they are all about my profession, than those relayed by Channels B and C.

This separation of the value of communication from the value of information logically means that they have separate (although related) worth in relation to power. The power of communication is different from the power of information.

Power is one of the most widely used words in the English language and it has a variety of interpretations. However, it seems widely agreed that power involves the ability to exercise control, to get others to do what they otherwise might not do were it not for your presence. But while it has been relatively easy to see the consequences of the exercise of power, it has been more challenging to describe the dynamic of power – how power actually operates. This dynamic has been viewed as the process by which it is determined who plays a game and by what rules.[5] Nye has directed attention to the specific resources that are important in the dynamic (e.g. population, territory, military forces, and mass communications capabilities) and how these various resources rise and decline in significance over time.[6] An earlier variation of this approach is E.H. Carr's admonition that there are three sources of power in international relations: military power, economic power and power over opinion.[7] In comparison, Susan Strange has focused attention on how these resources are used to extract outcomes. For her there are basically two types of power exercised in the international political economy: *relational power* and *structural power*. Relational power is the ability of A to get B to do something that B, without A's influence or coercion, would not otherwise do. In contrast, structural power is 'the power to shape and determine the structures of the global political economy within which other states, their political institutions, their economic enterprises and (not least) their scientists and other professional people have to operate'.[8]

Building on this foundation, we see that communications and power are related because communications is a resource that can be used in the exercise of power. To illustrate this point we can refer to the spread of American 'popular culture' (e.g. movies and TV programmes) worldwide. Nye has called it a source of 'soft power' for the United States. 'Of course, there is an element of triviality and fad in popular behavior,' he wrote, 'but it is also true that a country that stands astride popular channels of communication has more opportunities to get its messages across and to affect the preferences of others'.[9]

To continue the caveat expressed above, the value of communications to which Nye referred is different, of course, from the value of the information relayed by the media and channels. To precisely locate how information is a source of power we must ask questions about the nature of the information, the ability of the intended target to understand it, and the correlation between exposure to the information and expected outcomes from its being understood. Similarly, communications capabilities are not sources of power if the people over whom the power is to be exercised are not part of the communication process. The minimum that is required of them is the ability to receive. And even though communication, in its purest meaning, refers to sharing, it is interesting that the value of international communication to a country such as the United States does not necessarily involve others doing more than receiving. The process needs to be two-way only to the extent that the United States gets feedback that the intended action has taken place. So the millions around the world who are investing in satellite reception dishes are, in fact, unsuspectingly or not, buying into a process that gives others the ability to exercise power over them, both through communication and information.

To illustrate the points above, we can say that the power that comes from being the sole transmitter of TV news and entertainment to two million households in Africa with satellite reception dishes, for example, is distinctly different from the power derived from being able to include in the programmes relayed the subtle message that the Native Americans were savages preying on peaceful white people, instead of being a people trying to protect their land from thieves. The first source of power, although a precondition for the latter, does not automatically produce the second.

COMMUNICATION AND SCHOLARSHIP ON INTERNATIONAL POLITICS

The analysis above reveals that international communication is inherently strategic. But the literature of international relations in North America and Europe has historically been concerned with harnessing the strategic value of international communications technologies for maintaining a world order that, although peaceful, would still be on the terms of an elite of states. This view is in the literature implicitly and explicitly.

In North America and Europe, from early in the twentieth century, prominent writers on International Relations of diverse political complexions placed great hope in the idea that improved international communication would produce a world society that was at peace. For example, Graham Wallas wrote in *The Great Society* that 'Men find themselves working and thinking and feeling in relation to an environment which both in its world-wide extension and its intimate connection with all sides of human existence, is without precedent in the history of the world.'[10] In 1909 Norman Angell argued that modern telecommunications technology was a major factor contributing to why war would soon be futile:

> The complexity of modern finance makes New York dependent upon London, London upon Paris, Paris upon Berlin, to a greater degree than has ever yet been the case in history. This interdependence is the result of the daily use of those contrivances of civilization which date from yesterday – the rapid post, the instantaneous dissemination of financial and commercial information by means of telegraphy, and generally the incredible progress of rapidity in communication which has put the half dozen chief capitals of Christendom in closer contact financially, and has rendered them more dependent the one upon the other than were the chief cities of Great Britain less than a hundred years ago.[11]

In comparison, Quincy Wright, wrote that there was the emergence of a 'world society', the evidence of this being

> (i) instruments of communication and transportation and statistics indicating the degree of interdependence among members and of self-sufficiency of the whole; (ii) political organizations and institutions subordinating the members of the group to the whole; (iii) standardized behavior patterns indicating the degree of uniformity among the members; and (iv) acts and declarations of the members indicating attitudes toward one another and towards values imputed to the whole.[12]

Reflecting in the 1970s on these idealistic assumptions about international communication, Alastair Buchan argued that the hope that increased communication would augur well for international relations was also seized upon by those who panicked about the future of peace in the aftermath of the Second World War.[13] According to their logic, if the common man could communicate with his counterpart in another state without diplomacy, soldiers or traders mediating, there would be better international understanding and hence less conflict.

It is important to note that critiques of such assumptions were made even before they were proven wrong by historical events. Angell's view that improved methods of communication fostered an interdependent system of states was not shared by E.H. Carr 30 years later, as he wrote about a world on the verge of another war. In his realist critique of idealist views of world politics, Carr argued that international relations were essentially about power. States with power are the most able to pursue their objectives. Power in international relations is of the three kinds mentioned above: military power; economic power; and power over opinion. Propaganda – which Carr said was introduced by the Soviets as an instrument for conducting international relations – was the specific means by which a state gained power over opinion. Carr noted that power over opinion became a more important factor as the amounts of people involved in the political process increased:

> The radio, the film and the press share to the fullest extent the characteristic attitude of modern industry, i.e. that mass-production, quasi monopoly and standardization are a condition of economical and efficient working. Their management has, in the natural course of development, become concentrated in fewer and fewer hands; and this concentration facilitates and makes inevitable the centralized control of opinion. The mass production of opinion is the corollary of the mass-production of goods.[14]

But Carr's perspective was the exception. Many failed to ask questions about ownership and control, as the left-wing historian Carr did. There would be communication on whose terms? Would all peoples agree with the ideas being disseminated by those with the superior technologies of international communication?

As the century has progressed the concentration of control of mass communications technologies has increased and the imbalances in international communications capabilities among countries have widened. The relationship between international communication and power has become more glaring, and it is now more difficult for some to believe in the notion of international communications technologies fostering a harmonious 'global village' on the terms of a minority. Indeed, the aphorism 'global village' was coined in the 1960s by Marshall McLuhan, a literature and communications scholar from Canada, a country ranking among the wealthiest in the world, yet finding itself a communications neo-colony of its big, southern neighbour.

In 1967 Henry Comor asserted in the journal *Television Quarterly* that:

> American television has made the development of a Canadian cultural identity almost impossible....American television has destroyed television as an art. Canadians are often told their potential enemies are Russia and China. In my view, the US is a much more dangerous enemy.[15]

8   *International Power and International Communication*

Almost 25 years later, in the midst of the New World Information and Communication Order (NWICO) debate (see below), the same concerns were present in Canada. At that time, former chief of public sector broadcasting policy in the Canadian Department of Communications, David Gallick, was asking:

How can the CBC [Canadian Broadcasting Corporation] meet its objectives in the face of US DBS [direct broadcast satellites] being available to Canadians everywhere with the use of a C$300 receiving dish? ... With each day, there is less and less of a Canadian programming presence in the overall menu of television services available to most Canadians. It is a strong challenge to Canada's cultural identity and economic development. Perhaps it is not an overstatement to suggest it is a threat to Canada's sovereignty as well.[16]

I have shown elsewhere that Canadian concern about protecting its cultural sovereignty from the United States has been so great that it is one of the most important reasons why Canadians have been the most prominent researchers of problems in international communication.[17]

Research by Bruce Lannes Smith and Sara Fletcher Luther has shown that a main reason why such questions about ownership, control and imbalances were not posed by American scholars was because researchers' priorities were often shaped by the interest groups who funded them. There were three major deficiencies in the research evident in 1955, according to Smith:[18] there was great emphasis on the strategic importance of international communication, at the expense of studies into its values in the cause of peace; there was little attention to exploration of how the information processes of international organizations (e.g. UNICEF, WHO, FAO) could be improved; and no scholarship had been devoted to non-governmental forms of influence, such as films and textbooks. Smith noted that researchers in the field 'are often heard to say that the world impact of textbooks and of entertainment movies may well outweigh that of all governmental propaganda programs combined; but the writer has not been able to find a single major item of research on this'.[19] Smith described research that was being done almost exclusively in the United States and he noted that enquiry in international communication was being financed by four major sources: national governments; foundations; UNESCO; and transnational corporations. Writing about Communications scholarship in the US 30 years later, Sara Fletcher Luther argued that because scholars of communications attracted such institutional support, such funding shaped the research priorities and the assumptions they employed.[20] The literature had two main features: it paid little or no attention to questions arising from ownership and control of the media; and there was a large volume of data on *stimulus/response* – 'who say what, in which channel, to whom, with what effect'.[21] Fletcher Luther said the methodology of the Americans

> was based on their acceptance of the given framework of values; they seldom questioned fundamental mainstream beliefs and were seemingly unaware of their own role as stabilizers and legitimizers. By the mid-1930s, they were beginning to accept research support from the radio industry itself, as commercial communication interests sought to shape the theoretical context in which the social scientists worked, and the questions they set for themselves and society.[22]

By 1955 the Massachusetts Institute of Technology (MIT) already had a program of 'Studies in International Communication' financed by foundations,[23] and the 1960s and 1970s saw 'International Communication' become institutionalized in the United States as a sub-field of International Relations.[24] Although many scholars in international communication have been trained specialists in international relations (e.g. Mowlana),[25] many others who have contributed to the field's expanding body of literature over the years have come from sociology (e.g. Everett M. Rogers)[26] and psychology (e.g. Kaarle Nordenstreng).[27]

In the last 20 years 'critical' scholars in International Communication have emerged. Their research has focused on questions of ownership and control of international communication structures and has informed intellectual attacks on the United States' partiality to the so-called 'Free Flow' doctrine (see below). Their research differs greatly from the orthodox approaches because the critical scholars have not been content to view international communication as only a field which should be described and used to secure strategic advantage. Scholars such as Herbert I. Schiller, Kaarle Nordenstreng, Cees Hamelink and Armand Mattelart have viewed international communication structures as empowering some at the expense of others. They have sided with the disadvantaged in their research and have, as a result, supported arguments for a proposed New World Information and Communication Order (NWICO).

For example, although Hamelink agrees international communication involves *structures*, he notes that the 'old' structures – the ways in which international communication is organized in the world – have particular characteristics which must be the concern of the international communication scholar. These structures are:

- *oligopolistic*: their control is in the hands of a few large corporations
- *hierarchical*: the few talk to the many
- *synchronic*: the receivers are synchronized with the interests of the senders
- *bureaucratic*: there is a two-way flow but the quality differs with its direction; the top–bottom flow is decisive
- *authoritarian*: the experts' message carries prescriptive truth.[28]

Such a description asserts that international communication is unjust as it is presently organized. If there is to be justice there must be change in the present structures. The school of thought symbolized by Hamelink, Schiller and Nordenstreng, from the turn of the 1970s on, stands in contrast to the thinking about the role of communication in international relations represented by Angell, Wallas, Quincy Wright and others who wrote about international communication fostering interdependence in a world that was perhaps easier to theorize about because European colonialism dominated a great percentage of the globe.

COMMUNICATIONS NORTH/COMMUNICATIONS SOUTH

From early in the era of decolonisation, some political leaders of the new nation-states were aware of the strategic character of international communication and its potential to maintain informal empires. A very poignant quote can be found in Kwame Nkrumah's *Neo-Colonialism: The Last Stage of Imperialism* where the first Prime Minister of Ghana wrote that

> Even the cinema stories of fabulous Hollywood are loaded. One has only to listen to the cheers of an African audience as Hollywood's heroes slaughter red Indians or Asiatics to understand the effectiveness of this weapon. For, in the developing continents, where the colonialist heritage has left a vast majority still illiterate, even the smallest child gets the message contained in the blood and thunder stories emanating from California. And along with murder and the Wild West goes an incessant barrage of anti-socialist propaganda, in which the trade union man, the revolutionary, or the man of dark skin is generally cast as the villain, while the policeman, the gum-shoe, the Federal agent – in a word, the CIA-type spy – is ever the hero ....[29]

There Nkrumah was referring to the power of specific types of information, but he also saw power in the structures of international communication existing at the time when he noted that:

While Hollywood takes care of fiction, the enormous monopoly press, together with the outflow of slick, clever, expensive magazines, attends to what it chooses to call 'news'. Within separate countries, one or two news agencies control the news handouts, so that a deadly uniformity is achieved, regardless of the number of separate newspapers and magazines; while internationally, the financial preponderance of the United States is felt more and more through its foreign correspondents and offices abroad, as well as through its influence over international capitalist journalism. Under this guise, a flood of anti-liberation propaganda emanates from the capitalist cities of the West, directed against China, Vietnam, Indonesia, Algeria, Ghana and all countries which hack out their own independent path to freedom.[30]

In the era which saw the dissolution of formal empires after the Second World War, Kwame Nkrumah was among those who saw neo-colonialism replacing imperialism as a feature of the international political economy. Building on Lenin, he said neo-colonialism was imperialism at its last and most dangerous stage. Although the former colonies had gained their independence and the trappings of statehood, they were still being exploited by the old imperialist states by subtle mechanisms. These included control of the world markets especially in commodities; conditional aid agreements; monopoly control of strategic areas of the international market, such as the shipping industry; and domination of the means of international mass communication. Nkrumah argued that neo-colonialism was very dangerous because of its potential to generate armed conflict. The discontent which it caused produced 'limited' (or regional) wars among developing nations. Although limited war is an alternative to nuclear war, Nkrumah believed it would only be a matter of time before these local conflicts escalated into full-scale conflict between the superpowers.

This idea of the international structures of communication being key to the maintenance of informal empires was restated in 1983, 20 years after Nkrumah, by Michael Manley, who, in explaining why and how he lost the government of Jamaica a few years earlier, said

Our habits of dress, our sense of social hierarchy, our acceptance of monarchy can all be laid at the door of British colonialism and the skill with which empire fashions the mind of the governed. But America has never needed to precede its conquests by military action. Hollywood films, glossy magazines, canned television shows have all created a cultural invasion. This has proved more powerful than the attack of any army because it proceeds by stealth to occupy the corners of the mind and needs no fortress upon the ground to uphold its influence.[31]

One of the goals of Manley's *Struggle in the Periphery* was to document how the US government, overtly and covertly, systematically used the media to displace a government it did not like. Manley's government was particularly vulnerable to unkind international publicity because it was in charge of an economy heavily dependent on tourism as an earner of foreign exchange. Manley noted that

> Soon after the news that Jamaica was supporting Cuba (or Angola), a Kissinger confidante, James Reston of the *New York Times*, wrote a vicious and utterly inaccurate article about Jamaica. The article marked a turning point in Jamaica's image in the United States. Reston's wild charges about violence in Jamaica, the alleged presence of Cuban troops and Cuban secret agents, all added up to an impression of a Cuban takeover. This started off a chain reaction in the US press which never ceased until we were finally defeated in the elections of October 1980.[32]

These two examples, from the writings of Nkrumah and Manley, reveal that although political and intellectual elites in the North sometimes claim that their media and the market in movies and TV programmes are free of government control, the perspective on this international 'free flow' of information is somewhat different when viewed from the South. The view that the media and cultural products (e.g. books, magazines and movies) of the North are *de facto* tools in a form of dominance that has been given the various labels of 'cultural imperialism',[33] 'academic imperialism'[34] and 'socio-cultural colonization'[35] was one motivation behind the call for a NWICO. Two other imperatives for the South were: the need for redress of disparities – the North dominates book production, news flows, advertising and other forms of international communication; and the recognition of the key role that communication plays in national development.

Trying to understand and explore the perspectives of less powerful countries in the international communications structure is a complicated exercise because the inequalities in international mass communication are mirrored in the very structure of academic research and publishing. We get an appreciation of this by exploring first how ideas and information about international communication and international power are produced.

Apart from doing field research in the various countries, there are three main ways for a scholar in the North to get information and perspectives on so-called 'Third World' international communication problems actually written by persons from the 'Third World'. He or she can:

(1) Consult journals published in the North that make an effort to seek out and publish articles by scholars from the South. An example of this

is *Gazette*, the international journal for mass communication studies published quarterly by the Institute of the Science of the Press, Amsterdam. While other journals, such as the *Journal of Communication* in the United States, publish articles about and by people from the South, these journals are still mainly written by American and European scholars. It is not unusual to see several articles in one issue of *Gazette* written by Africans, Latin Americans or Asians. (2) Read reports of international institutions or of commissions convened by international organizations, such as the MacBride report[36] from UNESCO and the Maitland report[37] from the ITU. The remits of these commissions require that they consider a variety of perspectives and the obvious first way they do this is through making sure that an adequate proportion of their members come from developing countries. (3) Read the reports of debates on international communication at multilateral forums. The two forums where these debates occur regularly are Commission IV of the two-yearly UNESCO General Conferences, and the UN Committee on Information which debates problems in international communication and presents a report with recommendations to the General Assembly annually.

The positions from the South acquired through these three means are, with the exception of academic articles, almost always exclusively those of political elites who represent their countries at international organizations. In contrast, views from the West are not only available in larger quantity, but greater variety. The views of Western political elites are presented at the UN and its specialized agencies, but Western scholars, unlike their counterparts in the South, have a variety of journals in which to air their views and publish their research. Non-governmental organizations, such as the Zurich-based International Press Institute (IPI), the World Press Freedom Committee of the United States, the International Federation of Journalists (IFJ), based in Brussels, and the International Federation of Newspaper Publishers (FIEJ), and many others, are not only international lobbies, but they also provide forums for media-owners and journalists to discuss, organize and research their positions in ways not available to media elites in the South where such organizations often do not exist in abundance, and where they do exist they do not have the resources to send representatives to international conferences. A poignant illustration of this was at the UN's Second Roundtable on a New World Information and Communication Order, held in Copenhagen 2 to 7 April 1986. Of the 15 NGOs represented none were based in the South. Broadcasting Organizations of the Non-Aligned Countries (BONAC) was represented, but its delegate was a Yugoslavian journalist. In the NWICO debate the organizations with dispositions that could be considered alternatives to those of the Western NGOs were the Prague-based International Organization of Journalists (IOJ) and the London-based World Association for Christian Communication (WACC). These two organizations were represented, but as is often the case in debates of issues in international communication, the position of interests in the South, when not voiced by diplomats or politicians, are represented indirectly by sympathetic scholars and organizations from the North or, during the period up to the end of the 1980s, the Eastern bloc, rather than directly through their own NGOs. This distinction must be kept in mind in the interest of intellectual rigour because, in the discussion of international communication and international power, debates have not only taken place between countries of the North and South, but also between classes and interest groups within countries. And even though the disparities in international communication have been great, it has never produced a clear-cut simplistic scenario of 'have-nots' against 'haves'. For example, while India was a prominent member of the Non-Aligned Movement (NAM) and advocated the NWICO, one of its prominent publishers, Cushrow Irani, espoused the conservative views of the IPI (of which he was then Chairman) at the 1980 General Conference of UNESCO.[38] Irani had confronted the repressive press policies imposed by Prime Minister Indira Ghandi during a state of emergency in the mid-1970s. Ironically, Ghandi's administration, while it had such an attitude to the press, gave strong rhetorical support to UN policies aimed at redressing imbalances in global communication.

It must also be pointed out that even though Nkrumah and Manley wrote passionately about the role of communication in maintaining dependence, they did so along the way to explaining some problem that they considered larger. A striking feature of the intellectual output on international relations of thinkers from the South has been the relative lack of attention to international communication as an issue in its own right. The Non-Aligned Movement (NAM) placed and maintained the idea of a NWICO on the UN agenda. But most of the writers who have devoted their professional careers to studying the disparities of the international communication structure, and who are most often quoted in reference to such questions, are almost totally from the North, Kaarle Nordenstreng of Finland and Herbert Schiller of the United States being the most prominent of these. Indeed, this study is perhaps the first comprehensive study in book form of the disparities in international communication done by an individual from the South. This is not to say that there has been no Southern presence in the literature. Beltrán has documented the extensive number of studies done by Latin Americans on the impact of foreign TV programmes on their region.[39] Because dependency is considered a pattern of relationships in several areas, not just economic relations, the academic literature of Latin America, with its well-known attention to dependency, has of necessity paid attention to imbalances in international communication.

There is really no dispute that the ownership and control of international communication is often one-sided. The big questions revolve around what we should make of this scenario. It has been fashionable in some circles to glorify these disparities by arguing that international communication is the arena in which values, such as universal human rights and liberal democracy, are disseminated from the places that cherish them to backward, politically undeveloped regions. On the other hand, international communication has been viewed as a multi-layered structure, where the worldview of elite races, cultures and nations are imposed on others, and where questions related to the global power structure are not even allowed a hearing because all issues are framed by the powerful. This book hopes to show that the answers are never as simple as the above. The former view is an ethnocentric one that is often proved contradictory when juxtaposed against the domestic and international behaviour of the nation-states that profess these liberal ideals. The suppression of minorities and the use of covert action against democratically elected governments have hardly been in the best interest of promoting human rights or liberal democracy. The latter view is too simplistic because, as we will show in Chapters 3 and 4 especially, the domestic policies of many governments have actually been 'pull factors' in the spread of North American and European media. Furthermore, political repression in many countries has served to suppress in many instances the little output from writers, journalists and other intellectuals that can make the structure of international communication less one-sided.

In illustrating the complexity of the task of answering these big questions we will revisit repeatedly in the book the distinction we have made in this chapter between the power of communication and the power of information. When we talk about 'power over opinion', 'soft power', or other labels for the influence to be gained through communication, we are really referring to these two types of power operating in tandem. What is often termed 'the power of ideas' is really about the power of certain types of information, and it is distinct from the power of communication which refers to the media by which these ideas and other types of information are communicated. So our discussion in Chapter 2 of the rules by which international communication takes place is an analysis of the anatomy of the power of communication – an exploration of why and how the rules of international communication are laid down. In contrast, in Chapter 3 we devote considerable space to the analysis of the power of information when we show that the absence of international regimes for trade in cultural products and global news flows have been a function of certain assumptions in some powerful places about the power of information.

Apart from the distinction between the power of communication and the power of information, a second organizing principle employed throughout the book is the idea that international communication is essentially about those sectors covered by international regimes (i.e. telecommunications, the mails and intellectual property rights) and those that are not (i.e. trade in cultural products and global news flows). This is a distinction that is constructed upon the definition established in this chapter which notes that power is not only about getting others to do what they otherwise might not do were it not for your presence, but also about deciding the rules of the game. Indeed, embedded in my approach to the big questions is the assumption that this latter attitude to the definition of power is fundamental to understanding the anatomy of the relationship between international power and international communication. Chapter 2 illustrates that international communications regimes were created in some cases because there was little other choice. However, in Chapter 3 we show that there have been conscious efforts to avoid the creation of international regimes in some areas of international communication and that this posture by powerful states changed as the stakes changed – from abhorrence of state-devised rules for mass communication, based on the 'Free Flow' doctrine, to efforts to make trade in services and protection of intellectual property rights a part of the GATT regime.

Our attention to 'public diplomacy' in Chapter 5 is guided by the view that governmental public relations is one of the most significant, yet infrequently explored, dimensions of international communication. Public diplomacy, because of the capital intensity it requires, is an exclusive game restricted to relatively few countries who can play it on a global scale. At the same time public diplomacy embodies much of the ethnocentrism and contradictions that have marked the policies of the powerful states in the area of international communication. For example, while chiding small states for attempting to control the free press, many states have used broadcasting and other media to pursue their ends in international relations, such as undermining support for foreign administrations.

Our view – set out in Chapter 6 – is that the New World Information and Communication Order (NWICO) is a case study of what happens when the *status quo* of international communication is challenged. In it we find lessons for future attempts at transforming the structure of global communications. As a concept, the NWICO was never clearly defined, perhaps hinting at the severe complexity of international communication as a cluster of issue-areas. Another point is that postures to the NWICO were riddled with contradictions, all of which combined to ruin its viability. For example, governments guilty of suppressing free expression were at the same time ardent advocates of a NWICO. Also, the dice were loaded against the concept from the start because the chief means of relaying information about the NWICO – the international mass media based in influential countries – were also those most threatened by the prospect of reforming the *status quo*.The NWICO debate is a worthy case study because it embodies all the elements we discuss in the chapters preceding Chapter 6 – assumptions about the power of information that underlay the post-Second World War international order, defensive attitudes related to press freedom based on liberal-democratic ideals, conscious decisions to make certain sectors of international communication immune to multilateral rule-making, and the artificial division between the 'political' and 'technical' in the setting-up of international communications regimes. In other words, the NWICO was a power play in the arena of international communication.

The analysis of the NWICO debate is a useful *entrée* to Chapter 7 because, in attempting to answer our big questions, we are essentially thinking about the role of communication in world order. Order has been defined as a pattern of activity that sustains the primary goals of international society. Just as there was after the Second World War, there has been much discussion of a new world order following the collapse of Soviet communism in the late 1980s. Just what are those primary goals of international society? Peace? Liberal democracy? Social welfare? And what role does international communication play in first defining those goals and then maintaining that pattern of activity? The debates about international communication discussed in the book show that not all states agree that order should be the primary organizing principle in international relations. Indeed, equality and justice can conflict with order. An international system that is orderly is not necessarily one that might be considered just by all of its members.

Peace, equality, justice, democracy, religious freedom, an end to racial prejudice, and certain economic rights all seem like worthy goals to which a world order should be geared. However, peace has been the most elusive of values for the international system. Therefore, the recent theoretical and empirical finding that democracies do not go to war against each other is worthy of great scrutiny. Freedom of information – the right to hold and impart ideas – is intrinsic to the definition of liberal democracy. So it follows that if democracies do not go to war against each other there are certain implications for the theory and practice of communication. Based on our discourse about the relationship between international power and international communication, our approach to world order in Chapter 7 is meant to be a counterpoint to the fashionable ideas about the relationship between communication and democracy. It has been easy to conjecture a positive relationship between the spread of new communications technologies and the promotion of liberal-democratic ideals (or the spread of 'civil society', as this process is sometimes known). This approach, we argue, is problematic not only because it is inherently ethnocentric, but also because it ignores questions about ownership and control of communication and information. The discourse on world order is itself highly limiting. But even if we accept the premise that there should be a world order, and an order organized around the goal of civil society, we must confront the contradictions that have been very transparent in the field of international communication.

NOTES

1. The lexicographic references in this section are taken from *The Compact Edition of the Oxford English Dictionary* (New York: Oxford University Press, 1971).
2. A pioneer in the analysis of the role of communication in international relations is Karl Deutsch. See his *Nationalism and Social Communication* (Cambridge, Mass.: MIT, 1953; 2nd edn, 1966), and *Political Community at the International Level* (New York: Doubleday, 1954).
3. *The Compact Edition of the Oxford English Dictionary* notes that 'information' is rooted in the Latin *informare*, 'to give form to, shape, fashion, form an idea of, describe ...'. There is no mention in the definition of what Mowlana (below) refers to as the medieval Latin word *informatio*.
4. Hamid Mowlana, *Global Information and World Communication: New Frontiers in International Relations* (New York: Longman, 1986), pp. 3–4.
5. Stephen D. Krasner, 'Global Communications and National Power', *World Politics*, April 1991, p. 342.
6. Joseph S. Nye, Jr, 'Soft Power', *Foreign Policy*, No. 80, Fall 1990, pp. 153–171.
7. E.H. Carr, *The Twenty Years' Crisis* (London: Macmillan, 1939).
8. Susan Strange, *States and Markets* (London: Pinter, 1988), pp. 24–25.
9. Nye, 'Soft Power', p. 169.
10. Graham Wallas, *The Great Society: A Psychological Analysis* (New York: Macmillan, 1915), p. 3.

11. Norman Angell, *The Great Illusion* (New York: G. P. Putnam's Sons, 1913), pp. 54–5.
12. Quincy Wright, *A Study of War* (Chicago, 1942), pp. ii, 975–6, quoted on p. 3 of Alastair Buchan, 'Conflict and Communication', Colchester, 2 March 1971. The seventh Noel Buxton Lecture at the University of Essex.
13. Alastair Buchan, 'Conflict and Communication', Colchester, 2 March 1971. The seventh Noel Buxton Lecture at the University of Essex.
14. Carr, *The Twenty Years' Crisis, p. 134.*
15. Henry Comor, 'American TV: What have you done to us?', *Television Quarterly*, Vol. 6, no. 1, Winter 1967; quoted in Herbert I. Schiller, *Mass Communications and American Empire* (Boston: Beacon Press, 1971), p. 79.
16. David Gallick, 'Public Broadcasting and National Development in Canada', *Intermedia*, Vol. 13, no. 2, March 1985, p. 23.
17. See Mark D. Alleyne, 'Why Canada – the international dominance of Canadian communications research', *Intermedia*, Vol. 18, no.1, Jan.- Feb. 1990, pp. 12–19.
18. Bruce Lannes Smith, 'Trends in Research on International Communication and Opinion, 1945–55', *Public Opinion Quarterly*, Vol. 20, 1956, pp. 182–95.
19. Ibid., p. 188.
20. Sara Fletcher Luther, *The US and the Direct Broadcast Satellite: The Politics of International Broadcasting in Space* (New York: Oxford University Press, 1988), pp. 34–62.
21. Ibid., p. 45.
22. Ibid., p. 44.
23. Smith, 'Trends in Research', p. 186.
24. The first specialized degree program in International Communication in the US and one of the first in the world started at The American University, Washington, DC in 1968. See International Communication Program, *International Communication as a Field of Study* (Washington, DC: The American University, 1989).
25. See Hamid Mowlana, *Global Information and World Communication* (New York: Longman, 1986). This work, which aspires to be a comprehensive text on international communication, includes tourism, international academic conferences and student exchanges as all legitimate forms of international communication that should be studied along with more obvious forms such as wire services, broadcasting and publishing.
26. See Everett M. Rogers, *Communication and Development: Critical Perspectives* (Beverly Hills: SAGE, 1976); and his (with F. F. Shoemaker) *Communication of Innovations: A Cross-Cultural Approach* (New York: Free Press, second edn, 1971).
27. See Kaarle Nordenstreng and Tapio Varis, *Television Traffic: A One-way Street?* Reports and Papers on Mass Communication, No. 70 (Paris: UNESCO, 1974); and his (with H. I. Schiller) (eds), *National Sovereignty and International Communication* (Norwood, NJ: ABLEX, 1979); as well as his *The Mass Media Declaration of UNESCO* (Norwood, NJ: ABLEX, 1983).
28. Cees Hamelink, *New Structure of International Communication: The Role of Research*, ISS Occasional Papers No. 87 (The Hague: Institute of Social Studies, 1981), pp. 6–7.

29.   Kwame Nkrumah, *Neo-Colonialism: The Last Stage of Imperialism* (New York: International Publishers, 1965), pp. 246–7.
30.   Ibid.
31.   Michael Manley, *Struggle in the Periphery* (London: Third World Media in association with Writers and Readers Publishing Cooperative Society, 1982), p. 79.
32.   Ibid., p. 117.
33.   Johan Galtung, 'A Structural Theory of Imperialism', *Journal of Peace Research*, Vol. 8, no. 2, 1971, p. 93.
34.   Prime Minister Indira Gandhi, quoted in Tran Van Dinh, 'Non-Alignment and Cultural Imperialism', in *The Nonaligned Movement In World Politics*, ed. A. W. Singhan (New York: Lawrence Hill & Co., 1977), p.78.
35.   Karl P. Sauvant, 'From Economic to Socio-Cultural Emancipation: The Historical Context of the New International Economic Order and the New International Socio-Cultural Order', *Third World Quarterly*, Vol. 3, no.1, 1981, p. 57.
36.   International Commission for the Study of Communication Problems, *Many Voices, One World* (London: Kogan Page, 1980).
37.   Independent Commission For Worldwide Telecommunications Development, *The Missing Link* (Geneva: ITU, 1985).
38.   Kaarle Nordenstreng, Enrique Gonzales Manet and Wolfgang Kleinwachter, *New International Information Order Source Book* (Prague: International Organization of Journalists, 1986), p. 30. For a verbatim record of Irani's speech, see 'Belgrade Address by IPI Chairman Cushrow Irani', IPI Report, Nov., 1980, p. 16.
39.   Luis Ramiro Beltrán S., 'TV Etchings in the Minds of Latin Americans: Conservatism, Materialism, and Conformism', *Gazette*, Vol. 24, no.1, 1978, pp. 61–85.

2 The Structure of International Communication

If we accept the premise that the dynamic of power in international relations involves a process by which it is determined who plays a game and by what rules[1] (see Chapter 1), then the first stage in understanding the power of international communication must be seeing how the technologies and processes of international communication have been developed and under what rules. This history reveals that new means of transnational communication, and the arrangements for global cooperation around them, were both developed in the North American and European countries. Technology – the application of knowledge for a purpose – was developed to obviate problems experienced by these countries. The international regulations for these technologies were created by these states for their needs and applied in regions of the world over which they had dominion. The history of international communication, especially in the last 50 years, has also been a story of rules often being outpaced by the rate of technological development. It should have come as no surprise, therefore, that a number of states attempted a revolt against the structure of international communication in the 1970s and 1980s. Many countries were mere colonies when the technologies and international law for using them were created. So it was almost inevitable that questions would be raised sooner or later about the suitability for some countries of some technologies and related international laws governing their use.

International communication, in the context of this study, refers to processes and exchanges in eight areas: telecommunications; mail; intellectual property; advertising; news; movies and TV programmes; books and periodicals; and recorded music. A great degree of supranational rule-making and institutionalization has been evident in three of these areas – telecommunications, the mails and intellectual property rights. Indeed, the International Telecommunication Union (established in 1865) has the distinction of being the oldest international organization in the global system. The Universal Postal Union (UPU) originated with an international congress in Berne, Switzerland, in 1874. And although the World Intellectual Property Organization (WIPO) was only founded in 1967, the Paris and

Bern Treaties for the protection of intellectual property that the WIPO supervises were signed in 1883 and 1886 respectively. In contrast, the structure of power and rule-making in the other five areas is more complicated, with each not having a specific multilateral institution nor as coherent a regime. This chapter concentrates on the institutions and regimes for telecommunications, the mails and intellectual property rights. Chapters 3, 4 and 5 will deal with the other five areas.

FUNCTIONAL COMMUNICATIONS REGIMES

The ITU, UPU and WIPO are just three of a plethora of international organizations that mushroomed in the late 1800s and in the twentieth century. Cox and Jacobson note that there were 80 international organizations by the 1930s, but the number increased rapidly to reach over 200 by the 1960s. The growth of international organizations was encouraged not only by the very practical need to cooperate (especially in activities such as telecommunications and the post where there were few other options), but also by the popularity of a body of assumptions about international relations that came to be commonly known as *functionalism*.

The ITU and the UPU have been particularly important to functionalists who believed the primary goal of international relations – peace – would be achieved if the various forms of cooperation needed by states were delegated to a network of functional organizations.[2] The functionalist outlook can be stripped down to four basic assumptions:[3]

- All states have a harmony of interest that allows them to cooperate for mutual benefit.
- Political and technical matters (such as health provision, civil aviation and the mails) can and should be separated in international relations.
- There would be no recourse to war if economic and social welfare were achieved throughout international society.
- Functional organizations would have a positive spill-over influence on areas of international relations not yet covered by functional agencies.

The ITU and UPU, because of their relatively successful, non-controversial records, have traditionally been regarded as the best examples of functionalism at work.[4] In the same way they are the best illustration of the deficiencies of functionalism.

Before the specific rules related to telecommunications, the mails and intellectual property rights are analyzed for their value as resources for exercising power, it must be understood that the functional assumptions that created such organizations in the first place were themselves a reflection of a power dynamic. Functionalism assumes that order in international relations is a higher goal than justice and equality, a grave proposition for states and others who can cite many reasons why the international system can be viewed as unjust and unequal. The man considered the father of functionalist thought, David Mitrany, promoted the *principle of functional representation* which said that parties who are deemed insignificant in the broader scheme of international relations or whose stakes in an issue-area are relatively small can be excluded from decision-making. Small states would get 'working democracy' in lieu of 'voting democracy', and they would be consoled by 'an assurance of peace and a growing measure of social equality through the working of international service'. Mitrany justifies this by asserting that the 'formal principle of equality ... at best has never been more than a political fiction'.[5]

This idea of how functionalism as an organizational ideology is a source of conflict in international relations is expressed quite eloquently by Cox and Jacobson in Chapter 1 of their volume on international organizations (including studies of the ITU and UNESCO) when they state:

> Functionalism stresses developing collaboration among states with regard to specific objectives as a means of gradually eroding the authority of nation-states in favor of world institutions. Marxist and populist ideologies compete with functionalism as other broad interpretations of the aims and strategies of international organizations. International organizations are seen in the Marxist view as expressing power relations between socialist and capitalist blocs; to the populist, they appear as means of exerting pressure by the numerous poor on the few rich.[6]

In addition to the criticism above, functionalism in practice fell short of goals visualized. The three communications regimes, for example, never lived up entirely to the functionalist ideal. As long ago as 1963 a study by Kihl concluded that the ITU and UPU fell short of being the perfect examples of functionalism they seemed to be. Kihl attacked two of the functionalist assumptions as applied to the ITU – the idea that there was a clear separation between political and technical issues, and that members of a functional organization were motivated to cooperate through functional agencies because that was the best way to prevent war. On the latter, Kihl noted that

> It is obvious that the motive behind the nation states to institute cooperative action in the telegraph arrangement was not world-saving or

world-solving. They were mainly motivated by the desire to avoid inconveniences and difficulties which arise from the complex and diverse practice of bilateral telegraphic arrangements prevailing in the middle of the nineteenth century. Self-interest, therefore seems to be the powerful motive behind the act of nations to organize themselves into an international telegraphic regime.[7]

However, when political debate over the NWICO came to these organizations, the North seemed stunned that the business of the agencies could be taken up with issues of a non-technical (and therefore seemingly non-functional) nature. As Kinn has observed:

> To Western nations, it appeared that ITU Administrative Radio and Plenipotentiary Conferences during the 1970s and early 1980s had become mired in frivolous and peripheral political considerations which impinged on the delegates' ability to complete the technical work of the conferences. Negotiations traditionally restricted to purely technical and functional considerations were now shrouded in language referring to the 'New International Information Order,' or couched in demands for equitable access to resources declared to be the 'common heritage of mankind.' These conferences were subject to North–South struggles over the geostationary orbit and electromagnetic spectrum resources (orbit/spectrum resources).[8]

Similar sentiments were expressed in 1984 when Arab states, at the UPU's nineteenth congress in Hamburg, attempted (unsuccessfully) to have Israel expelled from the agency because of Israel's refusal to implement UN resolutions on the Palestinian question. An Israeli spokesman said it was 'a new attempt to politicize the special agencies of the UN', and, '[the] world should not allow these agencies to become another political arena for countries to act against Israel'.[9]

The WIPO also became a forum for political debate between North and South when attempts were made in the early 1980s to revise the Paris Convention. By 1980, when discussion of the revisions began, the Paris Convention was effectively protecting inequality in world research and development because although the South had 75 per cent of the world's population it owned less than 1 per cent of patents, and over 75 per cent of patents registered in Southern states were owned by nationals of the North.[10] The Group of 77 lobbied for greater discretion in the nature of the sanctions developing nations could impose on an owner who did not work a patent in a given country, and they wanted to be able to apply sanctions sooner. In contrast, the richer nations wanted to limit sanctions and allow more time for the working of inventions.

International institutions also reflect the global imbalances of power through their philosophies and bureaucracies. For the purpose of analysis we can adopt regime theory as an analytical tool. Although there are several theories about the role regimes play in international politics, Stephen Krasner's definition is the popular version of what international regimes actually are. This definition says that all regimes include four essential components: principles; norms; rules; and decision-making procedures.[11]

In the 1970s academic attention in the US turned to exploring international regimes as order-maintaining entities in international relations, based on a popular belief in the United States at the time that there had been an erosion of US hegemony. Regime theory became an analytical tool for exploring the post-hegemonic era and understanding what Keohane and Nye called 'complex interdependence'.[12]

Telecommunication and the mails confronted the modern states system with a dilemma. States could not communicate with one another without cooperating. Unplanned use of the radio spectrum would result in interference and telecommunications equipment had to be standardized in order for signals to be exchanged between them. Similarly, a set of principles, norms, rules and decision-making procedures were essential if mail was to circulate across the globe unhindered, especially through third countries. These compelling imperatives account for why these multilateral communications institutions are among the world's oldest.

There can be an obvious confusion between the concept of an international regime and an international organization. While not every international organization embodies and supervises the components of an international regime, it is difficult to conceive of a modern international regime without the presence of one or more international organizations to maintain it. For example, Cowhey has sought to explain the reform of the international 'telecommunications regime' by examining not only changes in the domestic telecommunications policies of states but also developments at what he considers the two primary organizations that maintain that regime – the ITU and INTELSAT.[13] Many writers on international communications regimes have therefore been able to find Cox and Jacobson's important study of decision-making and influence in international organizations instructive.[14]

The framework of regimes is very useful as a tool of comparison, because illustrations, such as Table 2.1, can be used to dissect these institutions and compare and contrast their component parts. The ITU, UPU and WIPO evolved during the twentieth century according to principles determined by the powerful states of North America and Europe that fashioned the modern international system. Principles common to all international institutions that are part of the United Nations system have included functionalism and the principle of nation-states being the only legitimate full members. Table 2.1 illustrates that, in addition to these basic principles, the institutions in the field of communications have had principles specific to their areas of purview. However, as technologies and

Table 2.1 Regimes in international communication

	ITU	UPU	WIPO
Principles	• First come, first served allocation of radio frequencies and satellite slots. • Universal Service.	• Universal membership to make a single postal territory for the reciprocal exchange of letter-post items. • Guaranteed freedom of transit for the mail of member states 'throughout the entire territory of the Union'.	• Intellectual Property rights are worth respect. • Creators must be able to have control over the use of their intellectual property. • Intellectual property rights are best preserved through coordination among states.
Norms	• Basic International telecommunications services are provided jointly by the facilities of two or more countries. • Telecommunications networks and equipment should be standardized. • Natural monopolies.	• Standardized international postal procedures (including rates, weights, sizes and restricted materials). • Priority to the needs of postal administrations in developing countries as a means to ensuring the efficiency of the entire postal territory.	• Each member state must give the same protection to the industrial property and copyright of citizens of other member states that it gives to its own citizens. • Copyright protection usually continues throughout an author's life and for 50 years after he or she dies.

Table 2.1 *continued*

	ITU	UPU	WIPO
Rules and decision-making procedures	• The ITU Convention is legally binding as international law. • The Plenipotentiary Conference is the supreme decision-making organ.	• The organic rules of Union are set out in the UPU's Constitution and General Regulations and are binding on all member states. • The universal Postal Convention and its Detailed Regulations are the rules governing the international circulation of mail. • The Universal Postal Congress that meets every five years and includes delegates from all member states is the supreme decision-making authority. It elects the Director-General and his deputy by simple majority, appoints the Executive Council and has the sole power to change the Universal Postal Convention.	• The WIPO's International Bureau is the central body supervising adherence to the two major 'Unions' (conventions) on intellectual property rights and no fewer than 15 other unions and agreements. • The supreme body is the General Assembly of representatives from all member states which has oversight over the International Bureau which is in turn run by a Director General. • There are two separate assemblies for signatories to the Paris and Berne Conventions. These two Unions elect Executive Committees and the joint membership of these two bodies makes up the WIPO's Coordinating Committee.

international politics have evolved, so have the principles and bureaucratic procedures of these institutions. For example, the ITU decided in 1992 to allow transnational corporations to become full members, a concession to the fact that private telecommunications equipment and service companies had become as powerful or more powerful than states in shaping the character of the international telecommunications market. Similarly, the norm of respecting 'natural monopolies' in the provision of telecommunications service was all but abandoned by the dawn of the 1990s because of deregulation and the fact that new technologies had facilitated tremendous competition due to the new capabilities of providing telecommunications services via cellular means, cable, and satellites (to name just some).

All three of these institutions have identical decision-making structures. Forums, meeting about every five years, for delegates from all member states are the supreme decision-making entities. For the ITU it is the Plenipotentiary Conference; for the UPU it is the Universal Postal Congress; and the General Assembly has this function in the WIPO.

Below are councils or committees, elected from among the delegates, that have annual oversight on the regime and organization between plenary forums – the ITU's Administrative Council, the Executive Council of the UPU, and the WIPO's Executive and Coordinating Committees.

Next are the specialized, technical arms. Because of the nature and vastness of its issue-area the ITU's structure of such bodies has been the most complex. For most of its post-Second World War history the two major technical organs were the International Radio Consultative Committee (CCIR) that studied and made recommendations in the area of radiocommunications (broadcasting) and the International Telegraph and Telephone Consultative Committee (CCITT), for exploring questions in telecommunications, especially about the standardization of equipment and services. The work of the CCIs was complicated because they appointed a number of 'Study Groups' for detailed consideration of specific issues (e.g. amateur satellite service, radio determination service, etc.). The International Frequency Registration Board (IFRB) recorded frequency assignments for international broadcasting and the orbital assignments for satellites, and it advised member states on the efficient use of the radio frequency spectrum and the geostationary-satellite orbit. In addition, periodically the ITU hosted 'World' and 'Regional' 'Administrative' conferences to regulate and discuss such issues as the provision of telecommunication services, the radio frequency spectrum and geostationary orbit and the provision of telecommunications aid.

This structure of the ITU's technical arms was altered by decisions made at the ITU's 'Additional Plenipotentiary Conference' in December

1992. On the advice of a High Level Committee (HLC) that spent over a year (January 1990–April 1991) reviewing the structure and functions of the Union, the CCITT, CCIR and IFRB were abolished.[15] The Plenipotentiary Conference was retained as the supreme authority of the ITU; however, the frequency of its meetings became every four years instead of every five. Also retained from the old structure were the Administrative Council and the General Secretariat. The combined technical work of the CCIs and IFRB, as well as the activities of the ITU to promote telecommunications development, were streamlined into three new sectors: Development, Standardization and Radiocommunication. The Radiocommunication Sector (including world and regional radiocommunication conferences, radiocommunication assemblies and a Radio Regulations Board) took over most of the work of the CCIR and the IFRB. The part-time, nine-member Radio Regulations Board actually replaced the full-time, five-member IFRB. The Standardization Sector (including world telecommunication standardization conferences) took over the work of the CCITT and the standardization work done by the CCIR.

The creation of the Development Sector was the third phase in a progression started in the 1980s that had seen first the making of technical assistance a line item in the ITU's budget, then the creation of a Center for Telecommunications Development (CTD) and later the setting-up of the Telecommunication Development Bureau (BDT). Although the establishment of a Development Sector, as one of the three functional areas of the ITU's work, might be viewed as an outcome of the pressures exerted by the South during the years of the NWICO debate, it is important to note that even as recently as 1992 there was still some dissatisfaction with the role the ITU was playing in telecommunications development.[16] Also, the reorganization was propelled as much (or more than) by the concerns of the North as by those of the South because, as the main funders of the Union, the rich countries had a vested interest in making the Union more efficient administratively and financially.[17]

The UPU and WIPO's technical arms have been more straightforward. Study and advice on problems related to postal administration are the purview of the Consultative Council for Postal Studies (CCPS). The UPU's International Bureau also serves the role of interpreter of the Union's Acts and can be a mediator in disputes between postal administrations. Because of the peculiarities of the issue-area and the weaknesses of the WIPO regime (see below), the WIPO's technical functions are more in the area of information clearance on intellectual property matters than standard-setting and arbitration. Over 50 per cent of the staff in the Berne bureau work with the four international registration services the WIPO provides in the fields of patents, trademarks, industrial designs and appellations of origin. In addition, there is a Permanent Committee on Industrial Property Information, and the WIPO supports with Austria the International Patent Documentation Center (INPADOC) in Vienna that maintains a computer bank of bibliographic data on patents for use by patent offices, industry and researchers.

All three regimes embody a 'development' component. They all participate in the UN Development Programme (UNDP). In the early 1980s (amid the debate over the NWICO) technical assistance was made a line item in the ITU's budget. And following the recommendations of the Maitland Commission on telecommunications development, the ITU established in 1985 the Center for Telecommunications Development (CTD) to promote investment in telecommunications in developing nations. The CTD was later superseded by the larger and better-financed Telecommunications Development Bureau (BDT) that came into being in 1990. With the decision in 1992 to have a Development Sector, the BDT became the administrative unit of the new sector. Although the UPU does not have a separate centre handling development, its activities in the area are handled out of the International Bureau because it administers projects financed by the UNDP, and there is a standing UPU committee on technical cooperation. The Permanent Committee for Development Cooperation Related to Industrial Property and its counterpart for copyright oversee the WIPO's technical assistance to developing nations. The WIPO's assistance is of a service nature, helping countries to create or modernize domestic legislation and government institutions to protect intellectual property rights; to accede to international treaties; and to have more specialists working in the field.

COMMUNICATIONS REGIMES AND THE POWER STRUCTURE

Although the creation of international regimes often means that member states must surrender some of their power to the jurisdiction of international organizations, in the case of international communication, the most powerful states have been able to obviate that problem by dominating the decision-making structures of the international organizations and using the regimes and institutions to legitimize policies favourable to them.[18] In the international communications regimes an elite group of states have been able to exercise such power in two main ways: (a) their dominance of technical expertise and consequent majorities on the technical committees that inform the work of the institutions; and (b) their financial support for the running of the international bureaucracies. The power of the purse has been a notable factor in the debates over international communication at UNESCO, where the US, the UK and Singapore withdrew, taking a sizeable chunk of the budget with them (see Chapter 6). However, budgetary support takes third place as a power resource to technical expertise and the large presence big countries have in telecommunications markets, international mail flows and the production of intellectual property.

In his seminal study of influence at the ITU Jacobson concluded that

> Influence goes to those states and private agencies that are technically prepared and that control the resources important in telecommunications, and extremely few meet these qualifications. Of course, these actors must be sensitive to the needs of others because they could always be voted down; but there is no substitute for technical knowledge and control of the physical resources involved.[19]

To back up his point, Jacobson gave the examples of the 1963 Extraordinary Administrative Radio Conference on space telecommunications and the 1964 Study Group VII of the CCIR. The US had the resources and expertise to spend two years preparing for the former, with the help of the RAND Corporation, Lockheed and General Electric (which allegedly at one time had over 200 people working on its study). It was no surprise that the conference's results were to the liking of the US. In the case of the latter, the US prepared 30 papers of the 53 before the Group, and the only other countries that offered papers were from the industrialized countries: the UK, West Germany, Czechoslovakia, Italy, Canada, Belgium and Japan. In the late 1960s more than 90 per cent of the vice-chairmen of the study groups of the international consultative committees were Western nationals.[20] By the 1980s, although there had been some changes, the North, with its advantage in high technology, still retained control of technical expertise for decision-making at the ITU.

Similarly, the extent of the United States' influence in the UPU can be gauged from an extract from the President's report to the US congress on the state's involvement in the UPU for 1984:

> On technical issues, the United States submitted 28 proposals for changes in the UPU Acts to enable the US Postal Service and its customers to engage in international mailings with greater ease and effectiveness. Of these proposals, 17 were accepted. The next EC [Executive Council] or CCPS will take up seven proposals for study. In addition, a very high percentage of proposals supported by the United States and sponsored by other administrations or UPU bodies was accepted. Major topics in this category dealt with strengthening international mail

accountability provisions in the UPU Convention, terminal dues on mail imbalances, international postage rates, transit charges, improved statistics on mail exchanges, and international express mail service.[21]

The influence of the United States in the UPU came from its large role in international mail flows. Comparative statistics for West Germany and the US serve to illustrate how the US dominated international postal traffic even among the industrialized countries. In 1979 516.7 million items were posted from West Germany for abroad, and that country received 666.7 million from other countries. In contrast, the statistics for 1980 supplied by the US gave a figure of 963.7 million items posted abroad, in comparison to 700 million received.[22]

In most international organizations financial assessments for contributions to their budgets are based upon states' ability to pay (as reflected through their GNPs) or the extent of their activities in the areas served by the organization in question. In this manner, wealth and communicative prowess can in many instances perpetuate power in international communication.

However, it is important to point out that no one country makes a singularly large contribution to any one of the three communications regimes in the way the United States did at UNESCO before it withdrew membership in the early 1980s. At that time the US accounted for 25 per cent of the budget of UNESCO and each of a number of other specialized UN agencies. In contrast, at the ITU, WIPO and UPU it is a small elite of countries that collectively make identically large contributions to the budgets of those international organizations. In the ITU's budget for 1993 five countries – Russia, the US, Japan, Germany and France – provided 40 per cent of the 166 707 950 Swiss francs that members states paid to the organization.[23] That five, plus the UK, contributed 8.55 per cent of the total income of all the intellectual property rights agreements administered by the WIPO in 1991. The percentage was smaller for the WIPO because 71.5 per cent of the International Bureau's income in 1991 was generated from fees paid by private parties making applications for registration under three of the many treaties administered by the WIPO – the Patent Cooperation Treaty (PCT), and the Madrid and Hague Unions.[24] The WIPO also has one of the smallest budgets of any UN specialized agency, and it was also privileged from the point of view that it had a surplus budget. For the 1992–93 biennium its income was 216 million Swiss francs (US$151 million) and its expenditure was 188 million Swiss francs (US$131 million).[25]

Unlike other UN Specialized Agencies, the UPU did not have a fixed mandatory scale for making member states pay, but instead had a voluntary system. So at the turn of the 1970s, for example, no member state paid more than 4.8 per cent of the UPU's total budget, including the

United States, the world's largest and strongest economy. The developing nations pressured the Executive Council in 1972 into recommending to the 1974 Congress that the size of the maximum contribution category be doubled from 25 to 50 units. But the US and other major contributors successfully insisted that the UPU's system of assessment remain voluntary, so even though the maximum amount a country could pay was doubled no country was obliged to assume the new highest limit.

However, an achievement of sorts for the South at the 1984 Hamburg Congress was the decision to permit member states designated by the UN as least developed to pay a rate of one-half of one contribution unit. This move effectively raised the size of the United States' contribution. The US assessment for 1986 became 1092 million Swiss francs (about 5 per cent of the UPU budget), an increase of over 152 000 Swiss francs (over 16 per cent) on the assessment for the previous year.[26]

In the case of intellectual property rights, the least institutionalized of the three regimes, influence has come not so much with the financial ability to underwrite the WIPO's bureaucracy or dominate technical committees in it, but with greater production of intellectual property and more elaborate domestic laws and systems for the protection of such property. Overall the WIPO has encroached on national sovereignty the least because of the nature of the issue-area itself and the looseness of the regime's rules and decision-making procedures. The regime was weak not only from the point of view of its very liberal rules but also because it was not until relatively recently (1967) that the regime was given a mechanism of maintenance through the setting up of the World Intellectual Property Organization. This weakness is due largely to the nature of the issue-area. One could argue that, on a scale of priorities for states, the protection of intellectual property rights would rank below the maintenance of telecommunications and the international flow of mail. Indeed, the idea of protecting such rights would be actually moot if there was no means by which intellectual property could be communicated from state to state. Also, there were no binding reasons to cooperate around intellectual property that necessitated creation and maintenance of an international regime because states could protect such rights in separate bilateral agreements or by incorporating them into related legislation.

The shortcomings of all the WIPO treaties is best illustrated with the example of what a WIPO document says the Paris Convention permits:

> each State is free: to exclude from patentability inventions belonging to certain fields of technology; to decide whether patents should be granted with or without examination as to their novelty and other criteria of patentability; to fix the duration of patents; to decide whether the right

to a trademark may be acquired by use or registration; to decide whether registration of trademarks and industrial designs should be effected with or without examination to determine whether they conflict with existing registrations; to fix the duration of the protection of industrial designs; to fix all the details of procedure and administration.[27]

Strict compliance to the very extensive laws some states have for intellectual property rights, requiring compensation for patents and copyright, would mean a further flow of valuable foreign exchange from poor to rich states.[28] But as the value of world trade with high intellectual property content (such as pharmaceuticals, computer software and TV programmes) increased in the 1970s and 1980s, the weakness of the WIPO regime became more of a problem. Larger states, with the leverage to extract penalties in other areas of international relations in the event of non-compliance, were able to put this issue on the agenda of international politics. This was done multilaterally through the attempt to make protection of intellectual property rights a part of the GATT, and bilaterally through threats in the negotiation of trade or aid agreements, such as the United States' forcing Caribbean countries to abandon video piracy or face exclusion from the Caribbean Basin Initiative.[29]

What we have shown in this chapter is that the first stage in understanding the relationship between international power and international communication is in seeing how the rules of the game are determined. The vagaries of world history combined to create a situation where the functional international system of nation-states and international institutions was set up by a minority of states for the majority. Functionalism as an organizational ideology values order ahead of equality. This premise helps us to understand why the regimes for international communication have been essentially dominated by states with the wealth, technology and expertise. To this list of power resources we must add that influence in the process of rule-making also goes to the heaviest users or biggest actors in an issue-area.

The decision to not create multilateral regimes is as much a manifestation of a power dynamic as is the process of creating and maintaining them described in this chapter. In Chapter 3 we dissect the assumptions and political imperatives that have until recently made multilateral rule-making of other areas of international communication a taboo prospect at the United Nations and elsewhere. It is in the area of trade in cultural products and global news flows that ideological assumptions about the power of information have been most manifest. Telecommunications, postal policies and intellectual property rights have been considered 'technical' areas, less accessible to non-specialists, but cultural products and news have attracted the most controversy because everyone feels a vested stake in them.

NOTES

1. Stephen D. Krasner, 'Global Communications and National Power', *World Politics*, April 1991, p. 342.
2. A classic statement for functionalism is David Mitrany's *A Working Peace System: An Argument for the Functional Development of International Organization* (London: Royal Institute of International Affairs, 1943). Also see Harrop A. Freeman and Theodore Paullin, *Road to Peace: A Study in Functional International Organization* (Ithaca, New York: Pacific Research Bureau, 1947).
3. See Young Whan Kihl, 'A Study of Functionalism In International Organization', PhD dissertation, New York University, October 1963. Kihl's study is an extremely astute attempt to test functionalist assumptions by exploring the records of the ITU and UPU.
4. For example, writing in 1949, Martin Zober (in a work pregnant with unquestioned functionalist assumptions) asserted that

> The Universal Postal Union is a non-political organization which confines its discussions to technical matters; it is in the interest of all the countries of the world to join this organization to keep in contact with the rest of the world quickly and inexpensively. The broad flexibility of the organization, the sanctions against violators of the convention, the equal voting power of all the countries regardless of size, the settlement of disputes by arbitration, the democratic expressions of opinion permitted at the Congresses, the coordinating activity of the international bureau, the willingness of the countries of the world to accept common standards in money, rates, and weights, and the high ideals of the delegates to the congresses, are all ideals toward which other organizations may well aspire.

Martin Zober, 'The Universal Postal Union: A Case Study in International Organization', PhD dissertation, University of Pittsburgh, 1949, pp. 2–3.
5. David Mitrany, *A Working Peace System: An Argument for the Functional Development of International Organization* (London: Royal Institute of International Affairs, 1943), pp. 29–30, quoted in Young Whan Kihl, 'A Study of Functionalism In International Organization', PhD dissertation, New York University, October 1963, n. 33, p. 29.
6. Robert W. Cox and Harold K. Jacobson, 'The Framework for Inquiry', in Robert W. Cox and Harold K. Jacobson (eds), *The Anatomy of Influence* (New Haven: Yale University Press, 1974), pp. 22–3.

7.   Young Whan Kihl, 'A Study of Functionalism', pp. 214–15.
8.   Robert A. Kinn, 'United States Participation in the International Telecommunication Union: A Series of Interviews', *The Fletcher Forum*, Vol. 9, Winter 1985, p. 40.
9.   'US Warns Arabs on Postal Ouster of Israel', *The New York Times*, 15 June 1984.
10. 'Big business gears up for the war over inventions', *South*, November 1982, pp. 59–60.
11. Krasner's definition is

> sets of implicit or explicit principles, norms, rules, and decision-making procedures around which actors' expectations converge in a given area of international relations. Principles are beliefs of fact, causation, and rectitude. Norms are standards of behavior defined in terms of rights and obligations. Rules are specific prescriptions or proscriptions for action. Decision-making procedures are prevailing practices for making and implementing collective choice.

Stephen D. Krasner, *International Regimes* (Ithaca and London: Cornell University Press, 1983), p. 2.
12. The three major characteristics of complex interdependence are : (1) multiple channels (e.g. conferences and NGOs) and rapid communications connecting societies; (2) the absence of a clear hierarchy of issues on the international agenda; and (3) military force is no longer as effective as it once was as a means to an end. Due to these characteristics, the political processes of complex interdependence are very different from those of a world that approximates more closely the pure realist paradigm. For example, because military force is less effective the old strategy of linking military might to other issues as a means of reaching ends becomes obsolete in relationships of complex interdependence. Militarily weaker states become more able to pursue *linkage* of unrelated issues in order to achieve ends. International hierarchy will be reduced as a result of this increased ability of weak states to pursue linkage in this way and lost to powerful states of military force as an instrument of linkage. Also, international organizations play an increasingly significant role in the politics of complex interdependence because they provide forums for building alliances, mechanisms for agenda-setting and means of direct communication. Robert Keohane and Joseph Nye, *Power and Interdependence*, 2nd edn (Boston: Scott Foresman, 1989), Chapter 2.
13. See Peter F. Cowhey, 'The International Telecommunications Regime: The Political Roots of Regimes for High Technology', *International Organization*, Vol. 44, no. 2, Spring 1990, pp. 169–99.
14. See Robert W. Cox and Harold K. Jacobson (eds), *The Anatomy of Influence* (New Haven: Yale University Press, 1974). Studies that have criticized or built on the findings of *The Anatomy of Influence* include Cowhey (see note 13).; Janis Doran, 'Middle Powers and Technical Multilateralism: The International Telecommunication Union', Middle Powers in the International System No. 4 (Ottawa: North–South Institute, April 1989); and Clare Wells, *The UN, UNESCO and the Politics of Knowledge* (London: Macmillan, 1987).
15. See International Telecommunication Union, *An Overview: The International Telecommunication Union* (Geneva: ITU Press and Public

Relations, March 1993); Gabriel Warren, 'ITU Takes a Promising "First Step" ', *Transnational Data and Communications Report*, March/April 1993, pp. 15–18; 'ITU Plenipotentiaries agree on a new ITU', *Telecommunication Journal*, Vol. 6, no. 2, 1993, pp. 55–62; High Level Committee to Review the Structure and Functioning of the International Telecommunication Union, *Tomorrow's ITU: The Challenge of Change* (Geneva: ITU, April 1991).

16.   For example, at the American Regional Telecommunication Development Conference in Acapulco (31 March–4 April 1992), Deoraj Ramnarine of the Caribbean Telecommunications Union quoted information from the ITU indicating that the Union's development activities dated back to the 1950s and US $1000 million had been spent on such efforts since then. He contrasted that with the admission by the chair of the HLC the telecommunications requirements of developing countries were immense. Ramnarine said all that money and time did not succeed in closing the gap because the smaller, poorer countries were not adequately represented in the decision-making bodies at the ITU. American Regional Telecommunication Development Conference (AM-RDC), Final Report, Vol. I (Geneva: ITU, May 1992), p. 66.

17.   See High Level Committee to Review the Structure and Functioning of the International Telecommunication Union, *Tomorrow's ITU: The Challenge of Change* (Geneva: ITU, April 1991), Chapter VI, 'Improved Management of the Union', pp. 41–9.

18.   Krasner identified five factors – 'causal variables' – that account for why states form regimes:

(1) *Egoistic self-interest.* This is of two varieties. (a) States are willing to form regimes if they are in a prisoner's dilemma – they have no other choice – as is especially the case with the provision of public goods. (b) Regimes are formed to further self-interest because they facilitate the flow of information and this allows more precise calculations of other actors' behaviour.

(2) *Political power.* Regimes are formed by the powerful to: (a) further the good of the system on the whole; or (b) to achieve the ends of one or more specific actors.

(3) *Norms and principles.* Based on the work of sociologists (e.g. Weber) and Marxists who conceive of a 'superstructure' that shapes human actions, Krasner notes that history, religion, and modes of production have provided certain norms and principles that make phenomena such as regimes natural courses of action. An example is the principle of sovereignty:

> Those areas where sovereignty is not applied are governed by vulnerable regimes or lack of regimes altogether. Sovereignty designates states as the only actors with unlimited rights to act in the international system. Assertions by other agencies are subject to challenge. If the constitutive principle of sovereignty were altered, it is difficult to imagine that any other international regime would remain unchallenged.

(These two last factors do not account for regime formation on their own, but are supplemental to those factors mentioned above.)

(4) *Usage and custom.* 'A pattern of behavior initially established by economic coercion or force may come to be regarded as legitimate by those on whom it has been imposed. Usage leads to shared expectations, which

38   *International Power and International Communication*

become infused with principles and norms.' For example, much of Western commercial law and the English common law is based on usage and custom. (5) *Knowledge*. This is not just any kind of knowledge, but the knowledge gained from social or 'pure' science that tells more about the human experience and fosters a degree of prediction. 'For knowledge to have an independent impact in the international system, it must be widely accepted by policy makers.' The international monetary system provides a good example of how knowledge and agreement on it can cause the formation of a regime and the reform of it. Drawing on the work of Benjamin Cohen, Krasner notes that

> the fixed exchange rate system agreed to at Bretton Woods was based upon understandings derived from the interwar experience and then-current knowledge about domestic monetary institutions and structures. States were extremely sensitive to competitive devaluation and were not confident that domestic monetary policy could provide insulation from external disturbances. It was much easier to accept a floating exchange rate regime in the 1970s because the knowledge and related institutional capacity for controlling monetary aggregates had substantially increased.

Stephen Krasner, 'Structural Causes and Regime Consequences: Regimes as Intervening Variables', *International Regimes* (Ithaca: Cornell University Press, 1983), pp. 1–21.

19.   Harold K. Jacobson, 'ITU: A Potpourri of Bureaucrats and Industrialists', in Robert W. Cox and Harold K. Jacobson (eds), *The Anatomy of Influence* (New Haven: Yale University Press, 1974), p. 74.
20.   Ibid., pp. 67–74.
21.   US Dept of State, *United States Participation in the UN: Report by the President to Congress for the Year 1984* (Washington, DC: Government Printing Office, 1985), p. 269.
22.   Universal Postal Union, *Memorandum on the Role of the Post as a Factor in Economic, Social and Cultural Development* (Berne: UPU, 1982), pp. 22–3.
23.   International Telecommunication Union, *An Overview: The International Telecommunication Union* (Geneva: ITU Press and Public Relations, March 1993), pp. 27–9.
24.   Arpad Bogsch, *Brief History of the First 25 Years of the World Intellectual Property Organization* (Geneva: WIPO), p. 95.
25.   Ibid., p. 76.
26.   US Dept of State, *United States Participation in the UN: Report by the President to Congress for the Year 1985* (Washington, DC: Government Printing Office, 1986).
27.   World Intellectual Property Organization, *WIPO: General Information* (Geneva: WIPO, 1990), p. 22.
28.   For a discussion of this problem in relation to the international music industry, see Roger Wallis and Krister Malm, *Big Sounds from Small Peoples: The Music Industry in Small Countries* (New York: Pendragon Press, 1984), p. 71.
29.   Aggrey Brown, 'Mass Media In Jamaica', in *Mass Media and the Caribbean*, ed. Stuart Surlin and Walter Soderlund (Philadelphia: Gordon and Breach, 1990), p. 19.

3 International Trade in Cultural Products

Although the three global institutions – the ITU, WIPO and UPU – have been the arena for the exercise of power by elite states through laying down the fundamental rules of international communication, the most prominent debates about international power through communication have been in those areas where multilateral institutions have been non-existent and where state sovereignty appears to be least threatened by supranational organizations. These sectors are global news flows, and trade in cultural products: movies, TV shows, books and periodicals, recorded music (phonograms) and international advertising. Here we must revisit the distinction we made in the first chapter between the power of communication and the power of information. News and cultural products can be relayed internationally via shortwave radio and satellite TV, but the power of these forms of communication appeared as an issue in the debates over international telecommunications at the ITU and the UN General Assembly during the 1970s and 1980s. In contrast, the controversies over imbalances in global flows of news and cultural products were also arguments about the power of information, that, of course, related to policies for shortwave and satellite communication, but were also separate questions as well.

UNESCO

The post-Second World War international system was founded on the notion that certain types of information are very powerful in the maintenance of the desired peaceful international system. And just as the UPU and ITU were established as the functional institutions for regulating international mails and telecommunications (respectively) along certain principles, the United Nations Educational, Scientific and Cultural Organization (UNESCO) was created as the functional organization to help the spread of these worthy ideas by encouraging states to cooperate in the fields of education, science, culture and communication.

The Conference of Allied Ministers of Education set up UNESCO, the constitution for which was signed in London on 16 November 1945. Article I(1) of UNESCO's constitution said its purpose was to foster peace and security by promoting collaboration among the nations through education, science and culture in order to further universal respect for justice, for the rule of law and for the human rights and fundamental freedoms which are affirmed for the peoples of the world, without distinction of race, sex, language or religion by the Charter of the United Nations.

Article I(2) listed the three main functions of UNESCO:

(a) Collaborate in the work of advancing the mutual knowledge and understanding of peoples, through all means of mass communication and to that end recommend such international agreements as may be necessary to promote the free flow of ideas by word and image;

(b) Give fresh impulse to popular education and to the spread of culture;

by collaborating with Members, at their request, in the development of educational activities;

by instituting collaboration among the nations to advance the ideal of equality of educational opportunity without regard to race, sex or any distinctions, economic or social;

by suggesting educational methods best suited to prepare the children of the world for the responsibilities of freedom;

(c) Maintain, increase and diffuse knowledge;

by assuring the conservation and protection of the world's inheritance of books, works of art and monuments of history and science, and recommending to the nations concerned the necessary international conventions;

by encouraging co-operation among the nations in all branches of intellectual activity, including the international exchange of persons active in the fields of education, science and culture and exchange of publications, objects of artistic and scientific interest and other materials of information;

by initiating methods of international co-operation calculated to give the people of all countries access to the printed and published materials produced by any of them.

Careful attention to the assumptions about the power of information that underlay the new world order in the 1940s is crucial in understanding the historical and intellectual context of the general *laissez-faire* situation related to global flows of news and cultural products. The very fact that these assumptions prevailed was in itself a reflection of a power dynamic at work, and this point was separate from the idea that the Free Flow of information doctrine that these assumptions buttressed allowed the imbalance in global flows of news and cultural products.

IDEAS OF POWER / THE POWER OF IDEAS

Freedom of information (the ability to hold and impart ideas), liberal democracy and notions of racial and gender equality, ideas very prominent in the preamble to UNESCO's constitution, were a reflection of the values that the Allied powers wanted to infuse into the new international system. They were not necessarily the values of the majority of the world's states that were not present at the postwar negotiating tables. So the constitution of UNESCO is essentially a manifestation of an attempt at universalism by the victorious powers. No matter how worthy the ideals appear, despite their cultural relativism, the Allied powers were nonetheless hypocritical, because these ideals did not often inform their behaviour. For example, the British and French in 1945 still had extensive colonies where censorship and racial discrimination were a way of life, and the United States, although it did not have as many colonies, maintained a domestic system of racial apartheid in which African-Americans were effectively disenfranchised and kept in the status of economic backwardness through the denial of many civil rights, such as equality of opportunity in education and employment. This major contradiction was in itself a recipe for the conflict over ideas that did occur within UNESCO and in other parts of the UN system in later years, as the membership of the UN expanded and those new members, many of them former colonies, took issue with the policies of the founding members and rebelled against the doctrine of 'Free Flow'.[1]

That 'free flow of ideas by word and image', laid down in Article I of UNESCO's constitution, was the principle that partly explains why the international regulation of global news flows and trade in cultural products was such an anathema in the post-Second World War order. According to Wells[2] the components of the doctrine were:

(a) belief in the idea that a multiplicity of independent media is one of the best guarantees of freedom;
(b) abhorrence of state control of the media on the grounds that it is one of the worst evils, even more undemocratic than concentration of media ownership in the hands of a few entrepreneurs;
(c) faith in the self-regulation of the media by media professionals, instead of external forces, especially governments;
(d) belief in the right of journalists to enjoy free movement and access to a variety of sources;
(e) faith in the view that the free market in information is in itself a barrier to imperialism of various kinds because it permits people to exercise free choice; and

(f) staunch support for the general maintenance of a free flow of information within and between states, free from regulation.

In addition to being a justification for the nurturing of democracy in civil society, the Free Flow doctrine was an intellectual response to the problem of maintaining the post-Second World War peace. The free flow of information among nations would serve to eliminate misunderstandings among men that were perceived to be at the heart of international conflict. Wells explained:

> Western spokesmen have worked from the position that, in the words of Clement Attlee as enshrined in UNESCO's constitution, 'wars begin in the minds of men.' More specifically, war was held by Western Allied leaders and by Western executive heads of the UN and UNESCO in the mid 1940s to result at least in part from lack of mutual knowledge and understanding between peoples which, in turn, was held to result to a large extent from manipulation of information flows by the State both domestically and across national borders. Peace, understanding and freedom of information from State control, nationally and internationally have thus traditionally been treated as interdependent principles. Indeed, the assumption of interdependence has tended to be reflected in a focus on the latter goal in which the primary end of peace, not explicitly recalled, has tended to become somewhat lost from sight.[3]

The UN Charter contained no explicit reference to freedom of information; however, Article 19 of the Universal Declaration of Human Rights (1948) asserted that

> Everyone has the right to freedom of opinion and expression; this includes freedom to hold opinions without interference and to seek, receive and impart information and ideas through any media regardless of frontiers.[4]

So important was Free Flow to the UN (as it was then composed) that it convened a Conference on Freedom of Information in the spring of 1948 in Geneva which attracted representatives from 54 states and lasted for a month. The Final Act of the Conference resolved:

> That everyone shall have the right of freedom of thought and expression; this shall include freedom to hold opinions without interference; and to seek, receive and impart information and ideas by any means and regardless of frontiers;
> That the right of news personnel to have the widest possible access to the sources of information, to travel unhampered in pursuit thereof, and

to transmit copy without unreasonable or discriminatory limitation, should be guaranteed by action on the national and international plane;[5]

It also said that governments had a responsibility to stem abuses of freedom of information by encouraging diversity of sources, and the Press had a 'moral obligation' to report facts and the truth.

LIBERAL-DEMOCRATIC AND LIBERAL TRADE THEORIES

These assumptions about the place of communication in peaceful international relations are rooted in (a) liberal-democratic political theory, and (b) liberal trade theory. These distinct origins have become so blurred over time that advocates of international press freedom, the Free Flow doctrine, and the benignity of the 'information age' have often not been able to tell the difference. Also, it has been easy to confuse these two distinct streams of thought because they are not the products of radically different political ideologies. The North American and European states that designed the new world order in the 1940s became defensive when the Free Flow doctrine was attacked because the doctrine was a manifestation of, on the one hand, a passionate belief in the principles of liberal democracy, and, on the other, ideas about liberal free trade. The imperatives of liberal democracy and liberal free trade largely explain why institutionalized regulation of international news and cultural industries has been taboo in the post-Second World War order. Another important explanatory factor is the fear many governments have about the potential power of the information relayed by news and cultural products. They are viewed as potential threats to religious and other cultural values, and to surrender national sovereignty in rule-making to supranational organizations in these fields has been seen as an affront to national identity itself. So it was only when international broadcasting by satellites, especially, made national borders permeable and other new technologies made piracy of cultural products a trade issue that there were some negotiations (at the Uruguay Round of the GATT) about creating international regimes governing trade in cultural products.

Although Wells[6] claims the 'liberal model of democracy', which assigns a critical role to the press, was 'classically expounded' by J.S. Mill in *On Liberty*, the Western liberal-democratic assumptions about the press pre-date Mill by over 200 years and are discussed in greater detail in John Milton's *Areopagitica* of 1644. Indeed, when Mill wrote *On Liberty* in 1859 he refused to discuss press freedom on the grounds that he felt these assumptions were so widely held that '[t]his aspect of the question,

besides, has been so often and so triumphantly enforced by preceding writers, that it needs not be specially insisted on in this place.'[7] Milton was perhaps the most celebrated of those 'preceding writers' who 'triumphantly' argued the case for press freedom. His *Areopagitica*, a speech, was a passionate plea for an end to the censorship caused by the Order of Parliament of 1643. The Order made it illegal to set up a printing press or publish anything without a licence from the government. The authorities were also given the power to destroy unlicensed presses, confiscate illegal literature and arrest violators of the law.

Milton gave a number of reasons why licensing and censorship were counter-productive. For example, objective truth is that which is tested by contrary points of view; in becoming the final judge on whom should be censored the government was assuming infallibility; and a censored populace might not be as enthusiastic to defend their government in times of foreign attack.[8]

While Milton was dealing specifically with licensing and censorship, Mill wrote about issues wider than, but including, the question of press freedom. In his introduction to *On Liberty* Mill noted how rulers had been viewed as having interests opposed to those of the masses and, as a result, societies sought protection through either the proclamation of rights or constitutional checks. But the era of representative government had revealed that there was the need for protection against another type of tyranny – tyranny of the majority. Based on this premise, Mill argued that there were three types of personal liberty: to hold ideas; to impart ideas to others; and to join with other individuals for various causes. An individual should be allowed to enjoy these freedoms to the fullest as long as no other members of society were harmed as a result. Mill concluded his argument by noting that the 'doctrine' of his essay was composed of two maxims: 'the individual is not accountable to society for his actions, in so far as these concern the interests of no person but himself'; and 'that for such actions that are prejudicial to the interests of others, the individual is accountable, and may be subjected either to social or legal punishment, if society is of opinion that the one or the other is requisite for its protection.'[9]

The body of notions about personal freedom and the role of social institutions (including the press) based on these ideas of Mill have come to be called liberal-democratic theory.[10] Under the theory democracy is seen as self-government through reasoned choice, whereby minority views have the potential of becoming those of the majority through rational persuasion. Prescription by autocracy is considered to be unhealthy. A cornerstone of this democratic theory is the quest for truth which is achieved by the competition of facts and ideas in a free market-

place; the continuing entry of new ideas and facts; freedom of each individual or interest to express their point of view; the tolerance of bias and eccentricity; and consideration of minority views. The theory, therefore, allows a central role for the press in the quest for truth. The three major functions of the press that can be identified under the theory are: (a) a channel for information; (b) a watchdog on government to stem the abuse of power; and (c) a conduit for the two-way flow of views between citizens and the State.

Although a major difference between domestic and international society is that international society has no central government, believers in liberal-democratic theory have found its assumptions about the liberating force of free communication also relevant in the analysis of international relations. New communications technologies, especially satellite TV, were seen as serving the same purpose in international politics as they do at the domestic level. Tyrannical behaviour can be exposed, dissident opinions can be aired, public opinion can be relayed back to governments (if only by the unscientific means of mass demonstrations). Over 40 years after UNESCO's founding, world events were illustrating this view even better, such as Cable News Network's (CNN) live broadcasts in 1989 of the student protests in China, and its live coverage of Boris Yeltsin's resistance to the attempted coup in the Soviet Union in 1991.

Since 1945 there has been conceptual fuzziness in discussions of the role of communication in international relations partly because liberal-democratic assumptions have been used to justify the doctrine of Free Flow even though upon closer examination it will be found that Free Flow is deeply rooted in liberal trade theory.[11]

The Free Flow doctrine was proposed for two major reasons. First, faced with the task of establishing and maintaining liberal democracy in the defeated states, the North Atlantic Alliance felt that an international order infused with liberal-democratic ideals about the role of communication and media was part of the solution. Second, notions about increased contacts between peoples being one of the best antidotes against war – ideas at the cornerstone of liberal trade theory – were seen as a vital ingredient to the new order if the peace was to be maintained. In other words, it is directly related to the view of liberal political economists that free trade lessens the likelihood of international conflict.[12]

War was viewed as resulting from lack of mutual knowledge and understanding between peoples which, in turn, was caused by manipulation of information flows by the states both domestically and across national borders.[13] So Free Flow would not only be essential to establishing democracy, but also to maintaining peaceful international relations. These

assumptions were apparently well-founded, as scholarship over the past 30 years has demonstrated. It has been found that democracies (carefully defined) hardly ever go to war with each other.[14] However, the spread of democracy is not necessarily the only precondition for international peace, because the same literature has not proven that a peaceful international system must, of necessity be composed of democracies.

It is important to recognize the roots of the Free Flow doctrine in liberal trade theory because from the time the US fought to have it enshrined in the postwar international order the Americans were well aware of the economic gains they would make if such a principle was made inviolable. The United States enjoyed comparative and competitive advantages in the international media industries and the markets of American companies in these fields would be protected and allowed to expand under the umbrella of Free Flow.[15] Schiller has reproduced a telling quote from William Benton, then Assistant Secretary of State, who gave the assurance in a State Department broadcast in 1946, that the State Department would

> do everything within its power along political and diplomatic lines to help break down the artificial barriers to the expansion of private American news agencies, magazines, motion pictures, and other media of communications throughout the world .... Freedom of the press – and freedom of exchange of information generally – is an integral part of our foreign policy.[16]

It does appear that the US stayed true to Benton's promise at the 1948 UN Conference on Freedom of Information. *The Economist* of 1 May 1948, reporting on the UN Conference on Freedom of Information, indicated that US advocacy of Free Flow was from the start linked to market imperatives, at the expense of the concerns of European and, in particular, developing nations. The magazine said most delegations got the impression that the Americans were seeking 'freedom of the market' for their news agencies and regarded freedom of information as an extension of the (then proposed) Charter of the International Trade Organization.[17]

GLOBAL CULTURAL INDUSTRIES

While the foreign policies of governments have shaped the environment for international exchanges of cultural products, the creation and distribution of such items on a worldwide scale have been the domain of large transnational corporations. Following the invention of such key technologies as still and moving photography, phonographs and radio in the late nineteenth and

early twentieth centuries, cultural industries gradually grew in size and economic significance to the point where, by the end of the 1980s, they were largely the domain of big companies, all based in either Japan, the United States or Western Europe, producing products for the entire world.

While most feature films were being made in Asia by the end of the 1980s, the most films traded internationally were made in the United States, and American film production was in turn dominated by seven major studios – Twentieth Century-Fox, Warner, Universal, Disney, Columbia, MGM and Paramount. By the end of the 1980s those seven studios made 85 per cent of the feature films exhibited in the States.[18] Meanwhile, the international market became more important to the financial well-being of those corporations. US theatrical distribution accounted for 75 per cent of their total revenues in 1979, but fell to 35 per cent by 1989 when the remaining revenues were coming from videocassette sales, cable TV, TV reruns, and foreign distribution.[19] With a product appealing to audiences around the world and supplied to foreign cinemas at a fraction of the cost of what it would take to produce films locally, American films were being blamed for the annihilation of film industries in some countries (such as Britain) and stunting the growth of such industries in other countries. For example, American films had a 95 per cent share of the British market and a two-thirds of the French by 1992.[20]

The imbalances in the movie trade were mirrored by those in trade in TV programmes. Many states introduced TV before being able to supply the shows, therefore, from early in the spread of TV worldwide, states with relatively large domestic production (such as the United States, Britain, France and Germany) have been the suppliers to many viewers around the world. This scenario became even more acute by the end of the 1980s when international satellite TV networks (e.g. CNN, MTV and BBC World Service TV) were circumventing national stations, relaying live not only the entertainment programmes that previously needed to be imported on film or videocassette, but also news and advertising. Even political leaders in countries with relatively large domestic TV production industries were complaining against the preponderance of American TV shows. According to President Mitterrand of France, European programmes accounted for only 20 000 hours of the estimated 125 000 shown annually on European TV.[21] The 'Television without Frontiers' directive of October 1989 set quotas on the amounts of foreign shows on West European TV during certain hours of the day, prompting the US to complain that the restriction contravened free trade and was as a result violating GATT rules.[22] The success of Latin American productions, especially the *telenovelas*, in penetrating foreign markets has been pointed to by

some as an example of the potential of other players to break the monopolies of American productions and make a lie of the argument that global TV is merely a reflection of cultural imperialism at work. But other observers have complained that diversity of sources does not necessarily mean diversity of approaches to production techniques and formats. In many cases the *telenovelas* and films made in other countries are merely different variations of the popular American soap operas or detective dramas, formats that have proven so successful around the world.[23]

The international music industry by the early 1990s was controlled by the so-called Big Six corporations, only one of them – Warner – American-controlled. RCA was owned by Bertelsmann of Germany, Polygram by Phillips of Holland, MCA by Matsushita of Japan, CBS Records by Sony of Japan, and Thorn-EMI was based in Britain. World production of gramophone records rose from 447 million in 1965 to 667 million in 1970, and to 963 million in 1976. The MacBride Report estimated in 1980, based on UN statistics, that two billion records and tapes were being sold annually, 85 per cent of them in North America and Europe.[24] But even though most recorded music sales were in North America and Europe, the large corporations still tended to dominate the phonogram industries in most other regions.[25]

The implications of such monopoly control in the music industry are great. The record producers catered to their largest markets in Western Europe and the United States, making it very difficult for artists from the South to be recorded and gain international exposure. A Swedish report noted that the companies concentrated on 'a few types of music, in particular "super hits" in pop music, Western art music, and disco music'.[26] However, the international music industry – with artists such as Bob Marley of Jamaica, the Bee Gees of Australia, and Miriam Makeba of South Africa – could still boast a more multicultural, multiracial and multinational array of stars than the film industry.

In advertising, while global agencies had become transnational corporations by the early 1990s they owed their growth to the existence of the transnational corporations that grew rapidly in number after the Second World War and which needed to advertise their products around the world. By 1990 the top 10 agencies worldwide – including WPP Group, Saatchi & Saatchi, Dentsu, and Young & Rubicam – were grossing $12.2 billion. Although the agencies had to abide by whatever laws were in force in each country where they had a presence, the content of international advertising is mainly determined by decision-makers at the headquarters of the international advertising agencies, a scenario that adds to the controversial notion that the structure of international communication is vertical –

conveying foreign images and ideas from the North to control the spending habits, popular culture and even self-perceptions of consumers in the South. But there was a trend in favour of more regulation in the 1970s and early 1980s and this was centred not in the South but in the advanced market economies, spurred by the consumer movement and suspicion of corporate advertisers. A variety of regulations have been in place to guard against problems as diverse as sexism, untruth, bad taste and even the introduction of foreign words to the native culture.[27]

The publishing industry (newspapers, magazines and books) was often the foundation on which many transnational corporations in film and other areas of entertainment built their power. Most of the world's books and other periodicals are produced in North America and Europe, even though there are significantly large publishing sectors in Asia, especially India. In 1970 over 75 per cent of the world's books (expressed in number of titles) were published in North America, Europe and the USSR. By 1987 this situation had changed only slightly, with those regions accounting for 67 per cent of book production. However, in 1987 those countries categorised by the UN as 'Developed' still produced nearly three-quarters of the world's titles (see Table 3.1). In most parts of the South readerships are small due to high rates of illiteracy and many countries are almost completely dependent on North America and Europe for educational books. The world's largest publishers are: Time-Warner (USA); Bertelsmann (Germany); Hachette (France); and News Corporation (Australia). A fifth major player was Maxwell Communications of Britain, but that empire collapsed in 1991 following the death of Robert Maxwell.

SUPRANATIONAL POLICY-MAKING

Table 3.2 is a description of the scenarios in the global flows of news and cultural products in terms of the criteria that make international regimes – principles, norms, rules and decision-making procedures. The table should be compared to Table 2.1 that describes the situations in those sectors of international communication where institutionalization is more developed. International cooperation on press freedom and news has been so ideologically charged and complex that it demands separate treatment in Chapter . However, in this chapter, it is important to examine the features common to all these sectors, including news.

Although there are no international organizations with the large briefs, or even the authority, of the ITU, UPU and WIPO in these sectors, the imperatives of commerce produced by industrialization and 'massification' in

Table 3.1 Distribution of TV, radio and books – 'developed' and 'developing' countries compared (1970 and 1990)

(Figures for 1970 are in brackets)

	Developed countries	Developing countries
Percentage distribution of population	(38.5) 23.1	(61.5) 76.9
Number of regular television transmitters*	(16 900) 74 000	(800) 13 810
Number of television receivers per 1000 inhabitants	(259) 492	(10) 55
Number of radio broadcasting transmitters*	(16 200) 25 850	(5 900) 12 000
Number of radio broadcasting receivers per 1000 inhabitants	(617) 1 023	(46) 176
Percentage distribution of book production	(86.6) 71.3	(13.4) 28.7

Figures are for 1987, the most recent year available.

Source: United Nations Educational, Scientific and Cultural Organisation. *Statistical Yearbook 1993* (Paris: UNESCO, 1993).

these five areas have created some norms and provided minor roles for some international organizations. Industrialization refers to use of these sectors to generate commercial profit. Massification is industrialization on a very large-scale basis, producing advertising, films, records and other cultural products for mass audiences.

Various fears in different countries about the subverting of indigenous cultures by these trends produced a scenario where the norms that developed actually served to undermine any move towards a genuine Free Flow principle that might have occurred. Therefore, Canadian legislation fixed 50 per cent as the minimum amount of Canadian-produced programmes Canada's TV stations had to air in prime time, and no international organization existed with the authority to prevent the Canadian government from taking the action on the grounds that it violated the Free Flow principle and was an unfair quota against exporters of TV programmes to Canada.[28] Similarly, advertising agencies wishing to film advertisements for broadcast in the US are required to get permission from actors' unions if no American actors are used, and contracts with the Screen Actors' Guild and the American Federation of Television and Radio Artists contain clauses against use of foreign actors unless absolutely necessary.[29] This is just one of a plethora of restrictions on the free flow of international advertising imposed by states in the name of protecting their economies, culture and workers.

In addition to the state, market practices have also shaped the norms in these areas. For example, to foster standardization in the international book and periodical markets, International Standard Book Numbering (ISBN) and International Standard Serial Numbering (ISSN) were introduced in the late 1960s and early 1970s through the International Organization for Standardization (ISO). Because each book or periodical has its own unique, internationally registered number, publishers, distributors, wholesalers, bookstores and libraries could use the codes to make more efficient operations such as fulfilling orders, electronic point-of-sale checkout, inventory control, processing returns, circulation/location control, file maintenance, library union lists and royalty payments.

Another example of a norm shaped by market practices is music licensing. After the passage of copyright legislation and rules (domestically and internationally) societies were established to be the clearing houses for royalties to musicians. For example, in the US the American Society of Composers, Authors, and Publishers (ASCAP) was formed in 1914 to enforce the performance-rights clause of the 1909 copyright law. ASCAP soon became one of the most powerful players in the US music industry by virtue of its monopoly as a mediator between composers and music publishers on the one hand and consumers on the other. Ryan has documented how this monopoly initially caused the exclusion from protection of certain musical genres thought to be inferior by ASCAP officials, such as Black and Country music.[30] Inroads into these prejudices were made when ASCAP's monopoly was broken by a competing society, Broadcast Music Incorporated (BMI). The equivalent of ASCAP in Britain was the Performing Rights Society (PRS). The norm of music societies spread from Europe and North America to other countries in alignment with international political relations. For example, Wallis and Malm have noted how branches of the PRS were set up in British colonies and remained even after independence.[31] However, this norm in relation to copyright had little or no effect on composers and performers in developing nations. For example, Harry Belafonte has acknowledged that the Caribbean songs he recorded, and from which he made millions, were in many cases the compositions of Jamaican, Trinidadian and Barbadian artists who were

Table 3.2 Nonregimes in international communication

	News	Advertising	Books and Periodicals	Films and TV Progs	Music
Principles	• National sovereignty guides international exchanges in these sectors.				
Norms	• Local and national media get international news from their own correspondents sent or posted abroad or from regional or international wire services. The five largest international wire services are AP, UPI, Reuters AFP and ITAR-TASS. All correspondents must obey the national laws of the countries from which they report.	• Determined by market practices in each country.	• ISBN and ISSN numbers approved by the international Organization for Standardization, give each book and periodical a separate identity. • Books are imported and sold according to the market practices in each country.	• Private entrepreneurs pay fees for the right to exhibit these. Use without paying is considered piracy by owners of copyright.	• Imported and sold according to the market practices of each country.

Table 3.2 Continued

	News	Advertising	Books and Periodicals	Films and TV Progs.	Music
Rules and-Decision-Making	• No international organization regulates the flow of international news. International press groupings, professional journalists' groups, the Red Cross and UNESCO have at various times established declarations of principles, norms, rules and decision-making procedures (e.g. UNESCO's Mass Media Declaration of 1978) but none has been binding.	• No international organization regulates international advertising. The industry must conform to the regulations of the state where it operates.	• No international organization regulates trade in books and periodicals *per se*, but the WIPO regime is meant to protect the intellectual property of authors, and the UPU's rates for printed matter impact on the viability of publishers. • Large book publishers use their economic clout to shape the character of the international market through the fees they offer writers, the types of books *(continued overleaf)*	• No international organization regulates trade in movies and TV programmes, but the US is the *de facto* hegemon through its dominance of the international market and the status the Oscars have as marks of excellence in international film. • The Motion Picture Producers Association of America lobbies for international trade practices favourable to US exporters, supported by the economic clout of the US.	• No international organization regulates trade in music cassettes, records and CDs, but the WIPO regime is meant to protect the intellectual property rights of performers.

Table 3.2 Continued

News	Advertising	Books and Periodicals	Films and TV Progs	Music
		they choose to publish, etc.	• The WIPO regime is meant to protect the intellectual property rights of film-makers.	

The US has found the WIPO regime inadequate in these areas and in 1986 started the effort, under the Uruguay Round, to put trade in intellectual property and services under the GATT. The GATT regime provides means for retaliation against international piracy in these and other areas (such as computer software). The major exporters in these areas are more concerned with strengthening *economic* rights rather than *cultural* rights, which are more the concern of countries that have a negative trade balance in the areas of books, periodicals, movies, TV programmes and recorded music.

never compensated or had sold their rights for pittances many years before he made their songs popular.[32]

The above example illustrates that prevailing norms in the international music industry have not necessarily been just. Norms lack the binding quality of rules. But no supranational rules exist to protect compositions (especially in poor countries) from piracy by foreign artists and companies, to prevent foreign entrepreneurs from undermining the TV production industries in other countries by unloading an abundance of relatively cheap programmes on those markets, or to even foster 'free flow' by preventing restrictions on the import of books and periodicals. Before the states of the South began to call for the existence of rules (with the main aim of protecting cultural sovereignty), it was the trade groups that lobbied for improvements in this area but with the aim of fostering *economic* rights.

Concerned about the damages to competition in the international music industry caused by high import tariffs, the International Federation of Producers of Phonograms and Videograms (IFPI) launched a campaign in 1972 to have UNESCO classify phonograms as 'cultural materials' on par with books. If such a status was accepted multilaterally the music industry could demand duty-free importation. The 1976 UNESCO General Conference did finally declare phonograms cultural materials. But the shortcomings of not having a binding international regime were evident in 1980 when an official of Polygram Records, dissatisfied with the slow pace of change, reasoned that it was 'unacceptable that pornographic books are treated as "culture" in many countries just because they are printed, and are consequently tax exempted or low-taxed, while a Beethoven symphony on records is taxed at luxury rates'.[33]

By the end of the 1980s the American entertainment industry was spending $6 billion a year domestically on the production of films, television programmes and prerecorded videocassettes, and on advertising in the US. The return in revenues from media use worldwide was estimated at $16 billion.[34] However, the revenues lost to illegal taping of videocassettes has been estimated by the industry to be several hundred million dollars annually. In 1990 estimated losses to American video producers due to illegal copying in France and Germany alone was estimated to be about $45 million.[35]

Likewise, in a study of international barriers done for the International Advertising Association (IAA) – the trade group representing advertising agencies – Boddewyn has noted that

Countries, like companies, lose millions of dollars when trade and investment in advertising are restricted by protectionist regulations.

Thus, Phillips, the Dutch multinational, estimates that it is wasting $1 million a year reshooting commercials that are not acceptable in such countries as Australia, Malaysia, and Venezuela.[36]

It is interesting that the IAA argued for a free flow with language ident ical to what might be voiced by diplomats , such as the following:

> One should be aware that such restrictions also threaten freedom of expression and access to foreign media guaranteed in such accords as the Universal Declaration of Human Rights, the Helsinki Protocols and the European Convention on Human Rights.[37]

By the mid-1980s these disparate concerns of the trade groups would crystallize into a campaign to bring these, what might be called, 'nonregime' areas under the world liberal trade regime – the GATT. But by making the service industries (including advertising) and piracy of films, books and other cultural products a trade issue, the United States was seeking to protect its economic rights, not *cultural* rights as was a major plank of the proposed NWICO. By the mid-1980s many industrialized countries (especially the US) were firmly in the post-industrial age and the nonregime areas were so significant to their economies, and their trade groups such effective lobby-ists, that it became clear that binding rules were needed to protect their markets. Gadbaw and Richards have explained the crucial nature of the campaign to the North by noting that US companies were estimated in 1986 to lose $25 billion annually because of piracy – 15 per cent of the US trade deficit.[38] An increasing proportion of world trade was taken up by goods utilizing intellectual property. For example, Gadbaw and Richards identify chemicals, books, electrical machinery and computers as goods with high intellectual property components. In 1947 (the year the GATT started) these goods (minus the then-absent computer industry) combined for 9.9 per cent of US exports. In 1986 (when the Uruguay Round started) all four areas were worth a total of 27.4 per cent of US exports.[39]

The WIPO regime had proven inadequate for protecting business interests in the cultural industries. In the US trade groups set up the International Intellectual Property Alliance in 1984 to lobby for better bilateral and multi-lateral procedures to protect American copyrighted works internationally. The members were: the Association of American Publishers (AAP); the American Film Marketing Association (AFMA); the Computer Software and Services Industry Association (ADAPSO); the Computer and Business Equipment Manufacturers' Association (CBEMA); the Motion Picture Association of America (MPAA); the National Music Publishers' Association (NMPA); and the Recording Industry Association of America

(RIAA). The members of the Alliance were said to represent 'more than 1,600 US companies accounting for over 5 percent of US GNP'.[40]

But the WIPO rules would not be abandoned entirely; instead they would be incorporated in the 'minimum standards' of intellectual property protection the Western states sought to be made part of the GATT's rules. The concept of nullification or impairment embodied in Article XXIII of the GATT would provide the link between the GATT and WIPO regimes. According to Gadbaw and Richards,

> The framework of the GATT agreement was built around the premise that the only legitimate commercial policy tool to regulate international trade was the tariff, and that tariffs would be subject to negotiation over time. If a country used a measure that was proscribed by the GATT, the country whose trade was thereby injured could claim that benefits to which it was entitled had been nullified or impaired.[41]

COMMUNICATION AS 'CULTURAL IMPERIALISM'

The economic rights that the main producers in the global cultural industries sought to protect were an issue distinct from the better-known debate at the United Nations over the protection of cultural rights. Net consumers of cultural products blame 'cultural imperialism' as the threat to these rights. Johan Galtung's Structural Theory of Imperialism is perhaps the discourse most frequently referred to in the field of International Relations in any discussion of forms of dominance through news, ideas and cultural industries. In light of this, it is quite important to point out that Galtung's conceptualisation of 'cultural imperialism' is sometimes quite different from that of thinkers in the South who have identified 'cultural imperialism' (or the other labels that approximate it) as a problem that would be addressed by a NWICO.

Nkrumah's idea of 'neo-colonialism' built upon Lenin's theory of imperialism. Nkrumah, therefore, remained true to a materialist conception of international relations. The new form of colonialism was a mere reflection of international (capitalist) economic relations. Neo-colonialism performed the vital role of maintaining that international capitalist system. During the NWICO debate this critique continued to be reflected in the writings of Herbert Schiller and Armand Mattelart.[42]

However, rather than viewing the control of information and ideas in the South as a part of the struggle by capitalist nations for global markets (as Schiller, Mattelart and others do), Galtung believes it is just another configuration of *power* relations taking place in the world all the time. In fact, what Galtung explicitly calls 'cultural imperialism' is one of five imperialisms he identifies in his discourse. These imperialisms characterise relationships between 'center' nations (those with power) and 'periphery' nations (those without power). In a relationship of 'cultural imperialism' the centre nations provide teaching to the periphery states which are dependent on them for scientific knowledge. 'Communication imperialism' is slightly different. It involves the domination by the centre nations of news and the means of international communication. The other three imperialisms are 'economic' (control of the means of production and processing industries); 'political' (the reliance on the centre nations for decisions and models of government); and 'military' (dependence on the centre for protection and weapons).[43]

The Structural Theory of Imperialism calls for imperialisms to go through three phases. The first phase, that Galtung labels 'colonialism', involves natives of the centre venturing out to the periphery to occupy territory. This seems to be what Lenin would term the 'imperialist' phase. In the second phase ('neo-colonialism') the periphery obtains independence, but the ruling elites of both centre and periphery maintain a 'harmony of interest' through their interactions in international organizations. The phase of 'neo-neo-colonialism' Galtung says would take place in the future, when the two elites would be unified through rapid international communication.[44]

Galtung's Structural Theory of Imperialism places great weight on international communication. It sees control of international communication as a distinct type of imperialism; and, apart from that idea, international communication – made very rapid and efficient through modern technology – enables the two elites (the centre of the Centre and the centre of the Periphery) to maintain their harmony of interest in the pursuit of all imperialisms.

This examination of Galtung's theory is important here because of its prominence in the field of International Relations, but it is significant that the foremost scholar of the Non-Aligned Movement (NAM), A.W. Singham, and Shirley Hune, after a 10-year study of the politics of the movement (1975–1985),[45] explained the concerns that led to the NAM to call for a NWICO in terms of 'hegemony' rather than Galtung-like 'cultural imperialism'. 'Hegemony' is derived from the writings of Antonio Gramsci and found its way into the jargon of social studies in North America and Western Europe following the publication in English for the first time of Gramsci's *Prison Notebooks* in 1971.[46] It refers to the process by which a dominant class not only enforces and maintains its power but, over a period of time, manages to gain endorsement from the subordinate class without the use of force because the power relationship is accepted as a popular ideology. Scholars in Cultural Studies, most notably Stuart Hall,[47] have identified the structure of communication as the mechanism through which hegemony is imposed.

Singham and Hune, after attending several NAM meetings over the 10 years of their study and interviewing many of the delegates, argue that the NAM, from the early 1970s, campaigned against hegemony in the international system. They point out that they use the term in quite a different way from American scholars of international political economy, such as Robert Keohane, who have written about the decline of American 'hegemony' in the international economic system.[48] This later concept refers to a hegemon as an actor that maintains order, and in the postwar international economic system the United States had the power to sustain such order because of its position as the leading creditor, the largest single market, the leader of the Western defence system, and so on. In contrast, by 'hegemony' Singham and Hune refer to an 'intellectual and moral leadership' that dictates the world-view and actions of subordinate states in the Western alliance system.[49]

Just as Galtung could identify a number of imperialisms, Singham and Hune refer to more than one type of hegemony: 'nuclear'; 'political'; 'economic'; and 'cultural'. It is here that Galtung's idea of imperialisms and the Singham–Hune notion of hegemonies converge because they, in essence, refer to forms of structural power. Hegemons, like states of the Centre, acquire and maintain power because of their control over alternatives. The USA and the USSR were therefore described as nuclear hegemons because they had a 'monopoly over the techniques of violence through nuclear weapons'.[50] Political hegemony is symbolized by the Western alliance system, led by the United States, to which newly independent states had been encouraged to belong. Economic hegemony is the clout TNCs and institutions, such as the IMF and World Bank have over the structure of the international economy. But Singham and Hune spend the most space discussing 'cultural hegemony'. This concept is essentially a fusion of Galtung's notions of cultural and communication imperialisms.

Singham and Hune believe that for non-aligned countries cultural hegemony is the hegemony 'most difficult to resist and combat'.[51] In a way similar to that in which the NAM has criticized TNCs and transnational banks for determining the domestic class structure of countries in the South (economic hegemony),

the movement is critical of its cultural counterpart, the Western dominated international communications system, for its inordinate influence on policies and options within non-aligned countries. The communications system is one sphere where the global superstructure and structure mesh. In describing this phenomenon at the national level Gramsci points out that there is a conscious attempt, especially by the ruling class, to determine the nature and values of the society by fusing the role of the structure (economy) with the superstructure (ideology).[52]

The international communications system exerts control in four basic ways. One way is that it determines economic choices by projecting the economic systems of the West favourably and ignoring their shortcomings, as well as influencing consumption patterns in the South through international advertising. Singham and Hune explain:

> The non-aligned world has experienced radical shifts ... in its food habits, largely as a result of advertising by the global communications systems. New food tastes, such as bread made of white, processed wheat flour, and powdered milk formulas for infants, are promoted as items of modernity and status. Such consumer items have not only altered the diet and nutritional level in the Third World, but have had a detrimental effect on the domestic economy since these purchases generally have to be imported with hard currency. These developments have contributed to a growing body of literature describing the impact of 'consumer ideology' on the political structure of non-aligned countries.[53]

The international communications system also can shape the domestic politics of countries. Western media promote governments favourable to the Western alliance system and besmirch those that are opposed. Singham and Hune also make reference to cases where Western intelligence services have used the communications system to overthrow governments in the South, such as in the case of Mossadeq in Iran and Allende in Chile.[54] Thirdly, the entire character of international politics is shaped by communications because the communications system has the power to define the nature of local wars and characterize the various participants. Here they refer to the often-quoted example of how anti-colonial groups are defined in the Western news media as 'terrorists', while those who defend the *status quo* are called 'freedom fighters'. Lastly, the international communications system often serves to create and perpetuate racial and cultural stereotypes. This idea is identical to that expounded by Nkrumah (see Chapter 1).

A number of criticisms can be made of the hypotheses about imperialism or hegemony as espoused by Galtung, Singham and Hune, and others. Unfortunately, the imbalances in global flows of news and cultural products, and the concentration of cultural industries in a few countries lend themselves to simplistic assumptions that: (a) news and cultural products have assumed ideological effects that are further reflected in the behaviour of individuals; and (b) there is little more than a compliant role for individuals and classes in the regions that are said to be subject to cultural imperialism. The logical outcome of these two observations is that more attention has to be paid to researching: (1) the effects of media on foreign cultures; and (2) the mix of government policies and social preferences that act as pull factors in the continued reign of the small group of TNCs dominating international cultural industries.

With regard to the former observation, Salwen has argued that a more informed understanding of what has been labelled 'cultural imperialism' could be attained if more attention was paid to researching the effects of foreign media products on audiences. Studies have shown these effects to be: minimal or limited; differential, in that effects vary according to gender, education and other correlates; or exerting influence only in specific kinds of ways, such as with 'cultivation analysis' which explores how foreign media cultivate certain distinct self-perceptions and views of other societies.[55]

What is interesting is that both proponents of the cultural imperialism hypothesis and more conservative thinkers, such as Nye, who speak in positive terms of Western influence through cultural products, assume effects that are not coherently researched or understood. In some situations exposure to an abundance of foreign media might mean little in the overall scheme of international politics, but in other instances, instead of subtly creating compliance, they can lead to mass rejection of the culture and policies of the state with which the foreign audience became so familiar through its cultural products.

While Galtung's reference to a 'harmony of interest' between elites in the 'core' and 'periphery' points to the significance of local factors favourable to the spread of Western cultural products, it is merely a cursory glance at the very complex mix of political relations, government policies, and cultural features that are pull factors. In many countries that are supposed to be the victims of cultural imperialism, political repression of writers, film-makers and others vital to developing national cultural industries has been so severe that many artists can only produce freely in exile, often in North America and Europe.[56] And while national industries are suppressed in other ways through lack of capital and poor economies of scale, imports of foreign film, video, music and other products are encouraged by some governments because they are taxed, bringing in much-needed revenues to government treasuries. Indeed, the more popular a film at the cinema might be, the more revenues it generates in taxes on tickets sold. By the late 1980s some governments in small countries were not only generating revenues for the popular films and prerecorded videocassettes, but were also cashing in on the popularity of North American cable channels by selling them for monthly fees, separate from the regular offerings carried by government-run services.[57]

So, ironically, although multilateral regimes have not governed exchanges of news and cultural products and national sovereignty has been greatest, these fields have lent themselves more to charges of cultural imperialism. The post-Second World War order was built on inflated hopes of the *power of information* and this power is often feared more than the *power of communication*. What this analysis also shows is that the ideas of liberal democracy and liberal trade have been powerful justifications for preserving the generally one-sided global flow of cultural products and news.

NOTES

1. Pierre de Senarclens, a former director of UNESCO's Division of Human Rights and Peace, explained the organization's predicament by the mid-1980s by describing it as 'the smashed mirror of the past illusions of the Western world [,] as well as the disturbing reflection of international society increasingly prone to division by religion, ideology, politics, and bureaucratic practice'. He used UNESCO's declaration on cultural policies of 1982 as an example of the ideological change that had taken place at the organization nearly 40 years after its founding:

    > [The declaration replaced] the concept of human rights by that of the 'rights of others.' It states openly that 'every culture represents a unique and irreplaceable set of values since it is by its traditions and the forms of its expression that every people can manifest its presence in the world most perfectly. Affirming cultural identity thus contributes to the liberation of peoples.' Such relativism is necessarily opposed to the universality that attended the founding of UNESCO, which postulated that certain values and traditions were incompatible with democracy, development, and human dignity.

    Pierre de Senarclens, 'The Smashed Mirror of Past Illusions', *Society*, Vol. 22, no. 6, September/October 1985, p. 9.
2. Clare Wells, *The UN, UNESCO and the Politics of Knowledge* (London: Macmillan, 1987), pp. 24–5.
3. Wells (see note 2), p. 26.
4. Universal Declaration of Human Rights, adopted by UN GA Res. 217(III)A of 10 December 1948 (UN GAOR 3(I)), Art. 19.
5. Final Act of the United Nations Conference on Freedom of Information, UN Doc. E/CONF.6/79 (1948), res. I, secs. 1–2.
6. Wells (see note 2).

7.   J.S. Mill (1859), *Utilitarianism, On Liberty and Considerations on Representative Government* (H. B. Acton, ed.). (London: Dent, 1972), pp. 83–4.

8.   John Milton (1644), 'Areopagitica', in Charles W. Eliot (ed.), *Essays, Civil and Moral and New Atlantis by Francis Bacon; Areopagitica and Tractate on Education by John Milton; Religio Medici by Sir Thomas Browne*, The Harvard Classics, Vol. 3 (New York: P.F. Collier & Son, 1909), pp. 383–407.

9.   Mill, *Utilitarianism*, pp. 162–3.

10. Wells (see note 2), pp. 24–5.

11. The classical expositions of liberal trade theory are found in Adam Smith (1723–90), *An Enquiry Into The Nature and Causes of The Wealth of Nations* (1776) and David Ricardo (1772–1823), *Principles of Political Economy and Taxation* (1817).

12. Gilpin summarized this thinking eloquently by noting that

    From Montesquieu's statement that 'peace is the natural effect of trade,' through the writings of John Bright and Richard Cobden in the nineteenth century, to contemporary theorists of functionalism and economic interdependence, liberals have viewed international economics as inseparable from politics and as a force for peace. Whereas politics tends to divide, economics tends to unite peoples. Trade and economic interdependence create bonds of mutual interest and a vested interest in international peace and thus have a moderating influence on international relations.

    Robert Gilpin, *The Political Economy of International Relations* (Princeton, NJ: Princeton University Press, 1987), p. 56.

13. Wells (see note 2), p. 26.

14. See Dean V. Babst, 'Elective Governments – a Force for Peace', *The Wisconsin Sociologist*, Vol. 3, no. 1, 1964, pp. 9–14; Dean V. Babst, 'A Force for Peace', *Industrial Research*, Vol. 14, April 1972, pp. 55–8; Steve Chan, 'Mirror, Mirror on the Wall … Are the Freer Countries More Pacific?', *Journal of Conflict Resolution*, Vol. 28, no. 4, December 1984, pp. 617–48; Michael W. Doyle, 'Kant, Liberal Legacies, and Foreign Affairs', part 1, *Philosophy & Public Affairs*, Vol. 12, no. 3, Summer, 1983, pp. 205–35; part 2, Vol. 12, no. 4, Fall, 1983, pp. 323–53; Michael W. Doyle, 'Liberalism and World Politics', *American Political Science Review*, Vol. 80, no. 4, December 1986, pp. 1151–69; Rudolph J. Rummel, 'Libertarianism and International Violence', *Journal of Conflict Resolution*, Vol. 27, no. 1, March 1983, pp. 27–71; Erich Weede, 'Democracy and War Involvement', *Journal of Conflict Resolution*, Vol. 28, no. 4, December 1984, pp. 649–64.

15. See Thomas Guback, 'Film as International Business', *Journal of Communication*, Vol. 24, no. 1 (Winter 1974), p. 95, for a documentation of US government assistance to the American film industry. For a chronicle of the rise in influence of Anglo-American media worldwide see Jeremy Tunstall, *The Media Are American: Anglo-American Media in the World* (New York: Columbia University Press, 1977).

16. *Department of State Bulletin*, 3 February, Vol. 14, no. 344, 1946, p. 160, quoted in Herbert I. Schiller, *Communication and Cultural Domination* (New York: International Arts & Sciences Press, 1976), p. 29.

17. Schiller, *Communication*, pp. 37–8.

18.   *The Washington Post*, 26 March 1989.
19.   *The Wall Street Journal*, 6 September 1989, p. B6.
20.   BBC World Service radio, *The World Today*, 0615 GMT, 25 March 1992.
21.   *The The Wall Street Journal*, 3 October 1989, p. A18.
22.   *The New York Times*, 6 October 1989, p. B1.
23.   The *telenovela* phenomenon 'exemplifies the creolization of U.S. cultural products', according to Omar Souki Oliveira. 'It is the spiced up Third World copy of Western values, norms, patterns of behavior, and models of social relations.' Omar Souki Oliveira, 'Brazilian Soaps Outshine Hollywood: Is Cultural Imperialism Fading Out?' in Kaarle Nordenstreng and Herbert I. Schiller (eds), *Beyond National Sovereignty: International Communication in the 1990s* (Norwood, NJ: Ablex, 1993), p. 119.
24.   International Commission for the Study of Communication Problems, *Many Voices, One World* (London: Kogan Page, 1980), p. 77.
25.   In one of the few studies of the political economy of the international music industry, Wallis and Malm have noted that back in the 1970s, when the 'six giants' numbered five, Polygram had 100 per cent control of domestic manufacture of gramophone records in East Africa, and EMI enjoyed a similar monopoly on the west coast of South America. Roger Wallis and Krister Malm, *Big Sounds from Small Peoples: The Music Industry in Small Countries* (New York: Pendragon Press, 1984), p. 81.
26.   Swedish National Council for Cultural Affairs, *Fonogrammen: Kulturpolitiken* (1979), quoted in Wallis and Malm, *Big Sounds*, p. 9.
27.   For example:

   In Austria and Switzerland … foreign expressions are allowed in commercials only if they are readily intelligible to a general audience. And in West Germany, foreign brand names are forbidden if they would cause confusion regarding the origin of the product. Thus a German advertisement could be run in English for a product made in the United States or the United Kingdom, but not for one made locally.

   S. Watson Dunn, 'International Advertising', in George Kurian (ed.), *World Press Encyclopedia* (Vol. 1) (New York: Facts On File, 1982), p. 66.
28.   'Bill Aims to Increase Canadian TV Programs on Stations in Canada', *The Wall Street Journal*, 13 October 1989, p. C17.
29.   J.J. Boddewyn, 'Freeing International Advertising', *Advertising Compliance Service*, Vol. ix, issue 17, 4 September 1989, p. 4.
30.   John Ryan, *The Production of Culture in the Music Industry: The ASCAP-BMI Controversy* (Lanham, Maryland: University Press of America, 1985), p. 132–3.
31.   Wallis & Malm, *Big Sounds*, Chapter 6.
32.   Ibid.
33.   H. van der Wal, 'Cost Development Trends in the International Record Industry', *Conference on the State's Role vis-à-vis the Culture Industries*, Council of Europe, CC-CONF-IC 19, Strasbourg, 1980, quoted in Wallis and Malm, *Big Sounds*, p. 72.
34.   Jack Valenti, 'Movies, Television, and Home Video [:] The Great American Trade Asset', in Motion Picture Export Association of America (MPEAA),

Trade Barriers to Exports of US Filmed Entertainment: 1992 Report to the United States Trade Representative (New York: MPEAA, 1922), p. iii.
35. John Maggs, 'Developed Countries Square Off on Property Rights at GATT Talks', *Journal of Commerce*, 21 November 1991.
36. Boddewyn, 'Freeing', p. 1.
37. Mary W. Covington, Executive Director, IAA, 'Preface', in J. J. Boddewyn, *Barriers to Trade and Investment in Advertising: Government Regulation and Industry Self-Regulation in 53 Countries* (New York: IAA, 1989), p. iii.
38. See R. Michael Gadbaw and Timothy J. Richards (eds), *Intellectual Property Rights: Global Consensus, Global Conflict?* (Boulder: Westview Press, 1988). See also, Edward A. Finn, Jr, 'That's the $60 Billion Question', *Forbes*, 7 November 1986, p. 40.
39. Gadbaw and Richards, *Intellectual Property Rights*, pp. 3–5.
40. See Gary M. Hoffman, *Curbing International Piracy of Intellectual Property: Policy Options for a Major Exporting Country (Report of the International Piracy Project)* (Washington, DC: Annenberg Washington Program, 1989), p. 30.
41. Gadbaw and Richards, *Intellectual Property Rights*, p. 44.
42. See, for example, Schiller's *Information and the Crisis Economy* (Norwood, NJ: ABLEX, 1984), and Mattelart's *Multinational Corporations and the Control of Culture* (Atlantic Highlands, NJ: Humanities Press, 1979).
43. Johan Galtung, 'A Structural Theory of Imperialism', *Journal of Peace Research*, Vol. 8, no. 2, 1971, pp. 91–4.
44. Ibid., pp. 94–8.
45. A.W. Singham and Shirley Hune, *Non-Alignment in An Age of Alignments* (Westport, Conn.: Lawrence Hill & Co., 1986).
46. See A. Gramsci, *Selections from the Prison Notebooks* (London: Lawrence & Wishart, 1971).
47. See Stuart Hall, 'The rediscovery of "ideology": return of the repressed in media studies,' in Michael Gurevitch, Tony Bennett, James Curran and Janet Woolacott (eds) *Culture, Society and the Media* (London: Methuen, 1982).
48. See Robert Keohane, *After Hegemony: Cooperation and Discord in the World Political Economy* (Princeton: Princeton University Press, 1984).
49. Singham and Hune, p. 342.
50. Ibid., p. 345.
51. Ibid., p. 350.
52. Ibid.
53. Ibid. pp. 350–1.
54. Ibid. p. 351.
55. Michael B. Salwen, 'Cultural Imperialism: A Media Effects Approach,' *Critical Studies in Mass Communication*, March 1991, pp. 29–38.
56. The Kenyan writer Ngugi wa Thiong'o has done a chronicle of his personal repression in *Decolonising the Mind: The Politics of Language in African Literature* (London: James Curry/Heinemann, 1986).
57. See Mark D. Alleyne, 'The Mass Media System in Barbados,' in Stuart H. Surlin & Walter C. Soderlund (eds), *Mass Media and the Caribbean* (New York: Gordon & Breach, 1990).

4 The International Politics of News

'Why should the United Nations pay attention to what is going on in Yugoslavia and pay no attention to what is going on in Somalia when people are getting killed in Somalia in a higher proportion than Yugoslavia?' he asked. One explanation is that public opinion was aware of what was going on in Yugoslavia. The limelight of media attention was on Yugoslavia, and nobody paid attention to Somalia. 'The day that [the media] began to pay attention to Somalia, we began to receive the support of the member states. Then they were ready to give us planes for transport and to provide more humanitarian assistance and the forces to protect it.' He warned that the same kind of situation could recur in the former Soviet Central Asian republics, which many fear are moving toward major ethnic warfare. 'Tajikistan or Armenia or Uzbekistan have the same problem as Somalia: They don't know how to reach the media or to do the lobbying,' he noted.[1]

In describing how international relief initiatives were mobilized, United Nations Secretary-General Boutros Boutros-Ghali provided a poignant illustration of the power of mass media and news flows in international politics. The structure of international politics is such that, although he used the generic terms of 'public opinion', 'media attention' and 'the media', the Secretary-General could only be speaking about specific media, catering to specific public opinion in specific parts of the globe. It would be nice if a newspaper with a circulation of 100 000 in Trinidad and Tobago covered fully the human suffering in Somalia's civil war, but that would not get the attention or have the impact of reportage in *The New York Times* or *Le Monde*, each with circulations in excess of one million and 300 000 respectively and published in countries with the resources to make a difference. These journalists, the institutions for which they work, and the information they report, play significant roles in shaping the agenda of international relations for governments, organizations and common citizens.

Political authorities of various ideological complexions all devise positions on news media and journalists very early in their rule and use their laws and monopolies on the legitimate use of violence to control the press. Murder, intimidation and censorship are an unfortunate features of life for journalists across the world.[2] At the same time, news media have the

66

means to project and protect their interests in ways not readily available to those that question their news values and other aspects of their operations. These features explain why global news flows are the most controversial aspect of international communication. For reasons that we will explore in this chapter and later in this book, governments and media associations have been unable to procure global rules for principles governing news media, protection of journalists and standards of journalistic performance. Indeed, journalism is one profession with a lot of influence for which there are no standard professional qualifications. In similarly influential professions, such as the law and medicine, admission to the bar or certification by professional boards are prerequisites to practice, but that is not the case with journalism, and such licensing of journalists is indeed anathema to liberal-democratic definitions of the press (see Chapter 3).

NEWS DEFINED

Because politics is about power, we say that the global flow of news is political: it reflects and determines the international configuration of power. The analysis of the relationship between power and news begins with the consideration of the concept of news itself. What is news? And on whose definition of news do we base our own definition?

The definition of news, or news values – what mass media see fit to report – has been found to be a key variable in understanding the politics of global news flows. Government officials and common citizens from small states often accuse the main disseminators of international news – i.e. the international wire services, the global TV networks and the Western elite press – of concentrating on 'negative' news about their countries. It seems that most of the news circulated about countries in Africa, Latin America and some parts of Asia is about natural and man-made catastrophes, a phenomenon that has been called a 'coups and earthquakes' syndrome.[3] It sometimes seems that there is a malicious attempt to stereotype these countries, and this attitude might be propelled by various factors, including racism, political ideology and ethnocentrism. In this way, international news is viewed as a weapon of those with power in the international system, a tool to maintain the *status quo*, at least in regard to the inferior status of some peoples and nation-states. But an alternative way of viewing the problem is to focus on the dominant definition of news. Such an approach locates the problem with the power of news values rather than with particular prejudices towards certain countries or groups of people. According to a study commissioned by UNESCO,

News in most media systems seems to be defined as the exceptional event, making coups and catastrophes newsworthy wherever they occur. It is not so much that the developing world is singled out for such 'negative' attention, but that the developing countries tend to be reported only in this manner. These countries are neither the source of, nor themselves apparently particularly interested in, presenting 'softer' news items. Third World media systems concentrate heavily on 'hard' news, and the tendency is that the smaller the amount of general coverage, the more it concentrates on a few topic areas and reflects the specific events of the time. News tends to stereotype all regions in some way or another.[4]

This particular definition of news controls the way journalists decide what is important. Regardless of where the definition was first devised, it has created a peculiar situation in which all journalists working for, or using material from, the major international media can be seen as accomplices, whether they be in New York or Lusaka. One writer described this mix of contradictions by explaining that

> Third World papers pay as much attention to the private lives of American celebrities, to the problems of drug-taking among American students, to the health of the American President, as they do to the comparable personalities and issues of their own societies. The news sent out from Latin America, Africa and Asia to the international agencies is sent by local agency offices and representatives who are often natives of the countries concerned. Yet the local journalist will send the New York office the material which he knows it wants; this is then retransmitted with the agencies' bulletins to the newspapers of the same region according to the presumed news priorities of those papers.[5]

The logical extension to this line of thinking is that even if the personnel and organizations relaying international news become more diverse there is no guarantee that the coups and earthquakes syndrome will go away. What must be changed also is the definition of news.

The observation quoted above also points to the relative lack of freedom that journalists in many regions of the world have in reporting about local personalities, issues and events. To avoid the sack, censorship, or even harassment and murder, many media workers in small countries devote much time and space to the readily available news from North America and Europe because such news is considered 'safe'. In contrast, investigative reports on government corruption, the private lives of local personalities or exploitation of consumers by merchants are 'unsafe' stories because they are too close to home. This situation is the product of a rather schizophrenic attitude of elites in many small countries to local and international news. An illustration of this is provided by a journalist from Ghana who noted that

> Castigation of the Western media is a regular feature of the state-owned media, for the anti-Ghanian views, supposedly directed by their governments. Yet ironically, when the Ghanian press criticises the Western leaders and system of government, it is with facts published in the same Western media. The fact that similar information published in Ghana about the government would be considered treason is conveniently overlooked. Most interesting of all, the least praise in the same Western press is proudly cited and broadcast.[6]

The recognition of the power of news values and the role of restrictions does not mean, however, that other factors such as ethnocentrism, racism and ideology do not colour international news. After news values are used to determine what is to be news, journalists often use vague, short-hand terms to describe complex issues and regions. The power of such parlance has become so strong that ironically a journalist used one such woolly generalization – 'Third World' – to express the anger that many feel when he declared: 'Third World states are persistently upset about being portrayed as poverty-stricken countries that are either pro- or anti-American.'[7]

THE STRUCTURE OF GLOBAL NEWS

In the case of global news flows, therefore, those with power are those who can determine the very definition of news. Power also rests with those whose voices and perspectives are heard the most. Figure 4.1 illustrates this hierarchy in the structure of global news flows.

The flow of news between regions varies *quantitatively* and *qualitatively*. As we noted in the preceding section, the quantity of news flowing from the richer countries of the North to the South greatly exceeds the quantity going in the other direction. We also noted above that the quality of news from South to North is lower than the reverse flow. In contrast, there are high quantitative and qualitative flows of news between the richer countries. The 'Big Five' international news agencies, the elite newspapers and magazines of North America and Europe, and now the global TV networks, such as CNN, have the vast majority of their foreign news bureaus concentrated in the 'major capitals' of the world, especially London, New York, Paris, Washington, Brussels, Tokyo and Hong Kong. Every day these offices generate millions of words, pictures (still and moving) and sounds to their head offices where they are packaged for

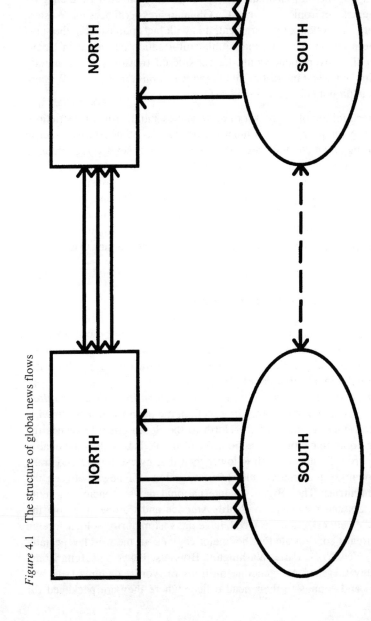

Figure 4.1   The structure of global news flows

North = the richer, industrialized states concentrated mainly in the northern hemisphere's regions of North America and Europe, and also including Japan.

South = the smaller, poorer states located mainly in the southern hemisphere and concentrated in such regions as Africa, the evening TV newscasts, radio reports and daily and weekly editions of newspapers and magazines. Also, an important distribution point for news in these countries are financial news services supplied to computer screens by such networks as AP/Dow Jones and Reuters.

The high quantitative and qualitative North–North flow can be contrasted with the South–South flow which is relatively low in quantity and quality. Unless there is a major natural or man-made catastrophe the average consumer of news in, say, New Delhi, will hardly have available to him or her as wide a choice of news about, say, Latin America, Africa or even other Asian countries, as he or she has about Western Europe or the United States. And even when the consumer of news in New Delhi gets news from other countries of the South this news is often of lower quality. By this we mean that a news story about a hurricane in the Caribbean, for example, might come only in words, without still or moving pictures. The quality of news flows is determined by how news is covered, and if there are few international news bureaus in these regions then it is less likely that information will be relayed in more ways than written reports from sources called on the telephone.

South–South flow is peculiar not only because of its very different quantitative and qualitative character, but also because it has a higher propensity not to flow directly. We can draw an imaginary triangle in the middle of Figure 4.1 with the tip of the triangle pointing upwards. Because all the major international news organizations are based in the North, news from Africa to the Caribbean, for example, often comes via London or New York. In the 1970s the Non-Aligned Movement and UNESCO encouraged initiatives, such as the Pan-African News Agency (PANA), the Caribbean News Agency (CANA), and the Non-Aligned News Agencies Pool (NANAP), to give journalists in these regions more editorial control over news from their regions and abroad, but none of these organizations have the resources to set up their own bureaus in distant capitals to obviate the triangular South–South flow, and the best these agencies can do is to mediate and re-edit the news supplied by the international wire services.

The journalists who define what is news not only see news as the exceptional event, but also what is important. So our description of the global flow of news is also a view of the perceived important sources of news and the major points of exchange for such information. Those who defend the character of global news flows argue that the international news organizations rightly pay more attention to the 'major capitals' because that is where the important news is produced. The assumption beneath this explanation is that the production of news is a reflection of the various configurations of international power. The international ramifications of decisions made in these capitals – especially in the areas of economic and military relations – are seen as justifications for the structure of global news. The logical extension to this line of thought is that the historical development of world political, technological, economic and military relations must be analyzed if we are to understand the character of global news flows.

Until the advent of global TV networks, the 'Big Five' news agencies were the dominant purveyors of international news. The story of why they were created, their historical relations with their home governments, and how they evolved does a lot to explain the relationship between international power and global news flows.

THE 'BIG FIVE' NEWS AGENCIES

News agencies are organizations which employ a number of correspondents in diverse geographic areas to report news to a central location where, for a fee, it is then disseminated, by electronic or other means, to a variety of newspapers, periodicals, radio and TV stations, diplomatic missions, business houses and other clients. Many news agencies are national in scope, concentrating their activities to the service of clients in their home states, even though they might employ correspondents in other countries. Examples of these are Japan's Kyodo news agency, China's Hsin Hua, and West Germany's Deutsche Press Agentur (DPA).

However, five news agencies tower above all others in terms of size and influence. Four of these (the 'Big Four') – the Associated Press (AP), United Press International (UPI), Agence France-Presse (AFP), Reuters – are based in the West; while the other, ITAR-TASS (Information Telegraph Agency of Russia – Telegraph Agency of the Soviet Union), is headquartered in Russia.

Table 4.1 gives an indication of the resources for news collection of these agencies and the size of their clientele.

It is common in discussions and writings on the international circulation of news to speak of the 'Big Four' instead of a 'Big Five' that includes TASS, because the Western agencies are not only the main source of international news for the media in the developing nations, but their reports are the chief means by which the power centres of the West are informed of developments in the Third World. Among the most prominent criticisms of the Big Four are that: their coverage of the developing world is 'crisis-oriented', providing good illustrations of the coups and earthquakes syndrome; their reports from the developing world are biased, and even racist, when referring to black countries, reflecting European and North American prejudices; and the dependence on them for international news by media in the poorer states is another manifestation of neo-colonialism.

However, as the table of statistics demonstrates, there is really a 'Big Five' if we include the Russian news agency ITAR-TASS, which was replaced in 1992 by ITAR (Information Telegraph Agency of Russia). TASS was historically not considered an international agency in the same league as the 'Big Four' due to its direct control by the state and as an instrument of Soviet domestic and foreign policy. But the coming of *perestroika* meant a new role for TASS, more approaching that of the Western agencies. Also, as our data reveal, it would have been a serious mistake not to include TASS in any study of the world's largest news agencies because in some statistical categories the agency was superior to the Western services. The term 'Big Five' has been used by UNESCO and others have followed UNESCO's lead and used it in discussions of global news flows.[8]

It is important when considering global newsflows to consider the fifth because: (1) at the centre of one aspect of the debates about news flows is the ideological argument over what should be the role of the media and news, and TASS should be considered if only because it has historically represented the antithesis of the Western news agencies' arguments that journalists and news flows should be free of government restrictions; (2) not to consider the role of TASS would be to ignore a significant dimension of the flow of international news, i.e. the audiences that TASS principally serves; and (3) TASS, in the person of its then Director, Sergei Losev, played an active role in the compilation of the MacBride Report, one of the most controversial documents of the NWICO debate.[9]

These five are special among news agencies for a number of reasons. They not only compile news from across the globe, but they also have clients in a number of other countries, in addition to their home states. They are very experienced in the task of collecting and disseminating news, most of them being in existence in one form or another since the 1800s (as we shall see below). Because they are so established they enjoy high credibility and so they are able to attract as clients the largest and most influential media in all countries of the world that have mass media systems of some kind. In the case of many newspapers or diplomatic offices, the international news agency, prior to CNN, was the only source of up-to-date information on international developments; and, if they are not the sole source of international news, they are most certainly the main conveyors of international news to all news media that cannot afford to maintain correspondents in remote parts of the globe.

The size of the Big Five translates into another reason why they are the most powerful actors in the global flow of news – their status as 'agenda-setters'. Boyd-Barrett lists four such agenda-setting roles of international wire services:[10]

(1) They determine on a daily basis what is considered to be 'news' because what they decide to relay accounts for a lot of what is printed and broadcast by their media clients.
(2) The amount of time and space the agencies devote to particular stories serves to rate material on a scale of importance and 'recommend' some stories to media editors, while downplaying others.
(3) The priority the wire services give to some events influences how editors deploy their own staff to cover these events in more detail.
(4) The standards of the international news agencies and the technological and professional help they give to other news agencies and media are agenda-setting in their very nature because they set codes of journalistic and international news-gathering conduct for organisations of less experience and stature to follow.

Although Table 4.1 is very useful in providing an idea of the relative size and reach of the 'Big Five', the first caveat is that some categories of statistics are in a state of constant change (e.g. daily number of words and exact number of correspondents). The total number of subscribers and number of countries served and covered also change but, obviously, not as frequently as the other categories.[11] It is also clear that the official statistics on output of words given by agencies do not lend themselves to good comparisons because some agencies do not count each piece of editorial matter once (as does Reuters), but matter can be counted more than once due to relays to several different regions and translations to different language services.

Compared to the three European agencies, the American agencies seem less international in reach, serving and covering relatively few countries, a feature that is to some extent the result of their not having as many old colonial ties. However, at the end of the 1980s all these agencies had subscribers and regular correspondents in the majority of sovereign states of the world.

Although all the international wire services had begun to invest heavily in new technologies and diversify their services by the mid-1970s, it was only in the 1980s that the true impact of the new technologies and diversification on the character of the agencies became clear. These developments caused questions to be raised about whether some agencies should still be described as *news* agencies, and, following from this,

Table 4.1 The 'Big Five' news agencies

Press[1] agency	Number of countries served	Number of subscribers (domestic & foreign)	Number of countries covered by correspondents	Number of words issued daily	Number of full-time correspondents in foreign countries
AP[2] (USA)	112	15 500	67	17 mill.	617
UPI[3] (USA)	100	6 000	81*	14 mill.	105
AFP[4] (France)	144	12 500	150	3 mill.	550
TASS[5] (USSR)	93	5 100	127	4 mill.	150*
Reuters[6] (UK)	137	29 310	77	300 000[x]	968[+]

*Denotes an approximation based on data from more than one of the sources listed below.

[1]Because the figures involved are often large and in a state of almost constant change, the wire services have in most cases provided approximations or rounded figures.

[2]Data on the Associated Press is extracted from *The Associated Press 1990 Annual Report*; AP, *The Associated Press: Origin, History And Development*, New York: 1987; and personal correspondence with Wendell Wood Collins, Director of Corporate Communications, AP, New York, 9 September 1991.

[3]Information on United Press International was gathered with the kind assistance of the UPI London Bureau, 1987; also see note 8 in the text.

[4]Data on Agence France-Presse is extracted from AFP, *From Havas to AFP: 150 Years of News Reporting*, Paris: AFP, 1985; from the information on France contained in the 1987 UNESCO data base on the world's wire services compiled by the Division of Free Flow of Information; and personal correspondence with Michel Saint-Pol, Vice-President, External Relations, AFP, 13 September 1991, and Michele Cooper, US Bureau Chief, 10 September 1991.

[5]Data on TASS (later renamed ITAR-TASS) is extracted from TASS, *From The First Days of the October Revolution*, Moscow: TASS (Main Secretariat), 1985; and from UNESCO, *World Communication Report* (Paris: UNESCO, 1988); and Leonid Kravchenko, Director-General, TASS, 'The Role of Regional Satellite Systems in Developing the Mass Media', Address at the Satellite Communications Users Conference – Separate Systems Update – Washington, DC, 24 October 1989.

[6]Data on Reuters is extracted from *Reuters Holdings PLC: Annual Report 1990*; Reuters (Corporate Relations Department), *Reuters: A Background and Chronology of Key Events*, London: 1990; personal correspondence with Robert Crooke, Director of Media Relations, Reuters America Inc., 29 August 1991, and with Daniel Brooksbank of the Corporate Media Relations Department, Reuters Limited, 10 January 1992. The figure for number of subscribers here refers to number of locations with terminals and printers receiving Reuter services. Reuters serves 205 000 video terminals.
[x]This figure may seem small compared to the figures for the other agencies, but it is based on each piece of editorial matter being counted once only.
[+]This total includes those involved in compiling data for Reuters' extensive financial information services.

whether it would not be more pertinent to examine global *information* flows because news has become a smaller and smaller proportion of the products the agencies sell.

The impact of diversification is manifested by the comparatively large number of full-time correspondents employed by AP and Reuters – the agencies that have diversified the most. The figures for these two wire services include the manpower deployed in the collection of financial data and other forms of information for their business clients.

History

International news agencies were established not so much to create an informed international citizenry as to make money. Their histories are characterized by struggles to secure and expand markets for their news, markets often delineated by the territorial limits of their home countries' empires or spheres of influence.

Of the five largest international agencies, three – AFP, Reuters and AP – were started in the 1800s, and of these AFP is the oldest. It celebrated its one-hundred-and-fiftieth anniversary in 1985, and claims to have been the world's first international news agency. AFP's origins date to 1835[12] when Charles-Louis Havas (1783–1858), a French entrepreneur, bought the Correspondence Garnier – a company that translated foreign newspapers – and started converting it into a news agency.

By the latter 1800s Havas was to encounter competition when rival international news agencies – in the form of Reuters in London and Wolff in Berlin – were set up. His competitors were the Germans Paul Julius Reuter and Bernhard Wolff, both of whom Havas had employed earlier and trained. These three agencies – Havas, Wolff and Reuters – would remain the premier news agencies of the world well into the twentieth century. But

Reuters and Havas outlasted the Wolff agency, which disappeared with the rise of Nazism in Germany and the coming of the Second World War.

Reuters began in 1850 when Paul Julius Reuter used 40 carrier-pigeons to fly stock-market prices between Brussels and Aachen to compensate for the deficiencies in the European telegraph network.[13] He moved to London in 1851 and continued his business in stock-price information, but this time sending it from London to Paris via the Dover–Calais submarine cable link. He gradually expanded to general news and increased his clientele to those other parts of the continent. The agency's reputation was enhanced considerably in 1859 when it was the first to transmit Napoleon III's Paris speech that was the prelude to war with Austria in that same year. It was also the first in Europe to carry the news of President Lincoln's assassination in 1865.

The Associated Press was set up as a cooperative among six New York newspapers in 1848. Until 1943 its constitution prevented new membership without the agreement of existing members, a restriction which led to hostility from other sectors of the press and caused the formation of rival agencies, including the one that was to become UPI.

In the 1800s AP differed from the European agencies not only in its restricted membership, but also in the fact that, unlike Havas, Reuters and Wolff, it was not a truly international agency because it did not collect its own foreign news and had no members in other countries. Havas, Reuters and Wolff had established an international news cartel between themselves by signing the Agency Alliance Treaty in 1869 under which they delegated to each other regions of the world for exclusive coverage and service. Reuter got the entire British Empire and the Far East; Wolff covered Scandinavia, Russia, Austria and its surrounding territories; and Havas gained the rights to the French and Portuguese empires, Italy and Spain. Reuter and Havas agreed to penetrate South America jointly. The agreement was made in an attempt to offset rising telegraph costs. It was the first of a series of contracts between the three agencies that would last well into the 1930s. AP joined the cartel in 1893 and got exclusive rights from Reuter to distribute news within the United States and US possessions, and to supply the European agencies with news from the US.

The cartel's virtual monopoly on the flow of international news was actually broken in the early 1900s by the agency that was to eventually become known as UPI. The 'United Press Associations' was formed by prominent American newspaper entrepreneur E.W. Scripps in 1907, to break AP's preponderance in the United States, a position that agency enjoyed because it was the only national news agency in the country at the time. Scripps' agency (unlike AP) placed no restrictions on who could become clients and sold its news to anyone who could pay. (Scripps is said to have detested the AP publishers because he thought they were conservative and capitalistic.)[14] Although the new agency initially abided by the international order the cartel had established and relied on the European agencies for coverage of other countries, 'UP' decided after 1912 that it did not want to be confined by the cartel and it would collect its own international news. UP's move proved a great success because it was helped largely by the Argentinean newspaper *La Prensa* which was willing to pay up to half a million dollars annually for the agency's international news. This success threatened to make UP the major American agency at the expense of the AP, and, as a result, AP gradually broke free from the cartel in order to be free to compete more effectively against the UP. Between 1918 and 1919 AP assumed responsibility for Latin America from Havas. The *de facto* end of the cartel came in 1930 when the Japanese agency, Rengo, agreed to distribute the AP service in Japan and AP declared that it would end its agreement with the European cartel.

Unlike the Western agencies, TASS did not originate as a private, entrepreneurial venture. It had its origins in two agencies: the St Petersburg Telegraph Agency and the Press Bureau of the All-Russian Central Executive of Workers', Peasants' and Soldiers' Deputies. Conflict between the two organizations after the 1917 revolution caused them to be merged into ROSTA Rossiyskoye Telegrafnoye Agentstvo – Russian Telegraph Agency). ROSTA had two departments: one for news and one for propaganda, and Lenin was among those who wrote for it. ROSTA became TASS after the declaration of the Soviet Union in 1925.[15]

TASS did not become a truly international news agency until after the Second World War. With the expansion of communist power in Eastern Europe and Asia, TASS became the dominant international news agency in those parts of the world (with the exception of Yugoslavia). However, it soon lost this dominance after Stalin's death in 1953 and the rise of the competing Chinese news agency, Hsin Hua, after 1951. TASS also lost its monopoly because its service was often unreliable and untailored to local tastes; the satellite communist states also felt a need to subscribe to some of the Western news agencies in addition to TASS.[16] The agency remained one of the leading international news agencies, however, because of its size, the vast number of its subscribers (including those in the newly independent states of the South who sometimes got the TASS service *gratis*), and the international role that TASS played as a mouthpiece of the Soviet state. TASS was directly controlled by the Council of Ministers of the USSR. Its Director was appointed by the Presidium of the Central Committee, and all its international contacts and agreements had to be approved by the foreign affairs ministry.

TASS's organization and the character of its news changed with the coming of *glasnost* in the 1980s when it began concentrating more on 'objective, general international information'.[17] Then in June 1990, the Soviet government passed a sweeping new Press Law which offered publishing rights to individuals, professional rights to journalists, and declared 'Censorship of mass information is not allowed.'[18] Gorbachev suspended the press law only a few months later, however, following media criticism of the crackdown in the Baltic region. *Perestroika* also placed a new demand on TASS to focus on 'what can be taken out of Western life and introduced into the Soviet Union'. This meant a less doctrinaire approach to Tass's international reporting.[19]

After Gorbachev's departure the very unusual occurrences in the former USSR profoundly affected the fortunes of TASS even more. On 22 January 1992, Russian President Boris Yeltsin signed Decree Number 37, creating the Information Telegraph Agency of Russia (ITAR) by merging TASS and parts of RIA-Novosti. RIA (the Russian Information Agency) set up in March 1991, was intended to be a joint-stock company. Private investment failed to materialize, however, and RIA was merged with state-supported Novosti, established by the Soviet government in 1961, as a second official news agency. Thus, rather than subsidize both RIA-Novosti and TASS, and to 'remove the unjustified duplication in work', a single agency, ITAR, was established by Yeltsin's decree to serve as 'the central state information agency of the Russian Federation whose activity is designed for the inner state and international audiences'.[20] It was decided that the TASS logo would remain in its news reports, as in 'ITAR-TASS', due to its worldwide recognizability. In a separate agreement, the heads of 14 national news agencies of former Soviet republics – also former branches of TASS – decided to cooperate in preserving ITAR-TASS's extensive information and communication structures in the post-Soviet area as well as to maintain its central data bank.[21] By 1992 ITAR-TASS had managed to pay all outstanding bills and held a two million rouble profit, putting it well on the way to becoming independent and self-supporting.[22]

Links with Governments

When governments of poorer, small states made calls at the UN in the 1970s for reform of the structure of international news, the influential media of North America and Europe dismissed these initiatives as raising the ugly spectre of government control over news. But the history of the international wire services reveals that these news organizations have never been completely free of relationships of some sort with their various home governments, for ensuring telecommunications links or for needed financial support. The agencies have patterned their international reporting very closely to the contours of power of their governments, as the specializations established at the time of the cartel reveal. And, in times of war especially, the strategic value of the wire services have not been lost on governments that have completely taken over some of the agencies.

Although TASS's ties with the Soviet government have been obvious, the European agencies and UPI have at various times in their histories not had the adversarial relationships with their governments that is the liberal-democratic ideal. About the time of United Press Associations' merger with William Randolph Hearst's International News Service (INS) in 1958 to form the United Press International, Frank Bartholomew, the UPI Chairman after the merger, said 'private enterprise with a profit incentive is the best guarantee of objective coverage of world news'.[23] According to this view, there is nothing inconsistent with the profit motive and the liberal-democratic ideal. However, there are contradictions in a news agency's aspiring for liberal-democratic principles while relying on its home government for financial support.

Charles-Louis Havas had personal connections with French government officials, and this more than likely played a part in the government's decision in 1838 to employ the agency to relay ministerial news to state agencies. In the interwar years the Foreign Ministry subsidised Havas in the wake of its losing markets due to competition from TASS, short-wave radio revolutionising the international transmission of news in the 1930s, and the end of the cartel. After the outbreak of the Second World War it was turned into the French Information Office. The agency was revived as Agence France-Presse after the war by former London correspondents and journalists of the Resistance. However, the turning-point was in 1957 when French law granted it editorial independence and financial autonomy. Nevertheless, to this day AFP has not been able to shrug off allegations that it is linked to French government interests, both domestic and foreign. The French government is still the major subscriber to the service.

Reuters entered an agreement with the British authorities during the First World War under which it 'transmitted a service of Allied war communiqués and official news financed by the government but kept separate from Reuters' own service.'[24] The agency was more successful than Havas during the Second World War in resisting official pressure. It achieved this by reorganizing itself in 1941 as a private company owned by the British provincial press. The ownership body became the Reuter Trust which 'provided that Reuters should never pass into the hands of any one interest group or faction, and that its integrity, independence, and freedom from bias should be preserved'.[25]

As part of a move to turn the company's financial fortunes around, UPI entered a US$2.5 million contract with the US government in 1987 to relay official releases outside the USA.[26] The agency had not turned a profit since the early 1960s and, after the Scripps family sold it in 1982, had gone through a succession of owners.

Although AP has never been in as desperate straits as UPI, Jean-Luc Renaud has documented US government assistance to AP's global expansion.[27]

The history of government relations with all the Big Five indicate that their home governments, for domestic and foreign policy considerations, are reluctant to stand by and let the agencies fail, especially if called upon to help. This suggests that predictions that the Big Five might decline to a smaller number due to the vagaries of the international marketplace for news might be somewhat off-target. However, the case of the former Soviet Union is an example of how the Big Five can contract to a lesser number if the home state actually ceases to exist.

Expansion and Diversification

The operations of the international wire services have been shaped by the vagaries of the international markets for news and information. A major feature of these markets is that 'hard news' – written breaking news of general interest – is an unprofitable area of business. This has forced all the wire services to diversify their output to include such other services as news photos, radio news, video services, and development of new technologies to improve the quantitative and qualitative transmission of news. In the 1980s the most lucrative of these diverse services was specialized news in the form of financial information. It was as though the history of international wire services had come full circle because international news agencies owe their origins to the need to supply financial news.

Reuters has best exemplified diversification at the international wire services. The milestones in the company's history from 1960 to 1990 had little to do with traditional news reporting and more with Reuters' diversification into the financial information sector. Some of these developments include: Reuters' pioneering of the use of computers to relay financial data across the world – the Stockmaster service – in 1964; the launching of Reuter Monitor in 1973 – a financial information system that gave subscribers access, via their own computer terminals, to a database of news and price information; and the starting in 1981 of Reuter Monitor

Dealing Service, a system giving dealers the ability to contact one another in seconds via their Reuter Monitor terminals.

By 1986 the media market accounted for only 9 per cent of Reuters' revenue, and although the company still ran one of the world's largest wire services, it was open to question whether Reuters could be defined as a news agency or a multinational corporation that sold news as just one dimension of its business. Over 50 per cent of Reuters' revenue in 1986 came from its very extensive dealing in financial data.[28] There were over 34 800 subscriber contracts for Reuter Monitor, involving about 71 500 computer terminals worldwide.[29]

Because the supply of financial data had become a lucrative field and Reuters was one of the most proficient in its collection and distribution, the 1980s were years of financial bliss for Reuters relative to previous years. For example, in 1964 (the year that the Stockmaster service was launched) Reuters made a net loss of £53 000 on a turnover of £3 583 000. However, between 1980 and 1984 annual revenue rose from £90 095 000 to £312 990 000, and profit after tax in 1984 was £42 209 000. That enabled the company to raise £52 000 000 of new capital (after payment of costs) from its floatation in June 1984.[30] Reuters' profits after tax in 1986 were £80.7 million, up by 47 per cent on the previous year's. By the end of the decade profits after tax had levelled off but were still sizeable – £208.4 million, an increase of 15 per cent on 1989. Throughout the decade the agency earned most of its revenue from services to the financial community, while sales to traditional media clients varied from a low of 5.9 per cent of revenue in 1988 to 6.6 per cent in 1990.[31]

Disgust with the increasing subordination of Reuters' news operations to financial services has been given as one reason why some senior Reuters journalists resigned from the organization in recent years – some of them going to set up London's new *The Independent* newspaper in 1986. Other forms of diversification have been in photos and video news. In January 1985 it bought UPI's newsphoto business outside the US and signed a 10-year newsphoto exchange agreement with UPI to swap its international photos for UPI's photos from within the US. In the same year Reuters bought a controlling interest in Visnews, the world's largest television news agency. By the latter half of the decade over 420 TV stations in more than 80 countries were subscribers to Visnews.[32]

Havas diversified into advertising as early as 1857, an area of the business that was to last well into the twentieth century. By the 1980s AFP had diversified into several areas of the information field, though not to as great an extent as AP, the most diversified of the Big Five. One of these new areas for the French agency is a data bank called AGORA. On

17 October 1984 AFP started its AUDIO radio service; and in January of the next year it launched its international Telephoto Service, Afp-Photo, employing a SYNTIN process that was developed by AFP for rapid transmission of news photographs via high-speed numerical circuits. In 1985 it entered the television market when it signed an agreement with Gamma Television Agency and *Le Monde* newspaper for the production of television news and feature programmes for an international clientele.[33]

AP, on the other hand, became an innovator in new information technology through its diversification. The agency's technological achievements include: the 1914 conversion from Morse to teleprinter transmission of news; the development of the CRT (Cathode Ray Tube) news writing and editing system in the 1970s; the introduction of the process called LaserPhoto for the transmission of newsphotos across the world; and the introduction in 1977 of what is known as the 'electronic darkroom', a computerised system for the rapid processing and editing of photographs.[34]

The uniqueness of Reuters' success in the 1980s is revealed in the fact that AP, the most successful wire service after Reuters, actually suffered a deficit in revenues in 1984. But AP, a not-for-profit cooperative, registered a pre-tax operating net surplus of US$5.4 million in 1985, and US$10.5 million in 1986. The increased revenue allowed AP to invest US$13.7 million in capital news technology in 1986.

Despite its problems with profitability, UPI also boasts a history of innovation in the information field. In 1935 it was the first agency in the US to start a news service for radio, and in 1958 it introduced the first radio network owned by a US wire service. It introduced the first fully automatic facsimile receiver, Unifax, in 1953; and in 1983 it started customised news selection services for broadcasters and newspapers – UPI Custom News and UPI Custom Data.

Like the other four, TASS diversified into news photos. It distributed photos to news agencies in socialist countries via an exchange arrangement called the 'Photointernational' ring. It exchanged its news photos with the non-socialist world through the communication lines of AP, UPI, Pressensbild and Kyodo. At one point there were over 200 subscribers (in 40 countries) to the photo service Photokhronika TASS.

A REGIME FOR INTERNATIONAL NEWS

The UN Secretary-General's recognition (quoted at the beginning of this chapter) that media are vital in marshalling 'public opinion', which in turn gets government action in relief efforts, suggests that mass media and the news they disseminate have a strategic character in international relations. Governments are very aware of this, and that is why they invest in national news agencies of their own and use mass media in their public diplomacy (see Chapter 5). But any resource that is strategic empowers some at the expense of others, and the history of global news flows has also been a history of attempts at multilateral rule-making to regulate mass media, journalists and the behaviour of others towards them. As we noted in Chapter 3, no separation can be made between political ideology and mass communication. All political ideologies embody certain assumptions about the role of the press. The rhetoric of liberal-democratic ideology, for example, advocates freedom of information and the marketplace of ideas, while the roots of Soviet communist policies toward the press were rooted in notions that journalists and mass media were party functionaries.[35] During the Cold War these antipodal postures made it difficult for the press to be even discussed and far less for ideas about a multilateral regime for international news to be proffered. What would be the principles and other features of such a regime? Who would set it up? The answer to the latter question would most certainly be governments because it is governments, representing their states, that are recognized as the full, sovereign members of the United Nations system. But for governments to set up and run an international regime regulating the mass media would contradict the liberal-democratic ideal of powerful members, especially the United States. Therefore, the result has been various declarations and other items of international law that have expressed the consensus of various groups of states at various points in time about specific principles related to the mass media, journalists and news. But national sovereignty in these matters has remained the rule and no state has surrendered its national sovereignty on any matter related to international news in the way that national sovereignty has been commuted in telecommunications, the mails and other fields of international interaction.

The attempt to have a New World Information and Communication Order (NWICO) was a case study of why it has been difficult to reform the *status quo* in international communication, and we will devote Chapter 6 to it, but here it is necessary to examine the types of attempts at multilateral rule-making concerning the circulation of news. These have been of four kinds: international law against propaganda; rules and declarations aimed at ensuring the safety of journalists; initiatives pursued by the media industry to gain protection from government censorship; and declarations sponsored by developing nation-states at UNESCO and the UN aimed at rectifying imbalances and injustices in the structure of international news flows.

(a) International Law against Propaganda

The experience of the Second World War and the growing use of short-wave broadcasting in the interwar years spurred states to take steps against propaganda. Preston[36] has identified a number of these: group libel became a recognised aspect of international law; the Kellogg–Briand Pact of 1928 that outlawed war also implied that incitement to war was criminal; an international right of reply was favoured by the International Juridical Congress in 1929 and by the International Federation of Journalists in 1934; the League of Nations established 'Radio Nations' to foster mutual understanding and good will; and, in the 1936 Geneva Convention on Broadcasting in the Cause of Peace, 22 nations agreed to 'insure that their transmissions do not constitute an incitement to war, or to acts likely to lead to war'. The three Axis powers and the US did not sign the convention on the grounds that their media were private and media houses could only be asked to volunteer. After the Second World War the UN adopted in 1952 the Convention on the International Right of Correction. Contracting states to the Convention agreed 'that in cases where the Contracting State contends that a news dispatch capable of injuring its relations with other States or its national prestige or dignity transmitted from one country to another by correspondents or disseminated abroad is false or distorted, it may submit its version of the facts ... to the Contracting States within whose territory such dispatch has been published or disseminated'.[37] Compliance was fostered by making states obliged to circulate corrections or else be denied the privilege themselves, and the UN Secretary-General was supposed to publicise non-compliance by particular states. The International Court of Justice was given power of arbitration.

(b) Protection of Journalists

UN initiatives to protect journalists begin with the recognition that the essential features of journalistic work are a 'human right'. This is contained in Article 19 of the 1948 Universal Declaration of Human Rights which says, 'Everyone has the right to freedom of opinion and expression; this right includes freedom to hold opinions without interference and to seek, receive and impart information and ideas through any media and regardless of frontiers.' International legal provisions dealing with the practice of journalism are in two main areas – the protection of journalists and codes of ethics – and all of these instruments begin with recognition of Article 19. A Draft International Code of Ethics for journalists was prepared by the UN Economic and Social Council in Resolution 442B (XIV) in 1952. The code said, *inter alia*, that journalists needed to ensure the relay of 'factually accurate' information, should be devoted to 'the public interest' and should avoid 'wilful calumny, slander, libel and unfounded accusations'. Article V said the Code was 'based on the principle that the responsibility for ensuring the faithful observance of professional ethics rests upon those who are engaged in the profession, and not upon any government'. This assertion was evidence that the balance of power in the UN at the time had caused liberal-democratic ideology to hold sway. In contrast, almost 20 years later, the Preliminary Draft International Convention on the Protection of Journalists Engaged in Dangerous Missions (transmitted to the General Assembly by the Economic and Social Council in its resolution 1597 [L], 1971) provided for journalists working in such situations to have 'safe-conduct' cards. The cards – bearing name, date and place of birth, habitual residence and nationality – would be a form of identification certifying that the carriers were professional journalists. Parties to the convention were to extend to holders of such cards 'the same protection of their persons as to their own journalists'. Such a convention, granting governments the power to certify the professional status of journalists, was a departure from the ideology regarding the press that prevailed in the early days of the UN. But, despite the expanded membership and consequent changed ideological climate, it is not difficult to see why nothing became of the Convention's provisions. The NWICO debate was to reveal that there were powerful interests, with the resources of money and their access to sources of publicity, who quickly mobilized to defeat any initiative that proposed government control of the press. Also safe-conduct cards would be a two-edged sword, identifying journalists for protection as well as harassment.

(c) Protection from Censorship

Non-governmental organizations, such as the International Press Insititute (IPI) and the Inter-American Press Association (IAPA), have existed as permanent bodies of agitation for the interests of the owners and executives of mass media that comprise their membership. A major concern of these institutions has been protecting mass media and journalists from the hostile behaviour of governments which comes in two main forms – censorship, and intimidation and harassment of workers. Press organizations lobby their cause by writing to offending governments, and to intergovernmental organizations to get attention, mobilizing their members to pursue campaigns in their editorial pages and broadcasts, and by publishing reports on the status of press freedom globally, regionally and nationally. They also pass various resolutions and other expressions of the collective will of their members that they hope will be heeded by governments.

The changed ideological climate toward press–government relations in the UN and UNESCO in the 1970s prompted media interests in the United States to form a new international non-governmental organization, the World Press Freedom Committee (WPFC), to wage ideological battle against forces whom they viewed as threatening to freedom. The WPFC's two declarations issued at Talloires, France, communicate what some media owners and executives wish to see in an international regime that would have the end of censorship as its fundamental principle.

According to its own literature, the WPFC was 'activated in May 1976 by a group of international journalists to unify the free world media for major threats that develop.'[38] By 1980 the WPFC was comprised of 32 journalistic organisations that provided the WPFC with 'a strong global voice against those who advocate state-controlled media; those who seek to deny truth in news; and those who abuse newsmen.'[39] But although its membership included the Caribbean Publishers and Broadcasters Association, the Japan Publishers and Editors Association and the Asia–Pacific Institute for Broadcast Training, the majority of the organisations were from the United States, and that country's private media supplied most of its funding and leadership. By 1980, Gannett, the largest newspaper chain in the US, had provided the biggest donation to the Committee (US$100 000). The WPFC used its funds for training projects in the South (such as $2000 on journalism textbooks in Kenya, and $10 000 on a seminar for business writers in Malaysia), publications that propagated the Committee's line on UNESCO's activities concerning communications,[40] and conferences such as those at Talloires.

The Declaration of Talloires was a product of the World Press Freedom Committee's Voices of Freedom Conference held in Talloires, from 15 to 17 May 1981.[41] Over 75 journalists and news executives from 24 countries in Asia, Africa, Europe and North and South America attended. Their Declaration said, *inter alia*, that:

> the free flow of information and ideas is essential for mutual understanding and world peace. We consider restraints on the movement of news and information to be contrary to the interests of international understanding, in violation of the Universal Declaration of Human Rights, the Constitution of UNESCO, and the Final Act of the Conference on Security and Co-operation in Europe; and inconsistent with the Charter of the United Nations.[42]

The Declaration also called for 'UNESCO and other intergovernmental bodies to abandon attempts to regulate the content of news and to formulate rules for the press'.[43] Instead, they urged that

Effort should be directed instead to finding practical solutions to the problems before us, such as improving technological training, increasing professional interchanges and equipment transfers, reducing communications tariffs, producing cheaper newsprint and eliminating other barriers to the development of news media capabilities.

The WPFC continued its battle to win over the media interests of the South in 1983 with its Talloires II conference. It was held from 30 September to 2 October, three weeks before the UNESCO General Conference in Paris. The 90 delegates that attended came from 25 countries, including 15 developing nations.[44] They drew up 'The List of Talloires' – 'a cross-indexed listing of more than 300 programs in 70 countries designed to equip journalists in developing countries with more professional skills'.[45]

The WPFC recognized the imbalances in global news flows, but it feared that attempts to solve the problem would lead to what it saw as the greater danger of government censorship. So transfer of news technologies and journalistic training went in tandem with resistance to censorship. But an alternative perspective on the matter posits that technologies and training bring with them their own values that might just reinforce the *status quo*. Either the WPFC was naive in not realizing the ideological nature of technology transfer and training or it was very astute in realizing that this was a way of co-opting any movement that threatened the interests of its members. A response from the socialist International Organization of Journalists (IOJ) to the Declaration of Talloires communicates the ideological divide that separated media interests of the era. IOJ President, Kaarle Nordenstreng, a Finnish writer and intellectual, regarded the Declaration as nothing more than another version of the 'Marshall Plan' strategy that was used by the United States in the late 1970s to neutralise the NWICO. The Declaration's call 'to abandon attempts to regulate global information and strive instead for practical solutions to Third World media advancement' received this characterization from Nordenstreng:

> Seen in the perspective of the media debate of the 1970s, this means, first, to turn attention away from a normative consideration of the content of communication and socio-political objectives which the media are supposed to serve and, second, to invite the media of the developing countries to co-operate with the private sector of the industrialized West in setting up, training, and maintaining their media infrastructure and personnel; in other words, 'trading ideology against cooperation'.[46]

(d) A Balanced, Just Global Flow

While principles relating to the outlawing of propaganda, censorship and repression of journalists had attracted multilateral attention for some time before and after the Second World War, attempts in the 1970s to set up regimes around the principles of balance and justice in global news flows were relative novelties in global media debates. In the heady years soon after decolonization and during the 'oil shocks', many small states, as members of the Group of 77 and the Non-Aligned Movement, demanded a New International Economic Order (NIEO) and a New World Information and Communication Order (NWICO) in tandem. The argument was that there were serious economic consequences to imbalances in the global news flows. As we have seen, the origins of the international news agencies as conduits for financial information reveal the symbiotic relationship between the international news structure and the structures of production. But, instead of viewing international news flows as the lubricants servicing efficient economic relationships, as the wire-service entrepreneurs might have done, the new, alternative view was that the imbalances in global news and information contributed to the problems of global economic inequalities and injustices. According to Sauvant, an information order dominated by Western values serves to undermine the goal of self-reliance because

> Under conditions of very scarce resources, the emulation of the socio-cultural systems and especially the consumption patterns of the rich home countries means first of all that the provision of basic foodstuffs, health services, clothing, housing, drinking water, education, reliable transportation and the like is neglected. It furthermore means that production processes tend to be utilised which actually may increase unemployment and underemployment; and that, in fact, resources are wasted in products subject to planned obsolescence. Moreover, to the extent that the satisfaction of foreign-oriented wants requires inputs from abroad, continuing dependence on countries and their institutions (especially transnational enterprises) that can provide these inputs remains almost unavoidable.[47]

Such ideas led to suggestions that transnational press organizations be subject to multilateral regulations. Adding to the momentum for this was the fact that North American and West European-based TNCs were under suspicion in the international political climate at the time and the proposed NIEO contained proposals for regulating them. The line of argument was that the international news agencies (specifically the Western Big Four) should be considered as multinational corporations before international law and should be subjected to the same rules and regulations that control international

monopolies. For example, the final report of the Non-Aligned Symposium on Information held in Tunis in 1976 stressed that there was a 'need for the non-aligned countries to look into the possibility of drawing up a common legislation for regulating the activities of the big press transnationals'.[48] The Declaration of the Ministerial Conference of Non-Aligned Countries on Decolonisation of Information held in New Delhi later that year said that the Non-Aligned countries should set up a Co-ordinating Council on information and communication issues to, *inter alia*, encourage 'Formulation of a common approach with a view to evolving an international code on the functioning and use of satellite communications, transnational press agencies and a code on direct and objective dissemination and free flow of information among various countries'.[49] In 1980 the resolution on 'The New International Information Order' passed by the fourth meeting of the Intergovernmental Council for Co-ordination of Information among Non-Aligned Countries, held in Baghdad, said that such an Order was based on, among other principles, 'the right of every nation to develop its own independent information system and to protect its national sovereignty and cultural identity, in particular by regulating the activities of the transnational corporations'.[50]

It was UNESCO's Mass Media Declaration of 1978 that attempted to reflect this extended collection of principles and was the most controversial proposal ever related to global news flows. Article VI declared that

it is necessary to correct the inequalities in the flow of information to and from developing countries and between those countries. To this end, it is essential that their mass media should have conditions and resources enabling them to gain strength and expand, and to cooperate both among themselves and with the mass media in developing countries.

The road to the Mass Media Declaration started in 1972 when the General Conference instructed the Director-General to formulate a set of principles 'governing the rise of the mass information media ... against propaganda on behalf of war, racialism and hatred among nations' and 'to strengthen peace and international understanding'.[51] Because of difficulties in finding a consensus on the wording of the document – especially resolving communist and Western attitudes to the press – the Mass Media Declaration took six years to draft before it was adopted by the General Conference. Keeping to the liberal-democratic tradition, Western media interests preferred that there be no declaration on the media at all; and categorical opposition to it came from the International Press Institute, Freedom House, the World Press Freedom Committee, the Inter-American Association of Broadcasters, Reuters and *The Times*. In its final form of 1978 the declaration was a slim document of only 11 articles called the

'Declaration on Fundamental Principles concerning the Contribution of the Mass Media to Strengthening Peace and International Understanding, to the Promotion of Human Rights and to Countering Racialism, Apartheid and Incitement to War'. These principles were meant to guide journalists the world over in the conduct of their profession. Although its passage can be regarded as a defeat of the West, Western opposition had still succeeded in moderating its content and so the Media Declaration was very descriptive in character instead of a normative document.

The other efforts at international law to reform global news flows mentioned above shared the fate of the Mass Media Declaration. The process of negotiation required for adoption by the UN produced documents that were so watered-down from their original versions (formulated at the Non-Aligned Movement and elsewhere) that they had little normative value.

The 1970s, in which there were rhetorical battles over global news such as had not been seen before and have not been seen since, concluded with the production of UNESCO's MacBride Report, a document which affirmed the supremacy of liberal-democratic values related to the press.[52] Although the report was criticized for containing proposals threatening to the free press, the real difficulty was not with the report but with the problem of multilateral decision-making for the mass media caused by states' refusal to surrender national sovereignty to international regimes. Even if the MacBride Report contained ideas entirely acceptable to media interests in North America and Western Europe it had little hope of being normative in scope.

CONCLUSION

While the case of international news reveals the power of information in international relations, this information is most powerful when combined with the power of communication possessed by certain kinds of media in specific regions. These media are the elite press, global television networks, and the international wire services, all based in the international power centres of North America and Europe.

What we have also shown in this chapter is how the structure of global news flows mirrors the structure of international political and economic relations. In the case of the 'Big Five' international news agencies the configuration of global political and economic power has shaped the ways in which they cover the world.

But the strategic role of news in international relations is more complex than a simple North/South divide, with rich countries using the structure of international news to control smaller, poorer ones. To understand the strategic value of news we must understand what are news values and the structures that co-opt those at the bottom of the global news hierarchy into defining news in specific ways. So how news is defined is an important explanatory variable for analysing the quantitative and qualitative character of international news.

There is no dispute over the fact that the quantitative and qualitative character of international news is imbalanced. The real quarrels have been over what should be done in the form of regime-creation or other actions by governments and media interests to change this scenario. Any global regime for news must cover the ideologically charged subjects of propaganda, government censorship, protection of journalists, and reform of the global imbalance in the flows of news and information. There have been various international laws and expressions of consensus by governments and non-governmental organizations on these issues at various times. But states have been unwilling to surrender national sovereignty in an area as strategic as news. Solving the problem of creating a more balanced flow of global news is also not as simple as providing more training and technologies for media workers in deprived areas. These processes replicate the hierarchies causing, and reflected by, the global news structure. Instead, a discourse such as the one presented in this chapter is the first stage in achieving lasting reform. No regimes for international news will last if they are created without clear understanding of the relationship between news and the other features of the international system valued by states and non-state actors. In particular, there is the direct relationship between news and political culture, including ideology, and the relationship between news and international power because of the very fact that news is a strategic entity in international relations.

NOTES

1. John M. Goshko, 'U.N. Chief Stresses Need For Money', *The Washington Post*, 22 November 1992, pp. A1, A33.
2   According to the Committee to Protect Journalists, 56 journalists were killed in the line of duty in calendar year 1993: 21 in Europe and the republics of the former Soviet Union; 14 in the Middle East and North Africa; 10 in the rest of Africa; eight in 'the Americas'; and three in Asia. As of March 1994, 126 journalists were in prisons around the world for reasons related to their reporting. Committee to Protect Journalists, *Attacks on the Press in 1993: A Worldwide Survey* (New York: Committee to Protect Journalists, 1994).
3. Mort Rosenblum, *Coups and Earthquakes* (New York: Harper & Row, 1979).

4. Annabelle Sreberny-Mohammadi *et al.* (eds), *Foreign News in the Media: International Reporting in 29 Countries*, Reports and Papers on Mass Communication, 93 (Paris: UNESCO, 1985), p. 52.

5. Anthony Smith, *The Geopolitics of Information* (London: Faber and Faber, 1980), p. 72.

6 Ajoa Yebo-Afari 'Watching the Media', *West Africa*, 31 August 1987, p. 1685.

7. Quoted in 'Tourist Journalists', *The Japan Times*, March 1981.

8. See UNESCO, *World Communication Report* (draft) (Paris: UNESCO, 1988), pp. 135–42. Anthony Smith in his *The Geopolitics of Information* (London: Faber & Faber, 1980) speaks of a 'big five' (p. 87). Richstad in 'Worldwide News Agencies – Private Wholesalers of Public Information', in Richstad and Anderson, *Crisis in International News* (New York: Columbia University Press, 1981), p. 243, has noted UNESCO's tendency to speak of a Big Five, but he argues that TASS and China's Hsin Hua 'do not measure significantly in the global flow of news' even though he points out that the communist agencies have the potential of 'increasing their global importance, and present some balance to Western reports'.

9. See Mark D. Alleyne, 'The Significance of the "Big Five" News Agencies in the New World Information and Communication Order Debate', M. Phil. thesis, University of Oxford, 1988.

10 Oliver Boyd-Barrett, *The International News Agencies* (London: Constable, 1980), p. 21.

11. The majority of statistics on UPI were compiled in 1987 with the kind assistance of the London bureau. Between that year and the time the statistics were last revised (February 1992) there is a great likelihood that the figures given would have contracted due to the agency's many problems. Many subscribers certainly dropped out in the late 1980s. However, we were unsuccessful in getting UPI to update our figures despite many attempts. By February 1992 it was also clear that the number of correspondents and countries covered by the new agency ITAR-TASS (see below), had contracted rapidly since 1990, but, due to the tremendous instability in the former Soviet Union, our sources within TASS could not provide specific updated statistics. For a discussion of the problems of UPI in the 1980s see Gregory Gordon and Ronald Cohen, *Down to the Wire: UPI's Fight for Survival* (New York: McGraw-Hill, 1990).

12. Anthony Smith, *Geopolitics*, p. 75. For more details on the history and development of Agence France-Presse see the typescript 'From Havas to AFP: 150 Years of News Reporting' (Paris, 1985).

13. For details of the history and development of Reuters, see: Reuters Holdings PLC, *Reuters: A Background and Chronology of Key Events* (London: Reuters, March 1987), and Jonathan Fenby, *The International News Services* (New York: Schocken Books, 1986).

14. See John C. Merrill, *Global Journalism* (New York: Longman, 1983), p. 334.

15. Smith, *Geopolitics*, p. 83.

16. Anthony Buzek, *How the Communist Press Works* (London: Pall Mall Press, 1964), pp. 188–9.

17. Personal interview, Yuri Levchenko, Chief Correspondent, TASS, London, 6 April 1988.

18. Francis Cline, 'Soviets Approve Law to Provide Press Freedoms', *New York Times* (13 June 1990), p. A1.

19.   Personal interview, Yuri Levchenko, Chief Correspondent, TASS, London, 6 April 1988.
20.   'Decree by the Russian Federation President on the Information Telegraph Agency of Russia', (22 January 1992). Complete text relayed by Federal News Service (Washington, DC, Federal Information Systems Corporation, 27 January 1992).
21.   Ludmila Alexandrova, 'News Agencies Agree on TASS Information Pool' (text). Moscow, TASS in English, 16 January 1992. *Foreign Broadcast Information Service Daily Report – Soviet Union*, 17 January 1992 (FBIS-SOV-92-012; p. 25).
22.   'Mikhail Poltoranin Meets the Staff of TASS (23 January 1992)', (TASS report), 24 January 1992. Translated with the kind assistance of Victoria Tsitlik.
23   Quoted in Fenby, *Internationa News Service*, p. 58. Also see Frank Bartholomew, 'Putting the "I" into UPI', *Editor & Publisher*, 25 September 1982.
24.   *Reuters: A Background and Chronology of Key Events*, p. 10.
25.   Ibid.
26.   See Bill McAllister, 'UPI Will Transmit US Agency's Material', *IHT*, 10 October, 1987.
27.   Jean-Luc Renaud, 'US Government Assistance to AP's World-Wide Expansion', *Journalism Quarterly* (Spring 1985), pp. 10–6, 36. Also see Margaret Blanchard, *Exporting the First Amendment: The Press-Government Crusade of 1945–1952* (New York: Longman, 1986).
28.   For details of Reuters' recent financial performance, see *Reuters Holdings PLC Annual Report* (most recent year).
29.   *Reuters: A Background and Chronology of Key Events* (London: Reuters, 1987) p. 3.
30.   *Reuters: A Background and Chronology of Key Events*, pp. 11–2.
31.   *Reuters Holdings PLC Annual Report 1990*, p. 20.
32.   *Reuters: A Background and Chronology of Key Events*, p. 6.
33.   'From Havas to AFP ...', p. 13.
34.   AP Corporate Communications typescript, 'The Associated Press: Origin, History and Development' (New York, 2 April 1987), p. 1.
35.   Lenin's so-called 'Twenty-One Conditions', presented to the Second Congress of the Comintern (19 July–7 August 1920) included: (a) strict guidelines for running the communist press; and (b) the stipulation that refusal to do propaganda work would be seen as resignation from revolutionary action.
36.   William Preston Jr., Edward S. Herman and Herbert I. Schiller, *Hope and Folly: The United States and UNESCO 1945–1985* (Minneapolis: University of Minnesota Press, 1989), pp. 26–7.
37.   Convention on the International Right of Correction, 1952, Article II (1).
38.   World Press Freedom Committee, *The Media Crisis ...* (Miami: World Press Freedom Committee, 1981), p. 107.
39.   Ibid.
40.   See *The Media Crisis ...*; and World Press Freedom Committee, *The Media Crisis ... A Continuing Struggle* (Washington, DC: World Press Freedom Committee, 1982).

41. See 'UNESCO Urged to Leave Press Alone,' *The Guardian*, 18 May 1981; as well as *The Media Crisis ...* and *The Media Crisis ... A Continuing Challenge*.
42. 'Declaration of Talloires' in Kusum Singh and Bertram Gross, "MacBride": The Report and the Response', *Journal of Communication*, Vol. 31, no. 4, Fall, 1981, pp. 113–15.
43. Ibid.
44. Thomas MePhail, *Electronic Colonialism*, Revised Second Edition (Beverly Hills: SAGE, 1987), p. 235.
45. Ibid.
46. Kaarle Nordenstreng, Enrique Gonzales Manet and Wolfgang Kleinwachter, *New International Information Order Sourcebook* (Prague: International Organization of Journalists, 1986), p. 35.
47. Karl P. Sauvant, 'From Economic to Socio-Cultural Emancipation: The historical context of the New International Economic Order and the New Socio-Cultural Order', *Third World Quarterly*, 1981, Vol. 3, no. 1, p. 59.
48. Kaarle Nordenstreng, Enrique Gonzales Manet and Wolfgang Kleinwachter, *New International Information Order Sourcebook*, p. 282.
49. Ibid., p. 287.
50. Ibid., p. 303.
51. See UNESCO 17 C/Res. 4.113 of 15 November 1972 (UNESCO 17 C/Resolutions at 70); and UNESCO Doc. 17 C/77 (1972).
52. Although the Report was criticized as hostile to a free press, in its text there are no proposals for regulating the 'Big Four' or censoring their news. The MacBride Report reflected the same liberal-democratic assumptions about the role of the mass media as those held by American media interests. This perspective was explicitly articulated on page 233:

> Freedom of the press in its widest sense represents the collective enlargement of each citizen's freedom of expression which is accepted as a human right. Democratic societies are based on the concept of sovereignty of the people, whose general will is determined by an informed public opinion. It is this right of the public to know that is the essence of media freedom of which the professional journalist, writer and producer are only custodians. Deprivation of this freedom diminishes all others.
> The press has been described as the fourth estate because full and accurate information on matters of public interest is the means by which governments, institutions, organizations and all others in authority, at whatever level are held accountable to and by the public.

In other words, each individual is free to choose for himself or herself; the only way an individual can make a rational choice is by having access to unadulterated information about his or her environment; the 'public opinion' formed by the collective choices of all these individuals is what should guide government action and determine the future of those placed in authority over the people. On page 234 the Report said restrictions on journalists not only damaged this social process but also hurt the profession of journalism itself because it can produce 'a situation in which honest journalists abandon the profession, and young people of talent decide not to enter it'. See International Commission for the Study of Communication Problems, *Many Voices, One World* (London: Kogan Page, 1980).

5 The Phenomenon of Cultural Relations

Lurking in the background of debates over trade in cultural products, transnational mass media and global news flows is the assumption that seemingly innocent items of entertainment, such as TV programmes and recorded music, are ideological tools of governments. These ideas make the relationship between international power and international communication seem even more sinister. Before governments of countries that are large generators of cultural products (such as France, Britain and the United States) can disseminate their own propaganda it seems that images of these countries, for better or worse, have been created in the minds of foreign populations. Some thinkers have explored how governments have actually deliberately used cultural industries, especially commercial movie production, to further their foreign policy objectives.[1] In comparison, the cultural industries of some countries can create certain images of some other nations or races, making it a task for these peoples to dispel stereotypes,[2] or creating pretexts for specific forms of international behaviour.[3] When governments decide to forsake the vagaries of mass media and international news to create and manage their own public relations they resort to 'cultural relations' and 'cultural diplomacy'.

The most poignant reminder of the significance of 'cultural diplomacy' or 'public diplomacy' in international relations can be got by tuning into the short-wave radio bands from any part of the globe at virtually any time of the day. Depending on where you are and when you are listening, you will hear a variety of radio stations in various languages, most of them owned by governments and broadcasting with the main goal of doing international public relations for those governments. The most extensive international broadcasters include the BBC World Service from London, the Voice of America, Radio Moscow and Deutsche Welle of Germany.

The term 'public diplomacy' was coined by the Americans to describe a means of conducting international relations that includes, but is not confined to, international short-wave broadcasting. The British refer to the same practices as 'cultural diplomacy'. Public or cultural diplomacy are one part of what are known as the 'cultural relations' of states.

In a book published in 1986 to help fill the void in International Relations literature caused by the neglect of cultural relations, the former Assistant Director-General of the British Council, J.M. Mitchell,

96

defined cultural relations as the 'fostering of co-operative relationships between cultural and educational institutions and individuals so that nations can interrelate intellectually, artistically and socially'.[4] This is in contrast to *cultural diplomacy* which is the 'involvement of culture in international agreements; the application of culture to the direct support of a country's political and economic diplomacy'.[5] Whereas cultural diplomacy is conducted only by government agencies, cultural relations are undertaken by both government agencies and private individuals and organizations. Cultural diplomacy is only one part of cultural relations.

The significance that states attach to cultural relations today can be gleaned from the fact that institutions such as the United States Information Agency (USIA), the British Council and the Alliance Française are now considered vital components in the successful execution of their states' international relations. Cultural relations makes maximum use of the means of international communication – international broadcasting, books, movies, TV programmes, periodicals, and other means. Governments have used these means as part of their cultural relations to win wars or gain favour in other states.

HISTORY

The use of cultural relations increased as means of mass communication were enhanced in the twentieth century and their strategic benefits, in times of war especially, were realised. The evolution of cultural relations and propaganda[6] was put quite succinctly by a British Committee of Enquiry in the early 1950s when it noted that

> To provide information about this country so that its policies would be understood and accepted abroad has always been part of the function of our diplomatic missions. In this sense information work is as old as diplomacy itself. But in the past it was enough for diplomats mainly to concern themselves with the small official world with which they were in personal contact. What is new is propaganda and counter-propaganda in the forms and on the scale which we now know. The necessity for this wider concept has come about with the development of mass methods of communications which can be used by Governments as a means of influencing public opinion in other countries in support of their foreign policy. Propaganda was developed to a high degree by the totalitarian Powers in the inter-war period and it was used on a vast

scale by both sides in the two Great Wars. Today virtually all countries, great or small, use this weapon in one way or another.[7]

International radio broadcasts by the Axis powers are the most infamous examples of the use of means of international communication for strategic advantage, particularly the programme supervised by Josef Goebbels which accounted to a large degree for the attachment of pejorative connotations to the term 'propaganda'. However, the fascist powers were not the first to broadcast internationally in foreign languages. The Soviet Union started broadcasts in English and German in the mid-1920s and was transmitting in about 50 languages and dialects by 1930. Lenin is said to have described broadcasting as an 'international newspaper'.[8]

When the Germans and Italians established schools and institutes[9] in various parts of the globe in the 1930s to maintain the allegiance of nationals and influence foreigners, they were employing techniques in cultural relations set in vogue by the French in the nineteenth century. After France was defeated by Prussia in 1871, the Alliance Française was started in 1883 so that France could invoke 'her cultural patrimony as a means of rehabilitation'.[10] The Alliance was to teach French in the colonies and elsewhere. It was followed 31 years later, in 1902, by the Lay Mission for non-religious teaching overseas. Third and fourth French institutions of international cultural relations came in 1910: the national office for school and university exchanges; and the Bureau for Schools and French Foundations Abroad (Bureau des écoles et des oeuvres françaises à l'étranger).[11] Because the French pioneered institutionalised cultural relations, this model that involved language teaching, 'education', exchanges, and even religion, was copied by the countries that adopted cultural relations in the twentieth century.

There was a marked difference between the crude forms of propaganda used during the First World War and before and the techniques employed later in the century. In the interwar years and during the Second World War the powers perfected their techniques by using the French model to make their strategies subtle and more pervasive. The methods used during the First World War were largely written propaganda messages, such as the pamphlets and books used by the British to get support in the US after two-thirds of American newspaper-owners were found to be neutral,[12] and the leaflets that were dropped from balloons over enemy territory.[13] Radio was used in war as far back as the Russo-Japanese War (1904–5) when it was employed in naval communication, and it was confined to the military sphere in the First World War. But it was only with Nazi propaganda of the 1930s that the institution of radio, which was previously regarded as a benign invention for domestic entertainment, became a weapon in struggles to influence public opinion.[14]

The experience of the Second World War and the growing use of short-wave broadcasting spurred states to take the steps against propaganda identified in Chapter 4. Preston[15] has identified a number of these: group libel became a recognised aspect of international law; the Kellogg–Briand Pact of 1928 that outlawed war also implied that incitement to war was criminal; an international right of reply was favoured by the International Juridical Congress in 1929 and by the International Federation of Journalists in 1934; the League of Nations established 'Radio Nations' to foster mutual understanding and good will; and, in the 1936 Geneva Convention on Broadcasting in the Cause of Peace, 22 nations agreed to 'insure that their transmissions do not constitute an incitement to war, or to acts likely to lead to war'. The three Axis powers and the US did not sign the convention on the grounds that their media were private and media houses could only be asked to volunteer.

In the late 1930s France was the only state with a 'cultural service' up to the task of combating Italian and German propaganda.[16] It was about that time that the British started institutionalised cultural relations. The British had disbanded their propaganda organization of the First World War but were persuaded to re-examine their position in the face of Nazi propaganda. UK propaganda during the First World War was handled by the News Department of the Foreign Office. The budget for such activities in 1918 was £2 million. That figure was scaled down immediately on completion of the war to £80 000, and Foreign Secretary Lord Curzon declared in 1919 that 'British propaganda in Foreign Countries shall, in future, be regarded as part of the regular work of His Majesty's Missions Abroad'.[17] In 1930 the Treasury began annual grants for 'books, lectures, films and miscellaneous minor services'.[18] Four years later a Committee of International Understanding and Cooperation was set up to coordinate the work of the General Post Office Film Unit, the Travel Association, the Department of Overseas Trade, and the News Department of the Foreign Office. This short-lived committee became the British Council, the first budget of which, in 1935, was £5000. The increased importance the British government attached to cultural relations, especially in the wake of war, can be gleaned from the rapid expansion of the Council's budget. It was £60 000 in 1937/38, £130 000 in 1938/39 and £2.1 million in 1944/45. In 1947 it had 53 institutes world-wide, seven in Egypt alone.[19]

The other form of British international cultural relations that would remain an institution in the UK's foreign relations from the 1930s onwards was the British Broadcasting Corporation (BBC). The BBC's Empire

Service was started in 1932, becoming the first regularly scheduled short-wave service in the world with 10 hours per day. The history of international short-wave broadcasting in the years between that milestone and the outbreak of the Second World War is fascinating because it reveals that international broadcasting expanded as conflict heightened. Between 1932 and 1937 the BBC added additional transmitters but it broadcast in no other language but English and never exceeded 17 hours per day on the air.[20] However, during those same years Russia, France and Germany experimented with external broadcasting in foreign languages, and Japan and Italy got their own international short-wave services in 1935. During this period the Abyssinian War and the Spanish Civil War provided the first occasions for the use of short-wave broadcasting as a weapon of political warfare. Largely in response to this occurrence, the BBC finally assumed broadcasts in foreign languages in 1937 with Arabic, Spanish and Portuguese. Two years later the number of these foreign languages increased to nine. In the meantime, Hitler employed broadcasting in the campaign against Czechoslovakia. The BBC reached its peak of wartime operations in 1944 when it was broadcasting in almost 50 languages, amounting to a total of about 130 hours daily from the total of 43 transmitters.[21]

After the war the British government decided to continue 'national propaganda overseas' with the aims of (a) supporting British foreign policy; (b) preserving and strengthening the Commonwealth and Empire; and (c) increasing British trade and protecting British investments overseas.[22] The Ministry of Information that had been set up for the war was abolished and replaced by a decentralised system in which British propaganda was conducted from the Foreign Office, the Commonwealth Relations Office, the Colonial Office and the Board of Trade, which all set policy; and from the 'operational' agencies of the British Council, the BBC and the Central Office of Information. Although the cold war, decolonisation and international economic difficulties were a challenge to British propaganda activities in the immediate post-Second World War period, by 1952 the 'Overseas Information Services' had been 'steadily whittled down', being effectively cut in half during the years since 1947 due to annual budget cuts and inflation. In 1952 these services accounted for 0.25 per cent (£10 million) of UK government expenditure.[23]

The Drogheda Committee enquired into British international cultural relations at the beginning of the 1950s and recommended a significant expansion. The 'broad pattern of information needs' set down by this committee indicates the detailed strategic thinking that surrounded Britain's approach to the use of the means of international communication as part of its foreign policy. The pattern broke the world down into seven parts: the 'Iron Curtain'; 'Asia'; 'United States of America'; 'Latin America'; 'Free Europe'; 'the Commonwealth'; and 'the Colonies'. The Committee advocated broadcasting as the 'only means of getting the voice of the West heard' behind the Iron Curtain.[24] Asia had to be a high priority for political and commercial reasons, and Britain should exploit the great demand to learn English in that region through the use of the British Council. 'The Communist threat required also political information work and broadcasting in this area.'[25] In the USA the British Council was not needed, in contrast, 'owing to community of language and cultural heritage', but there was the need for an efficient Information Service to explain British attitudes and policies. In Latin America, 'commercial publicity' was to be a top priority and the Foreign Office Information Service was the best medium to be used, supplemented by the Anglophile societies in the region, the British Council and the BBC. In Free Europe 'political and commercial publicity' was best conducted out of the various British embassies. Foreign language broadcasting was necessary only to those countries in Free Europe 'particularly exposed to the threat of Communist pressure'. In the Commonwealth the requirements differed from country to country but the BBC was the important link with all Commonwealth countries. In contrast, there should be a three-pronged strategy in the colonies: the use of the Information Services to explain the policies of the British government; the use of the British Council for adult education; and the BBC to provide news and transcriptions to local broadcasting systems in the colonies.

Despite its history of stops and starts, the UK's international cultural relations never again had the temporary and somewhat disorganised character of the interwar and war years. By the 1980s, the BBC was broadcasting in English and 36 other languages for almost 735 hours a week; the British Council had 116 libraries around the world and was assisting about 56 000 students overseas in learning English annually.[26]

Like the UK, the United States institutionalised its international cultural relations, after France and the Axis powers, in a late, reactive fashion, but, unlike that of the British, American international cultural relations enjoyed a steady expansion from the 1930s onwards and it was of an entirely different type. Preston asserts that US international cultural relations were less subtle. They aimed aimed at converting others to an American way of thinking rather than to listen to foreign concerns.[27] The US government opened a Division of Cultural Relations in 1938, followed two years later by the office of the Co-ordinator of Inter-American Affairs. Months after the attack on Pearl Harbor of December 1941, the Voice of America started broadcasts. The Office of War Information was also established in 1942, along with its overseas component, the US Information Service.

Whereas in Western Europe it was fascism that provided the spur for Britain to enter the propaganda war and institutionalise her cultural relations, the Cold War was the spark for the expansion of this new area of US foreign policy. In 1945, the year of the UNESCO constitution, the US had 48 cultural relations officers and 70 libraries in 30 countries.[28] About the same time there were 21 cultural centres abroad and 300 American schools in 'other American Republics'.[29] In 1946, while Stalin was according top priority to political indoctrination at home, Senator J. William Fulbright introduced Public Law 584 that started the famous international academic and cultural exchanges.

The major milestone in the history of US public diplomacy was the passage of the Smith–Mundt Act in 1948, the basic legislation authorizing United States informational and educational exchanges. In 1952 the US government spent over $162.8 million on these exchanges and other forms of international cultural relations, including $7.3 million in the Fulbright Scholarships. In addition, that year the Mutual Security Agency spent $21.7 million on 'overseas Information Work'.[30] Such activities got an even greater institutional character in 1953 with the setting up of the United States Information Agency (USIA), the jurisdiction of which covered the Voice of America. But while the VOA was overtly 'telling America's story abroad' (in the words of the USIA's motto), the Central Intelligence Agency (CIA) was covertly financing Radio Free Europe and Radio Liberty to pursue the cold war over the airwaves. Radio Free Europe was started in 1950 for broadcasts to East Europe. Radio Liberty started transmissions in 1953 to the various linguistic groups within the USSR. Both stations were based in Munich and claimed to be funded by non-governmental sources until their backing from the CIA was revealed many years later.[31]

The history of this battle of the airwaves during the cold war seems as intriguing as a spy novel. The Eastern Bloc jammed the VOA, Radio Free Europe and Radio Liberty. During the cold war the entire Eastern Bloc was allegedly engaged in blocking out broadcasts from the West. The Soviet Union alone is said to have used 2000 transmitters for the purpose of jamming. Poland allegedly spent £500 000 per annum on jamming before it stopped in 1956.[32] Floating transmitters in the Mediterranean were used to outfox the jammers, as well as a 'balloon campaign' that repeated the practice employed in the First World War of using balloons to drop propaganda leaflets in enemy territory. The balloon campaign started in 1951 and by 1956 was carrying 250 million copies of the leaflets.[33]

What is striking about the character of the international cultural relations of West Europeans, and of the United States in particular, was its self-righteous assumptions. Mitchell has noted that:

It used to be easier than it is now for intelligent Europeans to believe that their culture enjoyed such a superiority that its propagation was an obligation hardly less deniable than that of the good book. Even within living memory there have been cultural representatives who looked on the ability of foreign students to learn their language and mentality as a sign of grace: those students who could not progress so far were dismissed to outer darkness.[34]

This self-righteousness was also reflected in the terminology used to describe post-Second World War propaganda. In 1953, while arguing for US 'psychological warfare' to be a permanent feature of war plans, Hans Speier of the Rand Corporation, the research centre advising the Defense Department, noted that

It is significant that even the term 'psychological warfare' was used only by the military in designating their propaganda units, whereas the civilian agencies did not officially spread propaganda, but 'information and truth'.[35]

In other words, policy-makers in the United States and some other states of the North, approached international communication issues of the 1970s with this heritage of regarding their view of the world as being not necessarily ethnocentric. Even the writing of Mitchell, the former Assistant Director-General of the British Council, who has pointed out this ethnocentrism, reveals this myopia. After noting Marxist criticisms of Western 'cultural imperialism' in developing nations, Mitchell suggests that

In so far ... as the Western cultural presence and aid programmes are intended partly at least to erect a bulwark against communism, it is important to take the Marxist ideological ambitions seriously. Efforts in this direction will lack finesse unless they are based on an appreciation of the need to reach the semi-westernized intellectuals (e.g. schoolteachers, middle-rank officials and media personnel), who should constitute one of the most important target groups, standing as they do between the westernized elite and the diffused mass of the population. This task calls for greater resources than are available to cultural agencies alone. But these should play their part by appealing to the interest and sympathy of their own target groups among intellectuals.[36]

CULTURAL DIPLOMACY'S ELITE

Cultural relations as a means of pursuing international policy is extremely capital-intensive. For this reason only a handful of states are able to pursue government-sponsored cultural relations worldwide. These tend to be the states with extensive commercial and military interests: Japan, Germany, Russia, France, Canada, Britain and the United States. This does not mean that other states do not underwrite certain types of cultural relations. For example, well over 80 countries engage in international short-wave broadcasting.[37] But relatively few countries can maintain a full variety of programmes for conducting international cultural relations, the most well-known of which are language training, exchanges of persons, maintaining a global network of libraries and information centres, international radio and TV broadcasting, and distribution of books and periodicals.

Each member of this elite club of states organizes its cultural relations according to one of three possible models that have been identified by Mitchell: *direct government control*, where a department of government is set up for handling all the country's cultural relations, the best example being the United States Information Agency (USIA); *indirectly through non-governmental, autonomous agencies*, such as the British Council which has some autonomy even though it is mainly funded by the government; and a *mixed system*, such as Germany's, in which the 'government retains overall control but funds and contracts non-official agencies to operate independently within their competences'.[38] Whatever the institutional arrangement used, the money spent annually by each of the main states on international cultural relations alone is often greater than the national budgets of many countries.

Table 5.1 is a good illustration of capital-intensity of international public relations and the relative size of the programmes of three of these main players. The Japan Foundation and the British Council are non-governmental, autonomous agencies, while the Goethe Institute is part of the mixed system maintained by the Germans.

Although all three countries have economies large enough to support the most extensive cultural relations programmes in the world, it is striking how the budgets and size of the Goethe Institute and British Council dwarf those of the Japan Foundation. For example, the British Council's budget is almost five times that of the Japan Foundation, it has more than 20 times the staff, and it had 183 overseas offices in fiscal 1992 compared to the 15 of the Japan Foundation. The explanation of this situation is the fact that Japan entered the elite club of states with worldwide, institutionalised cultural relations much later than the Europeans and Americans. An

Table 5.1 Major foreign institutions concerned with cultural exchange

Fiscal 1992		The Japan Foundation	The Goethe Institute	The British Council
Budget		¥19.3 billion	DM334 million (¥27.3 billion)	£388 million (¥94.3 billion)
	comparative ratio	1	1.4	4.9
Staff		245	3431	4993
	comparative ratio	1	14.0	20.4
Overseas offices		15	147	183
	comparative ratio	1	9.8	12.2

Notes: 1. The Budget is given in 1992 values for the Japan Foundation and the Goethe Institute, and in 1991 values for the British Council.
2. The number of staff members for the Japan Foundation includes five government officials. The number of staff members for the Goethe Institute includes 750 language instructors.
3. The computation rate is that of the fiscal 1991 expenditures (DM1 = ¥82, £1 = ¥243)

Source: The Japan Foundation, *Overview of Programs for Fiscal 1992/ Annual Report for Fiscal 1991* (Tokyo: The Japan Foundation, 1993)

act of the Japanese Diet established the Japan Foundation in 1972 with an initial endowment of five billion yen. By August 1992 that endowment had grown to 94.9 billion yen.[39]

It is significant that Japan entered the club about the time its economy was emerging as one of the three most powerful in the world. As was noted in the previous section, international cultural relations is often used as a lubricant for external trading relations. In the context of Japan's expanding commercial links, the Foundation's brief was *inter alia* to, 'produce, collect, exchange, and distribute materials to introduce Japanese culture abroad and to promote international exchange, including books and other printed materials, films, slides, photographs, records, tapes, and other audio-visual materials'. Just as the endowment grew, the Foundation's programmes expanded. For example, in fiscal 1973 it sponsored the distribution of 34 feature films and the dispatch of 21 Japanese language specialists. By fiscal 1991 that number of films was 129, and the number of language specialists was 204.[40]

Although (as we will discuss below) institutionalised international cultural relations thrives on dependence, the bulk of money spent by the Japan Foundation and of institutions of cultural relations is not in the poorest parts of the world. Strategic, commercial and political concerns dictate that the major players devote the majority of their resources in the regions where they stand to gain the most. For example, in fiscal 1991 the three regions of the world where the Japan Foundation spent the bulk of its budget were North America (just over two billion yen), Southeast Asia (almost two billion yen), and Western Europe (nearly one and a half billion yen). In contrast, only about 193 million yen was spent on the continent of Africa.[41] This relative unimportance of Africa is also mirrored in the fact that the continent was not the site of any of the 13 cultural institutes, centres and liaison offices the Foundation maintained outside Japan in fiscal 1991.[42]

In contrast to the three institutions shown in Table 5.1, the United States Information Agency is a much more elaborate entity because it is the centralized government agency for the majority of the United States international cultural relations, including running international radio broadcasting stations, an activity that is not done by the Goethe Institute, British Council or the Japan Foundation. A similar pattern of priorities, based on strategic and other concerns, is depicted in the USIA's budgetary statistics for fiscal 1992. For example, in the budget of just over US one billion dollars, $36 million was spent on radio and TV broadcasting to Cuba alone.[43]

CULTURAL RELATIONS AND POWER

Using the distinction between the power of communication and the power of information introduced in Chapter 1, we can analyse the significance of cultural relations and cultural diplomacy in international politics. The awareness of the power of information has led governments to invest heavily in the various means of international communication. States with the wealth to maintain standing institutions for pursuing international cultural relations also gain the most from the power of communication. This is so because it gives them the power to manage the flow of information into, and sometimes out of, target countries or regions. Seen in this way, the power of communication is actually more important than the power of information because it determines the very effectiveness of information. Therefore, it is this power of communication in relation to international cultural relations that we analyse in greater detail in this section. The argument is that there are three scenarios which are the key configurations of the power of international cultural relations: (a) international cultural relations as a means of managing crises; (b) the tendency for some state-sponsored international broadcasting to become 'surrogate' domestic services for foreign publics; and (c) the way in which imbalance in the structure of international communication has facilitated the dependence of poor states on international cultural relations for information and education, almost as though information disseminated in this way is not part of the propaganda instruments of other states.

(a) The Management of Crises

As we have seen in the section above on the history of this tool, war has most often been the impetus for starting or reviving international cultural relations, especially cultural diplomacy. Military conflict is a rather straightforward example of what could be described as a crisis, but the definition is also a subjective one to be made by the state opting to use international cultural relations as a means of conducting its international relations. It is the potential for crisis to arise that explains the maintenance of standing institutions conducting international cultural relations even more than specific, identifiable crises. A good illustration of this is the case of commercial relations where states are conscious of how a good image is vital to keeping trading partners. That, no doubt, was in the minds of the Japanese as they emerged from defeat in the Second World War and established a powerful economy in the early 1970s. This analysis can be taken a step further with the observation that cultural diplomacy is a tool that is also used to create crises, or perceived crises, when it is in the interest of one actor to create such a situation.

This relationship with actual, prospective, perceived or created crises is the basic configuration of how international cultural relations is a resource for power in international relations. The two other configurations that we discuss below are both based on this fundamental observation.

The cases from the World Wars and the cold war discussed above were examples of the use of cultural diplomacy and propaganda in actual crises. In the case of military conflicts ('hot' wars), a way of studying the utility of cultural diplomacy has been to look at the difference between strategies directed at civilians and soldiers. For example, in his study of propaganda in times of military conflict, Speier has made the distinction between *tactical* propaganda, designed to break the will of enemy troops, and *strategic* propaganda directed at sapping the morale of enemy civilians.[44]

It can be argued that the cold war on many occasions provided the pretext for crises that were more perceived or created than *de facto* and cultural diplomacy has played a key role in constructing the stories of such crises. An example of this would be the proxy domestic conflict in Chile which is also an illustration of how covert intelligence activities have been linked with cultural diplomacy.

In the mid-1970s a congressional staff report discussed how the United States destabilized the elected government of socialist Salvador Allende in Chile using, *inter alia*, mass media and journalists. The congressional investigators acknowledged that in Chile the 'United States attempted to overthrow a democratically elected government' and that such activities 'appear to violate our international treaty obligations and commitments, such as the charters of the United Nations and Organization of American States'. The CIA reportedly spent millions financing *El Mercurio*, a Chilean newspaper opposed to President Salvador Allende; it orchestrated a statement by the Inter-American Press Association (IAPA) attacking the Allende government; and it sponsored trips to Chile of many foreign journalists to report unfavourably on the government.[45]

The revelations about Chile were just part of the broader fabric of cold war foreign policy-making that used the means of international communication as one of its most effective tools. In April 1976, the final report of the US Senate's 'Select Committee to Study Governmental Operations with Respect to Intelligence Activities' (the Church Committee) was published, revealing that the US media often knowingly or unwittingly worked for the CIA in collecting intelligence and manipulating domestic politics in foreign countries. Much of the information presented to the committee was kept classified (such as the chapter titled 'Espionage' and two sections of the chapter 'Covert Action of the CIA') but the final report of over 600 pages made it clear that use of the media was a significant part of US covert activities in other countries. The report noted that:

Until February 1976, when it announced a new policy toward U.S. media personnel, the CIA maintained covert relationships with about 50 American journalists or employees of US media organizations. They are part of a network of several hundred foreign individuals around the world who provide intelligence for the CIA and at times attempt to influence foreign opinion through the use of covert propaganda. These individuals provide the CIA with direct access to a large number of foreign newspapers and periodicals, scores of press services and news agencies, radio and television stations, commercial book publishers, and other foreign media outlets.[46]

In the case of Chile the United States was able to use covert action and public diplomacy to create a 'crisis' situation that provided a pretext for the overthrow of the Allende government. This was part of the broader scheme of institutionalized international cultural relations and public diplomacy that could be called upon on various occasions to serve the imperatives of foreign policy-making.

Raboy and Dagenais argue that labelling, or not labelling, certain situations as crises are 'ideological and political' acts, and, therefore, 'Making these choices and structuring the way they are presented in the public sphere has become one of the essential functions of mass media.'[47] For Raboy and Dagenais, 'the media–crisis relationship becomes a key factor in the struggle for democracy', and media 'constitute a contested terrain in the struggles surrounding conceptualization, definitions, and transformation of society in different parts of the world'.[48] The 1980s and early 1990s provided several examples of governments using public diplomacy and the careful management of journalistic coverage for strategic ends in 'crisis' situations. Reporters were not allowed to be present, or were present under very controlled circumstances during Israel's operations in Lebanon and Britain's war in the Falklands in 1982, the US in Grenada in 1983, the French in Chad in 1988, the US in Panama in 1989, and the Persian Gulf War in 1991/92.

(b) 'Surrogate' Domestic Services

The lesson from the conduct of cultural diplomacy via international broadcasting in the years since the Second World War is that institutions created to manage 'crises' often take on a purpose of their own quite separate from the original objectives. In various parts of the world the broadcasts of the BBC, VOA, Radio Liberty and Radio Free Europe became essential sources of information for audiences without comparable domestic radio stations or with unreliable, state-controlled media. The international radio of foreign governments is described as providing 'home service' or 'surrogate' broadcasting in such situations. Rampal and Adams have noted that even during the Falklands war many Argentineans listened to the BBC (the broadcaster of the enemy) for reports on the war; Iranians and Iraqis got their reliable information during their eight-year war from the BBC and VOA; and a key source of news about happenings in China for millions in the People's Republic of China during the democracy movement of May 1989 was the VOA.[49] So high are the reputations of these international broadcasters that friendly governments also retransmit their programmes on their domestic services; this was especially the case with the

BBC World (radio) Service in the former colonies of the British Empire after decolonisation.[50] The BBC benefited from such good will when it created its World Service TV in the early 1990s.[51]

The BBC and VOA have achieved reputations for 'objective' relays of news from inside and outside countries, and their roles as agents of cultural diplomacy are somewhat different from the services of RFE and RL which evolved to become means of intra-state communication. One observer has described their function by explaining that

> Unlike the BBC, the VOA and other international broadcasters, RFE/RL's programming concentrates almost entirely on internal events in the countries to which it is broadcast. ... The VOA's Polish service devotes around 20% of its feature programming to events in Poland or neighboring countries. RFE devotes over 70%. That's why when a VOA announcer uses the word 'we' he means 'we Americans,' but when RFE or RL announcers use that pronoun, they mean 'we Russians,' 'we Bulgarians,' etc. Listeners consider RFE/RL their stations, not those of a foreign government.[52]

The Economist estimated the annual cost of RFE/RL to be about $210 annually.[53] Both were set up in Munich by the CIA as anti-communist stations – RFE in 1951, broadcasting to Eastern Europe, and RL in 1953, beamed to the Soviet Union. In 1971 their ties with the CIA were cut and in 1976 their administration was merged as RFE/RL. By the early 1990s RFE/RL were broadcasting in six Eastern European languages, the three Baltic languages, in Russian and in 13 other languages spoken in the former Soviet Union. During their 50-year lives RFE and RL had also amassed in Munich at their research institute one of the largest collections in the world of research materials on the Soviet Union and Eastern Europe.[54]

This configuration of the role of cultural diplomacy shows that we must add another meaning to the definition of power. In the previous section we saw that power is the ability to define. The case of surrogate services suggests that power is also the ability to fulfil a need. If the American government was under any doubts about what the stations they supported in Eastern Europe meant to those countries they were reminded in the early 1990s when President of the Czech Republic, Vaclav Havel, in the wake of President Clinton's plan to abolish Radio Free Europe, wrote personal letters to leading members of Congress to whip up opposition to the President's plans.[55] A similar plea came from the former Soviet dissident, Elena Bonner.[56] The end of the cold war had removed the original pretexts for such broadcasts, but it had also shown how governments can gain influence over not merely time but a generation. The search for a mission of US international broadcasting in the post-cold war period created proposals for 'Radio Free China', a station that would become a 'home service' for the largest last remaining bastion of communism.[57]

(c) Dependence

The third configuration is similar to, but different from, the one discussed above. Institutionalised cultural relations and cultural diplomacy become part of a structure of international dependence. This is succinctly and poignantly expressed by Hachten who says,

> Generally, Third World nations are on the receiving end of public diplomacy because most lack the communication capability to compete globally. A partial exception has been the extensive radio broadcasting by a few developing nations – the Voice of the Arabs station under Egypt's Gamal Nasser, for example. On the other hand, many Third World nations have benefited from the cultural exchanges and educational assistance from developed nations – all aspects of public diplomacy.[58]

Without the resources to engage in international promotion on the scale of élite states and without large cultural industries of their own, many small countries, as Hachten observes, accept 'gifts' of books, scholarships and other tools of influence as forms of aid. Similarly, some governments actually rely on the foreign broadcasts of the élite players as means of communication to their people. Kunczik provides a quote from L.F. Kaemba, the information attaché at the Zambian embassy in Washington who admitted 'I have to work at times with the Voice of America. I may find it necessary to broadcast to Zambia and explain something that has taken place at the United Nations, perhaps in reference to the Zambia economic mission or within the Security Council. I pick up a phone and call someone with whom I have previously made contact at VOA and say, "At such and such a time can you let me broadcast to Zambia?"'[59]

It is very questionable whether this state of dependence is as beneficial as Hachten suggests because it means that many states are kept in the passive state of being receivers of the world-views of others. They cannot manage their public relations on a continuing basis as the richer countries can. What image-maintenance they do is often through North American and European PR and lobbying firms whom they usually hire for specific tasks. Kunczik gives a number of examples. In 1989, in the wake of allegations by Amnesty International of human rights violations in Turkey, the Turkish government hired Saatchi and Saatchi. The company was given a budget of £1 million for promotion in the UK alone. When the Socialists came to power in Greece in 1981, Prime Minister Papandreou hired the New York PR company, Fenton Communications Inc., for $6000 a month to help allay American fear about a socialist government. In 1982, in order to get Congress to agree, above Israeli opposition, to the sale of AWACS reconnaissance planes to Saudi Arabia, the kingdom paid $400 000 to Cook, Ruef & Associates Inc. In 1985 the UNITA rebels in Angola reportedly spent $600 000 on cultivating their image abroad. The Angolan government countered by hiring the PR company of Gray & Co. which also represented Japan, South Korea, Saudi Arabia, Canada, Turkey, Morocco and the Cayman Islands.[60]

CONCLUSION

Institutionalized international cultural relations became a regular means of conducting international relations for an élite club of states after the Second World War. The capital-intensity of international cultural relations has kept the number of states in this élite club small. They benefit from the power of communication and are positioned, therefore, to exercise the power of information.

The foundation of the link between political power and international cultural relations is how international cultural relations are used to construct or manage real or imagined crises. The spectre of a crisis – present, impending or probable – creates the pretext for the use of international cultural relations. Power is the ability to determine the very definition of crises. Institutionalized international cultural relations have also meant the further structuring of global communicative relations – the many dependent upon the few – as is illustrated with the cases of 'surrogate' broadcast services and states that accept the tools of international cultural relations as forms of aid.

NOTES

1.   The preponderance of American films abroad is partly due to the support the US government has rendered to its film companies. For example, the Webb-Pomerene Export Trade Act of 1918 allowed film studios that were competitors in the domestic market to obviate anti-trust laws and co-operate in international trade under the umbrella of the Motion Picture Export

Association (MPEA). Other forms of government support enjoyed by Hollywood that have been identified by Guback include the Informational Media Guaranty Program (established in 1948); the Revenue Act of 1971; and the Overseas Private Investment Corporation (OPIC) that was set up in 1971. According to Guback, Hollywood's dominance of the international film market has been encouraged by the government because the film studios 'are seen as a great asset to the US foreign propaganda program'. Thomas Guback, 'Film as International Business', *Journal of Communication*, Vol. 24, no. 1 (Winter 1974), p. 95.

2. See Kwame Nkrumah, *Neo-Colonialism: The Last Stage of Imperialism* (New York: International Publishers, 1965), pp. 246–7.
3. Michael Kunczik, *Images of Nations and International Public Relations* (Bonn: Friedrich-Ebert-Stiftung, 1990), p. 25.
4. J. M. Mitchell, *International Cultural Relations* (London: Allen & Unwin, 1986), p. 81. In the Introduction to this work, Paul Wilkinson, Professor of International Relations, University of Aberdeen, notes that: 'The reasons why the concepts of cultural relations, culture-clash, cultural imperialism, and cultural diplomacy are missing from the contents of our standard textbooks on international relations have nothing to do with their relative importance in the international system: rather they are a reflection of the uneven and incomplete development of the subject and, in particular, our contemporary preoccupations with the short-term shifts in the balance of power, alliances and foreign policy', p. x.
5. Mitchell, *International Cultural Relations*, p. 81.
6. I adhere to Mitchell's definition of propaganda – 'The diffusion of information and ideas, which may be true or false, in order to gain an advantage in a contest', p. 81.
7. Central Office of Information, 'Summary of the Report of the Independent Committee of Enquiry into the Overseas Information Services', (the Drogheda Committee) (London: Her Majesty's Stationery Office, April 1954), p. 4.
8. Colin Cherry, *World Communication: Threat or Promise* (New York: John Wiley, 1971, revised 1978), p. 109.
9. Here is a quote in Mitchell (pp. 32–3) from UK Foreign Office, 'Memorandum, Foreign Cultural Propaganda and the Threat to British Interests Abroad', FO P 823/160/150 (London: Public Record Office, 1937) that describes this dimension of Axis propaganda in the interwar years:

> Education is the basis of all organised cultural propaganda, and a special feature of its modern development is its determination to secure a hold on the education of foreign children at as early an age as the government of the foreign country concerned will allow. In this respect it may be said that the totalitarian State, abroad as well as at home, is following the example of the Church, though with a very different set of principles in view. In its full development, the organisation of German or Italian cultural propaganda in a foreign country begins with the schools. Very often pupils will be attracted to a German or Italian elementary school by the offer of education at a nominal fee or even gratis; thereafter they will proceed to a State School, in the curriculum of which every effort has been made to secure a privileged position for the teaching of German or

Italian. There follows a course either at a local university (at which there will always be a professor of German or Italian language and civilisation), accompanied by generous facilities (scholarships, free journeys, etc.) for travel or study in Germany or Italy, or else at a German or Italian university. Finally, for the former student or for others who may be interested, there is usually a club or institute with every social and intellectual amenity through which contact can be maintained with what should, by now, have become the student's spiritual home. To this may be added such further influence as may be exerted by the visits of prominent statesmen, artists or men of learning, the visits of theatrical companies, the showing of German and Italian films and the energetic advertisement and sale of German or Italian products of all kinds.

10.   Mitchell (see note 4), p. 23.
11.   Ibid.
12.   Ibid., p. 29.
13.   Ibid., pp. 51–7.
14.   Cherry, *World Communication*, p. 116.
15.   William Preston Jr, Edward S. Herman and Herbert I. Schiller, *Hope And Folly: The United States And UNESCO 1945–1985*. (Minneapolis: University of Minnesota Press, 1989), pp. 26–7.
16.   Mitchell (see note 4), p. 34.
17.   Ibid., p. 39.
18.   Ibid., p. 40.
19.   Ibid., p. 50.
20.   Central Office of Information, 'Summary of the Report of the Independent Committee of Enquiry into the Overseas Information Services', (the Drogheda Committee) (London: Her Majesty's Stationery Office, April, 1954), p. 41.
21.   Ibid.
22.   Ibid., p. 8.
23.   Ibid., p. 5.
24.   Ibid., pp. 8–9.
25.   Ibid.
26.   Central Office of Information, *Britain 1988: An Official Handbook*. (London: Her Majesty's Stationery Office, 1988), pp. 72, 427.
27.   Preston *et al.*, *Hope and Folly*, p. 31
28.   Ibid.
29.   Mitchell (see note 4), pp. 51–7.
30.   Central Office of Information (1954), p. 11.
31.   Mitchell (see note 4), pp. 51–7.
32.   Cherry, *World Communication*, pp. 111–2.
33.   Mitchell (see note 4), pp. 51–7.
34.   Ibid., p. 22.
35.   Hans Speier, 'The Future of Psychological Warfare', in *Reader in Public Opinion and Communication*, ed. Bernard Berelson and Morris Janowitz (New York: Free Press, 1953), p. 382.
36.   Mitchell (see note 4), p. 93.

37. For comprehensive information on these stations see Andrew G. Sennitt, *World Radio TV Handbook* (Amsterdam: Billboard Books, published annually).
38. Mitchell, p. 70.
39. The Japan Foundation, *Overview of Programs for Fiscal 1992 / Annual Report for Fiscal 1991* (Tokyo: The Japan Foundation, 1993), p. 13.
40. Ibid., p. 135.
41. Ibid., p. 132.
42. The countries where there were external offices of the Japan Foundation were: Australia, Brazil, Canada, France, Germany, Hungary, Indonesia, Italy, Malaysia, Mexico, Thailand, the UK and the United States. Ibid., p. 103.
43. United States Information Agency. *USIA Programs and Budget in Brief* (Washington, DC: USIA, 1993), p. 19.

The Reagan and Bush administrations devised Radio and TV Marti to be additional strategies, along with the trade embargo, to bring down the communist government in Cuba. But it was estimated that 'fewer than 1% of the Cuban population' had been able to view the service uninterrupted due to Cuban jamming and the technical problems of the station. See Alvin Snyder, 'Monday Memo,' *Broadcasting & Cable*, 9 August 1993, p. 62.

The United States government began broadcasting to Cuba on local frequencies without registering the station with the ITU or seeking the permission of the Cuban government. However, after noting that Radio Marti contravened ITU agreements, the North American Regional Broadcasting Agreement (NARBA), and the 1979 Geneva Convention, one writer, Youm, admitted that 'there are few clear-cut international agreements on how a nation's sovereignty can deal with intrusive broadcasting from outside without violating the basic freedom of human beings to receive and impart information with others'. Such a right is upheld by Article 19 of the Universal Declaration of Human Rights. Kyu Ho Youm, 'The Radio and TV Marti controversy: A re-examination', *Gazette*, Vol. 48, no. 2, September 1991, pp. 95–103.
44. Hans Speier, 'The Future of Psychological Warfare', *Public Opinion Quarterly*, Vol. 12, 1948, pp. 5–18.
45. John Marks, 'Media in the Third World,' *The Washington Post*, 27 August 1976, p. A25.
46. US Senate, *Final Report of the Select Committee to Study Governmental Operations with Respect to Intelligence Activities*, Book One, 94th Congress, 2nd session, Report No. 94–755 (Washington, DC: GPO, 1976), p. 192.
47. Marc Raboy and Bernard Dagenais, 'Introduction: Media and the Politics of Crisis', in Marc Raboy and Bernard Dagenais (eds), *Media, Crisis and Democracy* (London: SAGE, 1992), p. 3.
48. Ibid., p. 5.
49. See Kuldip R. Rampal and W. Clifton Adams, 'Credibility of the Asian News Broadcasts of the Voice of America and the British Broadcasting Corporation,' *Gazette*, Vol. 46, no. 2, September 1990, pp. 93–111.
50. Nelson described this practice after the cold war by noting that

The broadcasters are increasing their reach by what the Americans call 'placement' and the British 'rebroadcasting'. This involves broadcasting locally, using a variety of techniques, instead of depending only on short-wave transmission.

The one hour daily of VOA Armenian service is broadcast simultaneously on Radio Yerevan. An hour of the Ukrainian service is rebroadcast on almost the entire Ukrainian network. The BBC transmits by satellite two current affairs programmes of half an hour each of the Russian service each weekend, which are relayed on Radio Russia. They also relay a twenty minute feature programme once a week. RL likes to get entire programme schedules rebroadcast, says Gene Pell, President of RFE/RL. For example, the Ukrainian service is rebroadcast for six hours a day on six transmitters.

Michael Nelson, 'Why the "Big Three" Must Still Broadcast across the Old Iron Curtain', *Intermedia*, Vol. 20, no. 6, November–December 1992, p. 5.

51.   World Service TV was started in 1991. By 1993 it was a 24-hour news and information service disseminated by separate feeds tailored to the interests of its regional partners. For example, by early 1993 it was estimated to reach at least nine million homes in Asia via the Star TV satellite package delivered on AsiaSat1. Jeff Hazell, World Service TV's director of sales and distribution, said that that the mission of World Service TV was 'to be fully global by the end of 1993 using various joint venture partners' Meredith Amdur, 'BBC World Service TV looks west', *Broadcasting & Cable*, 19 April 1993, pp. 35–6.

52.   Malcolm S. Forbes Jr, 'Fact and Comment', *Forbes*, 7 June 1993.

53.   'Europe freed, radio signs off?', *The Economist*, 27 February 1993, p. 57.

54.   According to *The Economist*:

The institute is the largest archive, open to all, for East European, Soviet and post-Soviet studies. It employs more than 150 analysts. The institute's staff cut 1,500 newspapers from the ex-communist countries; keep the largest *samizdat* writings from the former Soviet Union; maintain a library of 120,000 books; and keep files covering several million items.

Though the ex-communist countries now have the freedom to run their own independent radio services, they often lack the experience or expertise to do so. Worse, in some countries governments still tend to confuse criticism with sabotage: under pressure, they still lean on their own broadcasters. Until a tradition of independent broadcasting is established the Americans might do well to let their own more balanced broadcasts continue. (Ibid.)

55.   Ibid.

56.   See Michael Nelson, 'Why the "Big Three" Must Still Broadcast across the Old Iron Curtain', *Intermedia*, Vol. 20, no. 6, November–December 1992 pp. 4–6.

57.   The proposal for Radio Free China came from the President's Task Force on US Government International Broadcasting. A majority on the panel believed that expanding VOA's broadcasts to China would not be enough because VOA is responsible for reporting on world events and US government policies and those goals would detract from giving daily coverage of

events in China. See R. Jeffrey Smith, 'Task Force Urges Creation of Radio for a Free Asia', *The Washington Post*, 17 December 1991, p. A10.

Fisher has noted the agonizing about the future role of United States international broadcasting in the post-cold war era which (including RFE/RL, Worldnet satellite TV, Radio and TV Marti, and VOA) was costing $844 million annually. In three years it was 'the topic of at least nine major reports by government task forces, commissions, councils and congressional committees'. Marc Fisher, 'From Communism to Clinton: U.S. Radio Free Europe Switches to New Focus', *The Washington Post*, 3 April 1993, p. A19.

58. William A. Hachten, *The World News Prism* (Ames, Iowa: Iowa State University Press, 1987), p. 92.
59. Kunczik, p. 187.
60. Ibid., pp. 21, 118, 123 and 128.

6 Reforming International Communication: The NWICO Debate

The discussion so far in this book has been an explanation of the structure of power as far as the role of information and communication are concerned in international relations. There now needs to be an analysis of exactly what happens when these structures are challenged. Such a task might contain objective lessons for those who are relatively powerless and are seeking change. At the same time it might show up serious shortcomings and contradictions in the arguments of those who shout 'cultural imperialism' and place most blame for the *status quo* on the shoulders of those with power.

Our use of functionalism and regime theory as methods of interpretation have already revealed how order, and not necessarily equality and justice, has been the axiological principle of the post-Second World War international system in general. The international order in the realm of economic relations was challenged in the 1970s through the movement for a New International Economic Order (NIEO). Similarly, the order that prevailed for international communication was attacked by those who called for a New World Information and Communication Order (NWICO).

In this chapter we will examine how the behaviour of state and non-state actors played a role in causing the NWICO's failure, and we will use the theoretical literature as our means of interpretation. We will take our discussion of regime theory a step further by exploring to what extent this theoretical literature serves to explain what actually happened. What this examination reveals is that to understand the dynamic of power in international communication it is not enough to focus on the character of regimes or the absence of regimes. The fate of efforts at change is also determined by the character of international negotiations and of foreign policy-making. By examining two case studies of foreign policy-making towards the NWICO by two states of the South we hope to provide a rich explanation of why change of the structure of international communication has been so slow in coming despite the obvious imbalances and inequalities.

THE NWICO DEFINED

After the United States and Britain withdrew from UNESCO in the early 1980s, the leadership of UNESCO changed in 1987 and the cold war ended with the collapse of the Eastern bloc, it became fashionable among scholars of international relations to speak of the NWICO in the past tense and to refer to it as another effort for global reform that failed.[1] However, the NWICO as a topic in international relations is a double-sided coin: while its significance as a means to real policy might be passé, it still remains as an artifact of the global discourse about the relationship between communication and power and as such the reasons for its failure will always remain salient as long as the implications of the communications revolution are subject to dispute.[2]

Although there was this clear link between the NWICO and the New International Economic Order (which was first mentioned in UN Resolution 3201 of May 1974), the two attempts at global reform differed on the very significant point that the NIEO was more coherently defined than the NWICO. From the time the term 'New World Information Order' was introduced into the diplomatic vocabulary in 1976 until the General Conference of UNESCO in 1987, when the Director-General of UNESCO was changed and the NWICO lost much of its support in UNESCO's bureaucracy, the NWICO was largely an undefined, vague concept that embodied global change in a diverse array of fields such as (but not exclusive to) telecommunications, news flows, intellectual property rights and international advertising.

There was a problem in finding a definition of the NWICO acceptable to all blocs of states. The Non-Aligned Intergovernmental Council for Coordination of Information passed a resolution on the 'New International Information Order' in June 1980 which sought to define the order, including calls for the regulation of transnational corporations and the 'right' of nations 'to use' their means of information.[3] The ideas in that document were reflected later in the year by UNESCO Resolution 4/19, passed at the twenty-first General Conference in Belgrade, which listed 11 objectives of the 'new world information and communication order':

   (i) elimination of the imbalances and inequalities which characterize the present situation;

  (ii) elimination of the negative effects of certain monopolies, public or private, and excessive concentrations;

 (iii) removal of internal and external obstacles to a free flow and wider and better balanced dissemination of information and ideas;

    (iv) plurality of sources and channels of information;

    (v) freedom of the press and information;

    (vi) freedom of journalists and all professionals in the communication media, a freedom inseparable from responsibility;

  (vii) the capacity of developing countries to achieve improvement of their own situations, notably by providing their own equipment, by training their personnel, by improving their infrastructure and by making their information and communication media suitable to their needs and aspirations;

(viii) the sincere will of developed countries to help them attain these objectives;

  (ix) respect for each people's cultural identity and for the right of each nation to inform the world public about its interests, its aspirations and its social and cultural values;

    (x) respect for the right of all peoples to participate in international exchanges of information on the basis of equality, justice and mutual benefit;

  (xi) respect for the right of the public, of ethnic and social groups and of individuals to have access to information sources and to participate actively in the communication process.[4]

The resolution's assertion that UNESCO's activities in the future should 'contribute to the clarification, elaboration and application of the concept of a new world information and communication order' was an indication of remaining uncertainty about the order's finer points as much as it was an allowance for Western reservations about wholehearted adoption of the order. Five years later, at the UNESCO General Assembly in Sofia, there was still no common agreement upon definition of the NWICO except that it was an 'evolving and continuous process', a compromise definition that was adopted to diffuse Western worries that the NWICO was too prescriptive and endangered press freedom.

Well before Amadou-Mahtar M'Bow's tenure as UNESCO's Director-General (1974–87) UNESCO was a forum for questioning the world information and communication order. A UNESCO meeting of experts on Mass Communications and Society held in Montreal in 1969 is noted as being the first international meeting at which calls were made for a 'two-way' or 'balanced circulation' of news.[5] A year later, a motion passed at the sixteenth session of the UNESCO General Conference recognized a need for UNESCO to help member states formulate communication policies and eventually led to publication of a UNESCO series on communication policies in selected countries.

Formal involvement of the Non-Aligned Movement (NAM) in the quest for a new information order dates to 1973. The Non-Aligned Summit in Algiers of that year recommended the formation of Non-Aligned News Agencies Pool as an alternative to the 'Big Five' news agencies, and it produced an Action Programme for Economic Cooperation which pointed to a link between colonialism and communication and the need for the South to act in unison to redress the existing imbalances, a position that was to be reiterated by Non-Aligned conferences and delegates from the South at international organizations throughout the 1970s.[6] In essence, it was held that control of information flows from North American and European centres was a component of neo-colonialism; colonialism by its very nature sapped the resources of the colonized for the benefit of the colonial centre and reduced colonized peoples to a position of peonage in the international system; multinationals based in the old colonial centres were the agents of colonialism – or, more correctly, neo-colonialism; hence, there was a need to end the free-for-all which the multinationals enjoyed. This basic hypothesis explains why there was a direct link between the NWICO and the proposed New International Economic Order (NIEO).

At almost every top-level meeting of the NAM the idea of a NWICO continued to occupy considerable attention. There was a declaration on it at the Non-Aligned Foreign Ministers Conference in Belgrade in August 1978, and it took up several paragraphs of the Political Declaration issued by the Sixth Non-Aligned Summit in September 1979 in Havana, Cuba.

The force of numbers the new states had in the UN system also effected rhetorical and policy changes at the UN General Assembly and UNESCO. The General Assembly voted to support the idea of a NWICO in Resolution 33/115B on International Relations in the Sphere of Information, passed on 18 December 1978. At UNESCO, the MacBride Report – the most comprehensive assessment of the world's information order – was presented to the General Assembly in 1980, and from that year on its recommendations were used to guide UNESCO's aid activities in the field of communication. Western governments – and the Western press, which by then had become active participants in the debate – had serious reservations about the Report and UNESCO's world communication policy. These differences were to account in part for the withdrawal from UNESCO of the USA, Britain and Singapore a few years later. The twenty-first General Assembly of UNESCO in 1980 also gave final approval for the setting up of the International Programme for the Development of Communication (IPDC) which was to be a fund for financing communication development projects as a means of correcting the imbalance in the distribution of the world's communications resources.

Although relatively few scholars of International Relations *per se* have directly focused on the NWICO,[7] there has been no shortage of approaches to the NWICO from the media scholars who have been the ones to examine it using language not entirely unfamiliar to students of International Relations. For example, Colleen Roach[8] has concentrated on the NWICO as a case study in US foreign policy making, especially towards UNESCO. Giffard[9] has used it as an opportunity to evaluate American media coverage of UNESCO. Sauvant,[10] Nordenstreng[11] and Schiller[12] have preferred to regard the NWICO as an anti-colonial struggle aimed at bringing (in Sauvant's words) 'socio-cultural emancipation' to the South. Singham and Hune's seminal work on the Non-Aligned Movement [13] has given great prominence to the NAM's concerns about world information and communication, and the NWICO is seen also as an anti-colonial struggle, but, more importantly, a struggle crucial to the NAM's overall strategy for global reform. Two scholars of International Relations, Finkelstein[14] and Wells[15], have seen the NWICO as a manifestation of larger problems confronting the UN system in the late 1970s and during the 1980s. And for the foreign policy-makers of the US and Britain who took their countries out of UNESCO, the NWICO was a clear manifestation of the still improperly defined concept of 'politicization'.[16] Unfortunately, the literature on the NWICO has been of little explanatory value to understanding the dynamic of change in international communication despite these many perspectives. Too much attention has been focused on the *formal* features of the debate over international communication – the passage or non-passage of resolutions at UNESCO or the UN General Assembly, and various international 'declarations' by governmental and non-governmental organizations – at the expense of the *technical* – for example, revolutions in new international communications technologies, changes in the structure of international production and trade, and the distribution of power within the international regimes and organizations regulating international communication. A good example of the shortcomings of this literature is Mowlana and Roach's article that attempts to show how the 'movement for a NWICO has continued'. Their evidence is a listing of a variety of resolutions and other statements passed by a variety of organizations such as the International Organization of Journalists (IOJ), the South Commission, the MacBride Roundtable and the UN General Assembly. No mention was made of specific results that might have stemmed from this rhetoric, such as increased funding for communications infrastructure in the South or changed policies and business practices by the powerful transnationals in communications. Illustrative of the approach is the following passage:

In this, the post-Unesco phase of the NWICO, support for the movement has ... been primarily taken up by non-governmental and professional organizations. In the forefront of these organizations has been the World Association for Christian Communication (WACC), a long-time backer of the movement. In October 1989, the WACC's first international congress adopted the *Manila Declaration*, whose 'new vision for the 1990s' emphasized the historical experience of the last 15 years, namely the communication imbalance analyzed in the MacBride Report. The Declaration gave priority to communication as a people's right, stressing 'the principles of communication for the 1990s should be based on the power of the people going beyond the formal processes of party politics' and calling for the use of media technology for the 'empowerment of the people.' It also called for a 'revolution in social values and priorities to create a new media ecology, and recommended action for the empowerment of women through communications.'[17]

THE DEFEAT OF THE NWICO

The emphasis on rhetoric, as is illustrated in the preceding quote, can lead down incorrect paths to understanding why the NWICO failed. Although UNESCO was the rhetorical forum for the cluster of reforms known as the NWICO, the first step towards understanding the fortunes of the NWICO is the realization that UNESCO had no authority as an international institution to make the reforms. As we have shown in the preceding chapters, international communication is composed of a number of issue areas characterized by varying degrees of institutionalization. But although Article 1 of UNESCO's constitution said that it was to 'Collaborate in the work of advancing the mutual knowledge and understanding of peoples, through all means of mass communication and to that end recommend such international agreements as may be necessary to promote the free flow of ideas by word and image', UNESCO was not given the means nor the authority to establish binding norms and rules in international communication.[18] Instead UNESCO was conceived by the Western states that created it as a vehicle for promoting universalist ideals via a free flow of information that would be an antidote to communism and fascism as well as fashion the post-Second World War order according to their terms − the fewer rules there were controlling information flow, the better.[19] It has also been a 'forum'[20] organization for the issue-areas of international communication, and it has also existed to provide the very valuable service of compiling statistics on various forms of international communication.[21] UNESCO could do little better than to suggest the creation of arrangements or organizations that could make and apply rules, or UNESCO could relay proposals for reform to the specialized UN agencies equipped to deal with the pertinent issue-areas.

These shortcomings make it difficult to describe UNESCO as a 'regime' for international communication, capable of effecting the changes demanded by the South. Although there are several theories about the role regimes play in international politics, Stephen Krasner's definition is the popular definition of what international regimes actually are. This definition says that all regimes include four essential components: principles; norms; rules; and decision-making procedures.[22] We applied this theory to international communication in Chapters 2 and 3. This framework is very helpful in organizing the variety of issue-areas covered by the NWICO and analyzing the dynamics of the movement for change in international communication. The proposed NWICO was essentially an effort to reform the three communications regimes and create new regimes where none existed.

Reform at the WIPO

The South's concern relating to the WIPO regime was that the system of copyrights and patents was too restrictive, preventing the flow of technological discoveries to the South from the North. Because national sovereignty was the strongest in this regime it is important to note that the practice by states of protecting copyrights and patents were more the source of the problem than the extremely liberal international regime. Overall, the WIPO has been the least effective regime because of the nature of the issue-area itself and the looseness of the regime's rules and decision-making procedures. Enforcing intellectual property rights is not as essential an activity as telecommunications and mail, especially in situations where states have little to lose because they have few or no patents, trademarks or copyrights registered. The shortcomings of all the WIPO treaties is best illustrated with the example of what a WIPO document states the Paris Convention permits:

> each State is free: to exclude from patentability inventions belonging to certain fields of technology; to decide whether patents should be granted with or without examination as to their novelty and other criteria of patentability; to fix the duration of patents; to decide whether the right to a trademark may be acquired by use or registration; to decide whether

ORB(1) (or the 'First Session of the World Administrative Radio Conference on the use of the geostationary-satellite orbit and the planning of the space services utilizing it') was to agree on a principle, while ORB(2) was to discuss how the principle would be implemented. ORB(1) saw the South arguing for *a priori* allocations of 'parking slots' for satellites and frequencies to specific countries even if those countries did not yet have the technology. For its part the North argued that such allocations would restrict the development of the technology by leaving idle allocations that could be in use. Another argument was that technological improvements would obviate the problem of saturation. This benefit of telecommunications R & D allowed ORB(1) to produce a new 'dual' principle that incorporated elements of both FCFS and *a priori* principles. Some bands would be allocated to states *a priori* (with each state being guaranteed at least one orbital position for domestic service), while other bands would be determined via 'improved procedures' that involved abandoning the old procedures of the ITU's Radio Regulations in favour of 'periodic multilateral planning meetings'.[28]

Reform at the UPU

Although the UPU was criticized for harming small-circulation publications because the discount it allowed for printed materials and the bottom rate for air mail were expensive,[29] international postal rates were not at the top of the South's proposals for reform of the UPU regime. The South sought reform in three main areas: terminal dues; the Union's scheme for apportioning its expenses on member states; and aid for developing their postal infrastructures.

Terminal dues are the reimbursement paid by corresponding postal authorities to countries that receive substantially more mail than they send out. Because the Western industrialized countries were by far the major source of mail circulated worldwide, the South sought to maintain a system that gave them maximum compensation. In 1971 the US argued that terminal dues should be calculated based on the difference between costs incurred for services instead of by simply multiplying the excess weight of incoming mail by a rate (per kilogram) fixed by the UPU. However, the position of the US was in the minority when a questionnaire circulated by the UPU in 1972 decided (65 to 18) in favour of the calculation by excess weight.[30]

But although the system was not changed throughout the 1970s and 1980s, it would remain a controversial item on the agendas of the annual Executive Council meetings and the five-yearly Universal Postal

Congresses because the rate per kilo had to be revised to reflect inflation and increased costs of mail handling. For example, the 1979 Rio Congress approved a large increase, changing the rate from 1.50 gold francs (about 60¢) per kilo to 5.50 gold francs (about $2.15). The change, effective 1 January 1981, produced 'substantially increased costs' to the US Postal Service because at about that time the United States' international mail volume was 964 million pieces annually, far exceeding the total volumes of many countries of the world.[31]

On the other issue of contributions to the UPU's costs, the South was not as successful. Unlike other UN Specialized Agencies, the UPU did not have a fixed mandatory scale for making member states pay dues according to their means. So at the turn of the 1970s, for example, no member state paid more than 4.8 per cent of the UPU's total budget, including the United States, the world's largest and strongest economy. The developing nations pressured the Executive Council in 1972 into recommending to the 1974 Congress that the size of the maximum contribution category be doubled from 25 to 50 units. But the US and other major contributors successfully insisted that the UPU's system of assessment remain voluntary, so even though the maximum amount a country could pay was doubled, no country was obliged to assume the new highest limit.

However, an achievement of sorts for the South at the 1984 Hamburg Congress was the decision to permit member states designated by the UN as least developed to pay a rate of one-half of one contribution unit. This move effectively raised the size of the United States' contribution. The US assessment for 1986 became 1092 million Swiss francs (about 5 per cent of the UPU budget), an increase of over 152 000 Swiss francs (over 16 per cent) on the assessment for the previous year.[32]

With regard to the third issue, of aid (or 'technical assistance'), the UPU was reluctant to go as far as the ITU and UNESCO and appoint international commissions to study the problems and establish separate institutions within its structure to supervise aid for development. The imbalance in the world's postal infrastructure at the height of the NWICO debate is reflected in statistics for 1977 which show the industrialized countries having 2923 post-offices for every 10 000 people compared to 993 for the developing nations. Ten years later there was little improvement, with the figures being 2743 and 945 respectively.[33]

By the turn of the 1970s the UPU provided technical assistance in two ways: by participating in the UNDP; and through its own voluntary Special Fund. However, the US did not participate in the Special Fund and there was only just over $500 000 in money available for technical assistance through the UNDP. An attempt to augment these resources by making each member donate to the Special Fund each year a fixed percentage of its regular contribution was defeated before the Executive Council through the initiative of the United States in 1970. At the 1974 Lausanne Congress an attempt to create a separate Council for Technical Assistance within the UPU was also defeated and the Congress reaffirmed that the UNDP would remain the primary source of postal development funds. But the Congress was the first to discuss technical assistance in a separate committee.

Although nationals from the South were at the helm of the UPU for most of the 1970s and all of the 1980s,[34] a major obstacle for the South in getting reform of the regime was its lack of a significant presence in the technical arm of the UPU (a scenario that was mirrored at the ITU). The Lausanne Congress recommended that developing nations participate more in the work of the Consultative Council for Postal Studies (CCPS), and a study done by the CCPS found later that 'the contribution of these countries had considerably improved'.[35]

In contrast, although the issue of terminal dues was something of a defeat for the US, it still managed to maintain structural power over the UPU regime by membership of the Executive Council, top positions in the CCPS and its position as a leading generator of international mail.[36] For example, even though the US exhausted its limit of two successive five-year terms on the Executive Council in 1974 (and its efforts to scrap the rule preventing another term failed), it was elected to the CCPS by the Congress that year. It was then elected chair of one of the CCPS's seven committees, making it eligible for a vice-chairmanship of the entire CCPS; and, under a new rule passed by that Congress, the US, as a CCPS vice-chair gained the right to attend Executive Council meetings as a non-voting observer.[37]

The extent of the United States' influence can be gauged from an extract from the President's report to the US Congress on the state's involvement in the UPU for 1984:

> On technical issues, the United States submitted 28 proposals for changes in the UPU Acts to enable the US Postal Service and its customers to engage in international mailings with greater ease and effectiveness. Of these proposals, 17 were accepted. The next EC [Executive Council] or CCPS will take up seven proposals for study. In addition, a very high percentage of proposals supported by the United States and sponsored by other administrations or UPU bodies was accepted. Major topics in this category dealt with strengthening international mail accountability provisions in the UPU Convention, terminal dues

on mail imbalances, international postage rates, transit charges, improved statistics on mail exchanges, and international express mail service.[38]

Creating New International Communication Regimes

As we have shown in Chapters 3 and 4, international rules and institutions governing global news flows and trade in cultural products have been poorly developed or entirely non-existent. In many areas a new order for communication and information would mean the setting up of international regimes where the principle of 'free flow' would be moderated by the observance of other principles, such as cultural sovereignty and equal exchange.

This effort at regime creation for global news flows came in the form of the Mass Media Declaration (see Chapter 4), but it failed due to ideological clashes among governments and systematic, organized opposition from Western media interests. This hostility from the world's most influential mass media also had the impact of stigmatizing the entire concept of a NWICO.[39]

Opposition to the NWICO from the advertising industry, though not as elaborate as that of the mass media, was just as hostile. Shortly after the MacBride Report was released, the President of the American Association of Advertising Agencies, Leonard Matthews, in an article in *Business Week*, claimed the report was part of 'a calculated attempt to set the stage for a nightmarish system of trade barriers, of propaganda agencies, of managed news, and of advertising bans, all aimed at uplifting the masses by depriving them of their right to see, hear, discuss, and buy whatever they want'.[40] Months later, in 1982, at UNESCO's world conference on cultural policies in Mexico City, the advertising industry organized to show its opposition to what it feared might be the MacBride Commission's consequences. The industry's journal, *Advertising Age*, reported that

> International officers at US ad agencies are fearful this is the next step in the battle to impose the commission's recommended restrictions on advertising and press freedom on Third World governments. A coalition of ad agency associations is meeting with the US delegation to brief them on the issues; Mexican agencies and advertisers are standing by to air their views against it.[41]

That coalition included the American Association of Advertising Agencies, the European Advertising Agency Association and the International Advertising Association. They got support from the World Press Freedom Committee.

About the same time the advertising industry was lobbying against measures UNESCO could adopt, the US government demonstrated in a highly publicized controversy that it would side with industry to protect the free flow of international advertising even against attempts to curb it in the interest of world health, and even when its position got no support from any other states.

At issue was the lucrative international baby formula industry which was expanding its sales in the South during the 1970s through consumer advertising and marketing practices that included the distribution of free samples. While breast-feeding was becoming more popular in the North it was declining in the South due in part to the fact that the use of formula was viewed as a symbol of progress, even though mother's milk was superior for infants' health. In 1979, after finding that there was an estimated 10 million serious cases of malnutrition or diarrhoea each year due to improper use of baby bottles and infant formula and that as many as one million infants died annually from diseases related to poor feeding, the World Health Organization and the United Nations Children Fund (UNICEF) developed a set of guidelines for advertising and promoting breast milk substitutes. But in 1980 there were 650 violations of the guidelines, prompting the WHO to draft a commercial code for adoption by WHO member states.[42] The vote on the code at the WHO in May 1981 was 118 in favour and one against – the US. The US based its stand on the grounds that the code would be a restriction on freedom of speech and free trade. It was the posture advocated by a lobby of three corporations that together were said to account for $150 million or 15 per cent of the world market.[43] In protest, two top officials with the US Agency for International Development (AID), Eugene Babb (a nutritionist), and Dr Stephen Joseph (a pediatrician), resigned.

But, while interests in news and international advertising organized against the NWICO, the reason why the reforms the South wanted in the 'nonregime' areas did not come was due more to changes in the global political economy than to the lobbying of special interests. By 1987 regime creation in the 'nonregime' areas was about protecting their economic rights, as far as the North was concerned, and the onus was on the South to regain the initiative by injecting cultural concerns into any negotiations on these issues at the GATT. In effect, the new configuration of the debate was about reconciling a problem of regime reform with the need for regime creation because the North was motivated to have these areas covered by the GATT regime, given the shortcomings of the WIPO.

The confusing mix of concerns about money, culture and intellectual property related to the shift is poignantly expressed by Wallis and Malm in their work on the international music industry. They note:

Small nations are under pressure to abide by numerous international conventions and agreements, many of which have been developed to suit the interests of the larger, richer nations. The diplomatic hiccups hampering cooperation between the industrialized nations and the third world, the call for a new 'world information order' or discussions within UN organizations such as GATT regarding Third World economies illustrate how hard it is to change the established order of things. A music copyright system based on the concept of an individual being solely responsible for the creation of a work might not be suitable for a society where composition is a collective activity and where the creative results are traditionally regarded as general property in the 'public domain'. For many small nations, strict adherence to international agreements such as the Berne or Rome convention [on copyright] might merely lead them to pay out a lot of money to the Boney Ms and ABBAs of this world, and not get very much in return. International bodies, such as the World Intellectual Property Organization (WIPO) encourage adherence. But for small countries with foreign currency problems any net outflow of cash is not welcome, whatever the morals involved.[44]

The above quote speaks about a fascinating complex of issues that complicate regime creation in the 'nonregime' areas. While the South wanted regimes that would protect their 'cultural sovereignty' through restrictions on the flow, NWICO advocates stayed clear of suggesting that the new regimes created should also protect economic sovereignty in these areas by imposing rules and penalties for unauthorized use of copyrighted material. Indeed, in the 1980s, while calling for a NWICO, the South was complaining that the WIPO regime was too restrictive on the grounds that patents and copyright kept advanced technology and information needed for development away from the South. Wallis and Malm note that strict adherence to the regime would also result in outflows of scarce foreign exchange in the form of royalties back to the North.

These concerns meant that the South had to be very careful how it advocated new regimes in the areas of books and periodicals, the international music industry, and the flow of movies and TV programmes especially.

With industries in these areas that were becoming of increasing significance to the health of the total economy, the US especially could not ignore the issue of economic rights. By the early 1980s the US led the way in linking the free flow of such cultural products to any bilateral concessions it would make in international trade and aid. This culminated in the proposal to include intellectual property and trade in services under the GATT as the Uruguay Round began in 1986. In this way regime creation for a NWICO was effectively upstaged.

One of the earliest bilateral measures taken by the US was the rider put on the bill for the 'Caribbean Basin Initiative' (a set of trade and aid concessions) as it passed through Congress in 1983. The rider said that the President could deny the bill's benefits to any country guilty of pirating material broadcast by satellite. This was done after Jamaica's government-owned TV station was found to be retransmitting American TV shows without paying user fees to the distributors.[45]

Under the Trade and Tariff Act of 1984, the President had to consider a country's record on intellectual property rights protection when deciding on eligibility for the Generalized System of Preferences (GSP), and whether a country's actions are 'unjustifiable' or 'unreasonable' according to Section 301 of the 1974 Trade Act.

In 1985 the US government filed a trade case under Section 301 of the 1974 Trade Act against the Republic of Korea and Taiwan for their failure to provide adequate intellectual property protection. That same year, in response to restrictions the South Koreans placed on American movies, the US threatened retaliatory tariffs on South Korean videocassette recorders and succeeded in opening that market to Hollywood.[46]

The Reagan administration's *Intellectual Property Rights Policy Statement* (7 April 1986), argued that better protection of intellectual property rights would make all states more competitive, and the failure to protect intellectual property rights creates inefficiencies in world trade. A year later, as the GATT talks were underway, the Senate's 1987 trade bill (S. 1420, 100th Cong., 1st Sess.) provided for: Foreign Commercial Service Officers that would monitor and report on the intellectual property procedures in foreign countries; the setting up of an Intellectual Property Training Institute to train nationals from the South in intellectual property issues; and the granting of aid to promote R&D capabilities in developing nations.

By making intellectual property a trade issue the United States effectively exerted structural power because it was the world's largest market. The cases of Jamaica and South Korea cited above are good examples of how the options of Southern states in the 'nonregime' areas were limited by this new chapter in the life of the global political economy.

THEORETICAL EXPLANATIONS

In Chapter 2 we criticized functionalism as an organizational ideology for a peaceful international system on the grounds that: (a) it valued order above other principles; (b) its assumptions that political and technical matters could be separated were flawed; and (c) states were motivated to cooperate more out of individual self-interest than perceived harmonies of interest with other states. It is ironic that while such points were factors motivating some states to attempt reform of international communications regimes, they also account for why it was so difficult to create new regimes. For example, the FCFS principle at the ITU was attacked because it compromised equal access to satellite telecommunications; however, there was not similar enthusiasm for principles and binding rules governing intellectual property rights where states eagerly pursued their self-interests by guarding their national sovereignty.

Although it is clearly useful to organize our analysis of the South's attempt at global reform of the structure of international communication through the prism of regime theory, the literature on international regimes must be used carefully and modified because of its excessive preoccupation with the concerns of the North. Not enough research has been done applying the theoretical framework to the role of the South in international relations. In the so-called 'neo-realist' view of Krasner, when regime theory is applied to the South's behaviour in international relations it is found that those countries want 'authoritative' regimes. However, our case study of the NWICO finds that even though the South largely wants stronger regimes, their goals are not so much international order but equality and justice.

The major problem with using the idea of international regimes as conceptual frameworks in the analysis of international relations is that the literature on regimes has been in disagreement on what is the role of regimes in international politics. Realists and neo-realists (such as Keohane, Nye and Krasner) tend to treat regimes as (in Krasner's words) *intervening variables* between the international power structure and desired outcomes. On the other hand, a writer such as Oran Young has viewed regimes as *autonomous variables*, international political phenomena in their own right that perform functions in the international political system that cannot be done by states. Another criticism is that theories of regimes are inadequate for explaining failed attempts at regime creation and reform because they pay little attention to the role of bargaining among states in the life of regimes.[47] A third problem is the inattention of theories of regimes to the role of domestic imperatives in regime formation, maintenance and change.[48]

However, even the critics of regime theories do not deny the fact that regimes do exist. The disagreement has been over why and how they are formed, why they change, and their importance to the overall analysis of international political economy. Even Susan Strange, who has made the most provocative critique, has not denied the existence of regimes.[49]

Krasner identified five factors – 'causal variables' – that account for why states form regimes: egoistic self-interest; political power; norms and principles; usage and custom; and knowledge.[50] An analysis of existing or proposed regimes involves not only a look at the principles, norms, rules and decision-making procedures, but also these causal variables. These five factors identified by Krasner were later incorporated by Rothstein in his regime analysis of the NIEO and the proposed Integrated Program for Commodities (see below).

The example of the NWICO reveals that an explanation of why regimes are formed cannot afford to be ahistorical. All causal variables seem plausible when applied to the formation of the three regimes in international communication – telecommunications, mail, and intellectual property – because they were created in the 1800s by the then predominant states. However, the fact that these regimes were found wanting by the new members of the expanded international society almost immediately after decolonization and that these new states wanted to create even more regimes in international communication suggests that *international* regimes can only be created at times when consensus in an issue-area can be fostered among the international community of sovereign states. It is highly questionable whether the ITU regime (with the FCFS principle), the UPU regime (with the controversial scale for terminal dues) and the WIPO regime (requiring the majority of states to compensate the few for use of copyright and patents) could have been formed if as many regions had sovereignty as they did by the 1970s. And it is also doubtful whether having 'nonregimes' would have been an acceptable state of affairs.

A second but related observation is that our viewing the NWICO as an attempt to address imbalances in global news flows, international advertising, the music industry, and trade in books, movies and TV shows tells us that states seek to create regimes when they feel vulnerable and want regimes to foster equality and justice. This idea is related to, but not the same as, egoistic self-interest because while State A might succeed in getting a regime that ends a prisoner's dilemma and enables it to better understand and predict the behaviour of other states, it does not follow that the new regime will necessarily be just or foster an equal flow of information for all.

A third observation that can be made based on the experience of the NWICO is that even though norms and principles and usage and custom played a part in the formation of the established regimes, they were not strong variables in the effort to create regimes in the 'nonregime' areas. Even though there was the perceived need to rectify imbalances in international communication, exactly what the principles and norms guiding the

new regimes would be was never clearly expressed. In addition, the principle that all the 'nonregime' areas had was 'free flow'. This principle had
become part of the established 'usage and custom'. Because the NWICO
aimed at overturning this principle usage and custom did not figure as a
causal variable.

Egoistic self-interest and knowledge also help to account for the existence of regimes in international communication; however, it is power that
has attracted a considerable amount of attention as a factor shaping the
institutions that maintain the international political and economic structures. Strange has argued that the possessor of 'structural' power does not
have to resort to coercive force and the exercise of relational power to
advance its interests because structural power is a subtle, and little understood, means of limiting the range of choices open to those subject to that
power.

The NWICO is a good example of how structural power works, especially the exercise of structural power via the Knowledge Structure.
Indeed, it can be argued that any kind of attempt to change the *status quo*
in communications is much more difficult than in other issue-areas
because information and communication are themselves sources of power.
The states and non-state actors in news and cultural industries that mobilized to kill the NWICO exercised structural power because their very
industries controlled knowledge, beliefs and ideas. Therefore it is no
wonder that after the biased press coverage of UNESCO, the Conferences
at Talloires and the activities of the advertising lobby in the US, that the
NWICO became stigmatized, making it harder to gain moral or financial
support for its objectives. States with close trading, military and political
ties with the US were lukewarm at best towards the NWICO. This is
further evidence of structural power at work. To support or not support the
NWICO were foreign policy choices that had to be made considering the
consequences. States would not join the NWICO bandwagon if such a
move threatened the close ties they enjoyed with powerful states that were
opposed to the NWICO. Structural power not only operated against
regime creation, but also regime reform. If Strange's urging that structural
power must be more properly understood is taken to its logical conclusion
then any strategy of regime reform or creation must include ways to
obviate barriers that will possibly be erected by the holders of structural
power in their attempt to maintain the *status quo*. This point must be given
serious attention in the case of North–South relations because what the
debates over the NIEO and NWICO clearly revealed were that the imperatives of the two sides are often inconsistent with each other, and the South
often had no answer to resistance it encountered from the North.

In addition to supporting Strange's structural approach to international political economy, the case of the NWICO also backs up Robert Rothstein's assertion that the consideration of regime formation must pay great attention to negotiation and bargaining strategies.[51]

Lessons learnt from an analysis of the failure of the NIEO are useful in understanding the poor success of the NWICO. An observation of Rothstein is that a major weakness of the NIEO was that it did not reflect a coherent set of norms and principles. This assertion is striking when the NIEO is compared to the NWICO because the NIEO was much more coherent a strategy than the NWICO.

Rothstein's premise was that both the proposed NIEO and Integrated Program for Commodities were quests by the South for new regimes, and he used Krasner's conceptual framework of causal variables as part of his strategy to assess the relative success of the two efforts.

Based on this examination of the causal variables, Rothstein came to two conclusions: (a) the South devoted inadequate attention to considering the resistance their proposals would encounter and what would be necessary for the NIEO to succeed; and (b) their bargaining strategy was faulty because they over-emphasized development at the expense of concerns important to the North, and any strategy that does not emphasize mutual benefit is likely to fail.[52]

With the IPC Rothstein found that the causal variables were more precise, but the attempt at regime creation also failed at the bargaining stage. The G77 did not spend time devising a strategy that would prepare it to deal with the structural power of the North that would be mobilized against proposals unacceptable to the North, and a strategy that would keep the coalition together under the stress of the negotiations.[53] UNCTAD *politicized* the negotiations.[54] Negotiating as a group was also not necessarily the most efficient means because the economists and other experts could not provide answers satisfactory to such a broad political coalition; secondly, the G77's promise of satisfying the demands of all of its members fostered proposals that were often too ambitious; and the negotiations for the G77 were actually in the hands of 'a small oligarchy of delegates and staff members of a few international institutions'.

Rothstein finds that although the two efforts were in essence attempts at regime formation, the South did not conceive of them as such and missed out on the benefits to be gained from employing the conceptual framework of regimes. However, he also concluded that there were serious shortcomings of regime analysis itself. Specifically, causal variables are imprecise; and more attention needs to be placed on the relationship between causal variables and international bargaining. He even suggests that bargaining strategies should be regarded as intervening variables between regimes and outcomes.

The negotiation and bargaining for the NIEO and the NWICO were similar but also different in a number of ways, however. In both cases the South sought branches of the UN system that were concerned with the issue-areas in question and were even favourable to their position. However, the histories of UNCTAD and UNESCO in relation to the South were vastly different. UNCTAD was established in the 1960s to actually cater to the needs of the South. In contrast, the North created and used UNESCO to foster the principle of free flow under the misguided assumption that a free flow of information (on the North's terms) would create a community of mankind. UNESCO was never conceived as a lobbying organization for the South. It should be no surprise, therefore, that the North was hostile when the correction of imbalances in news, advertising, trade in publications, records, movies and TV programmes were put on UNESCO's agenda.

Explaining the reform of regimes is different from accounting for their creation in one major way. The discussion of reform includes factors internal to the regimes and the international organizations that maintain them. Therefore, a comprehensive analysis of why regimes change or fail to do so must discuss the internal dynamics of regimes in addition to external factors such as power and self-interest.

Keohane and Nye have suggested four models of regime change, arguing that change is often the product of more than one model working together. These four models are:

(1) *The Economic Process Explanation.* Under this model, regimes change when: (a) more sophisticated economic activity makes traditional regimes obsolete; (b) there are domestic demands for economic welfare issues; (c) increased economic interdependence brings so many benefits that reform of regimes is hard to resist.

(2) *The Overall Power Structure Explanation.* Rules change when the overall power configuration of the actors in a regime changes.

(3) *The Issue Structure Explanation.* The state or states with the most power in a particular issue area determine the rules of the game. (This is based on the fundamental assumption of complex interdependence that, although there is no hierarchy of issues, there is a structure of issues with states having various degrees of power and vulnerability from one issue-area to the next.)

(4) *The International Organization Model.* Although international organizations solidify rules and norms and make it difficult for even power-

ful states to change rules, 'organizationally dependent capabilities' – such as voting power, ability to form coalitions, and control of élite networks – will become the key factors determining regime change.[55]

Following on from the argument presented in the previous section that negotiation and bargaining are crucial variables, the attempt at reform through the NWICO demonstrates the salience of the International Organization Model very well.

It was at the ITU that the NWICO demanded the most significant and extensive changes. However, the general quest for equality and justice in international communication was felt at the UPU as well. But at the WIPO regime the developing nations wanted to make an already weak and loose set of rules and decision-making procedures even weaker on the grounds that the regime was (in the words of Masmoudi) 'too restrictive'.[56]

The decision-making procedures within the ITU and UPU regimes illustrate well the important role of such internal factors referred to by the international organization model. Although by the 1970s the developing nations were a clear majority in the ITU and UPU they could not get their way on most issues because they were still under-represented on the technical bodies that studied and resolved problems. These technical arms were the Study Groups of the CCIR and CCITT of the ITU and the UPU's Consultative Council for Postal Studies. It is significant that the one issue before these two regimes of great concern to the South that was decided by a simple majority vote went the way of the South. That issue was the UPU's decision in 1972 to calculate terminal dues by weight. However, the other problems – the geostationary orbit, an equitable scale for apportioning the UPU's expenses, and aid – were not decided in such a fashion and did not produce a similar result.

A good explanation of why there was such limited success on the other issues before the ITU and UPU is supplied by the Issue Structure Model. The North, particularly the US, dominated R & D and usage of satellites and hence could call the shots in the debate on the GSO. A poignant illustration of this was when the US refused to sanction the *a priori* principle for Region 2 at the 1977 Broadcasting WARC. Similarly, as the largest generator of mail and a major source of financial aid, the US maintained structural power over the UPU regime.

The models do not only account for the failures of the South, but also for some successes. For example, the Overall Power Structure Model accounts for why development became a component of all three regimes in the period after decolonization. Although the new nation-states did not possess a great degree of structural power, their entry into the regimes changed their overall power configurations. As far as the smooth functioning of the UPU regime was concerned, their postal infrastructures had to be developed if the 'single postal territory' itself was to be efficient. New states without up-to-date telecommunications technologies could not be part of the global telecommunications network and this was the concern of all states because local telecommunications companies could never boast of being able to provide universal service. Similarly, states without the expertise and technology to protect intellectual property rights could not be meaningful participants in the WIPO regime that thrived so much on the principle of reciprocity. In sum, development had to be a component of the international communication regimes if they were to be truly global in nature.

The Economic Processes Model describes almost perfectly what happened when the North sought reform by trying to incorporate certain principles and norms of the intellectual property regime into the GATT. Indeed, Gadbaw and Richards' accounting of the move strikingly mirrors what is suggested by the model even though their discussion is not about regimes *per se*. Five factors account for the increased dissatisfaction with the WIPO regime and the consequent thrust for reform at the Uruguay Round:

(1) An increasing proportion of world trade is taken up by goods utilizing intellectual property. For example, Gadbaw and Richards identify chemicals, books, electrical machinery and computers as goods with high intellectual property components. In 1947 (the year the GATT started) these goods (minus the then absent computer industry) combined for 9.9 per cent of US exports. In 1986 (when the Uruguay Round started) all four areas were worth a total of 27.4 per cent of US exports.

(2) The single world marketplace created by rapid communications has spurred appetites in foreign countries for goods which are then fair game for pirates who cash in on demand by creating counterfeits.

(3) New technology has made it possible for the easy, high-quality mass-copying of audio and video recordings, resulting in losses through piracy to the music and film industries.

(4) The increasing costs of R&D to create original products make it more attractive for others to 'free ride' on the R&D of others by selling counterfeit goods, often at much lower costs than the products of the inventors.

(5) Existing laws in many states do not cover, or are vague about, very new creations, such as semi-conductor chips, computer software and biotechnology.[57]

These factors actually serve to illuminate the idea of vulnerability and the quest for equality and justice as significant constants in efforts at regime creation and reform. It can be argued that the North wanted trade in services and intellectual property rights included in the GATT because it was vulnerable and it realized that the new technologies that facilitated piracy had very unfair consequences for its creators and industries in related fields. However, as has already been argued, while the aspirations of the South in the 'nonregime' areas were aimed at preserving *cultural* rights, the North made its move solely with the aim of protecting *economic* rights.

TWO CASE STUDIES

So far it has been convenient to speak in generalities about upholders and reformers of the power structure of international communication. While such generalizations are convenient for broad theoretical explorations, they must be refined in order to attain a comprehensive explanation of the difficulties in reforming international communication.

It has been fashionable to depict that NWICO debate as largely a struggle between a coalition of developing countries promoting the NWICO and a group of Western industrialized states (smaller in number but more powerful) that were hostile to the idea. However, just as all nations of the North were not as antagonistic to the proposed NWICO as the US and the UK,[58] the NWICO did not enjoy enthusiastic support from all nations in the South, or even all members of the NAM. For example, President of the International Organization of Journalists (IOJ), Dr Kaarle Nordenstreng – a supporter of the NWICO who has written extensively on the topic – has noted how Sri Lanka, Tunisia, Venezuela, Jamaica, Egypt and Malaysia have been described by the Western media as 'moderates' at various times in the NWICO debate due to their willingness to seek compromise with the North or their (non-governmental) representation at the anti-NWICO Talloires Conference in 1981.[59] Another scholar, Joon-Mann Kang, of the University of Wisconsin-Madison, has gone a step further and done a study seeking to account for South Korea's 'ambivalent' attitude to the NWICO.[60]

It has been clear that the structural power the US and UK had as major underwriters of UNESCO and the UN system generally served to sabotage the movement, especially when those two countries decided to quit UNESCO. Also, as detractors of the NWICO pointed out during the course of the debate, many states that were ardent advocates of the NWICO caused justifiable suspicion of the proposals' supposed lofty ideals because these states were well-known violators of human rights and press freedom. However, the dynamic of internal and external imperatives that are more the stock in trade of foreign policy analysts than communications scholars have not been explored in any of the post-mortems on the NWICO so far.

This section focuses on the dynamic of foreign policy-making with regard to communications in two countries of the South. A comparison of the attitudes of Barbados and India reveals that, although both countries have relatively little power in the structure of international communication compared to Western states, the character of their external political and economic relationships and the nature of their domestic media systems are the two key variables that determined their postures towards the NWICO, as Kang has found to be the case with South Korea. States that are very reliant on one or a few countries for security, aid and the bulk of their foreign trade are constrained from wholeheartedly supporting measures for radical reform of the international order, especially proposals opposed by their more powerful defence and economic partners. States that are regional powers of their own and whose political, defence and economic relationships are more diffuse are less constrained. Domestic media systems are important to external policy towards the NWICO because the NWICO debate provides an excellent example of how powerful actors in such systems, with vested interests in the outcome of the debate, lobbied governments in favour,[61] and against,[62] the concept.

Barbados and India Compared

Because Barbados and India differ so vastly in territorial and population size it seems almost ridiculous to compare the two countries, but in the event of roll-call votes at the UN General Assembly and at General Conferences of UNESCO, each country, regardless of size, has only one vote. Although the developing countries usually vote as a bloc at the UN under the umbrella of the Group of 77, in the mid-1980s when the battle over the NWICO came to a head and there was pressure from the West (particularly from the US) for the UN to reform its agenda, some developing nations weakened the voting bloc behind the NWICO by voting against the concept or abstaining at the General Assembly, or (as Singapore did) actually following the lead of powerful allies and leaving UNESCO. While India has been consistent in its support of the NWICO, Barbados (although a member of the NAM) has had a lacklustre attitude to the proposal at best.

Barbados, an island of 166 square miles, has a population of 256 000, making it one of the most densely populated countries in the western hemisphere. (Singapore is not much larger than Barbados, but its 224 square miles must support a population of over 2.5 million.) It was a British colony from 1627 to 1966, and as a result its parliamentary system of government and its legal system are derived from Britain. But, unlike

Britain, Barbados has a written constitution. This document, like every other constitution in the English-speaking Caribbean (except that of Trinidad and Tobago), does not explicitly guarantee freedom of the press. White notes that in these constitutions

> press freedom is guaranteed by implication in so far as 'freedom of expression' is interpreted to include 'freedom to hold opinions and to receive and impart ideas and information without interference.' Whether impliedly or expressly guaranteed, freedom of the press is a right which is guaranteed to every person and it does not matter whether that person is a natural person or an artificial person such as a company.[63]

In addition to the vague constitution, Barbadian journalists are constrained by laws of libel and defamation that date back to colonial times at the turn of the century. This ensures that there is hardly any investigative reporting in Barbados because the law does not distinguish between public and private individuals (as does US law) and innuendo is enough to bring a libel suit. As one of Barbados's two daily newspapers noted:

> Judges have criticised the law they have to administer. Successive Governments have ignored such criticisms and pleas to change it. Sometimes, but not always, the present law suits politicians because it stifles investigative journalism. It is [,] for example [,] a truism that a Barbadian Watergate could never be exposed under the present libel laws.[64]

In Barbados's common law tradition the laws relating to the media can be updated and liberalized through legal precedent, but Barbadian media enterprises have been reluctant to bring test cases before the courts. This docility is partly due to the nature of the media system's political economy. By 1987 Barbados had two daily newspapers, five radio stations and one TV station.[65] On the island broadcasting is a semi-monopoly of the government. The state owns the TV station and two of the radio stations, while the remaining media are subject to near-monopoly control by the powerful Nation Publishing company, which owns the largest daily, *The Nation*, and two radio stations. Because legal constraints on the press protect political élites, successive governments have not been enthusiastic about changing the *status quo*, while the media institutions with power preferred to channel their resources into economic expansion and increased profit-making. For example, between 1979 and 1987 *The Nation* moved from being solely devoted to publishing newspapers to owning two radio stations, a magazine and a travel agency. This expansion was also assisted to some degree by links that *The Nation's* management forged with the US-based conservative organization, the World Press Freedom Committee, which sponsored training courses for *The Nation's* staff.[66] The World Press Freedom Committee is very well known as an opponent of the NWICO; indeed, it was founded in the mid-1970s to lobby against NWICO-related initiatives at UNESCO such as the Mass Media Declaration (see Chapter 4). The media is clearly good business for any corporation that has a near-monopoly in Barbados because the penetration of the mass media is very high. Literacy is 98 per cent;[67] by 1989 262.7 television sets and 878 radios were in use; daily newspaper circulation was 155 per thousand people.[68]

The two political parties that have governed Barbados successively since independence have both set 'national economic development' as the main goal of the country's foreign policy. Barbados is very sensitive, therefore, about pursuing acts of foreign policy that might upset its external trade and its tourism industry, the leading provider of foreign exchange. Receipts from tourism in 1987 were US$354 million.[69] The Barbados national budget in 1991 involved expenditures in excess of US$920 million.[70] Figures for 1991 show that 30.2 per cent of the 394 200 tourists to Barbados were from the United States.[71] The United States also accounted for 12.8 per cent of Barbados's exports, and 33.4 per cent of its imports.[72] Although Barbados likes to affirm its national sovereignty, it also points out that 'the U.S. has legitimate security and strategic concerns in the region and [Barbados] will do nothing to jeopardize those concerns'.[73] The closeness of Barbados's ties with the US was illustrated in 1983 when Barbados joined in the invasion of Grenada.

In contrast to Barbados, India has a population of over 850 million on a sub-continental land area of just over 1 million square miles. Because of its parliamentary system, another legacy of British colonialism, and its vastness, it is considered the world's largest democracy. India also has a written constitution, but, like Barbados, freedom of the press is mentioned by implication. Mundt notes that

> While freedom of the press is not explicitly guaranteed, it has been judicially determined that the freedom of speech and expression clause – Article 19(1)(a) – includes press freedom. However, it is not an absolute freedom, for Article 19(2) qualifies it somewhat: 'Nothing in sub-clause (a) of Clause (1) shall affect the operation of any existing law, or prevent the State from making any law, insofar as such law imposes reasonable restrictions on the exercise of the right conferred by the said sub-clause in the interests of the security of the State, friendly relations

with foreign states, public order, decency or morality or in relations to contempt of court, defamation or incitement to an offence.' Thus the government can restrict freedom of the press with cause, subject to judicial interpretation of the reasonableness of that restriction.[74]

Such a legal foundation, that gives the government more or less *carte-blanche* supervision of the media, governs the second largest media system in the world after the United States. There are over 13 000 newspapers and other periodicals published in India. While the government has shares in some publications and owns publications of its own, the print media are largely in private hands; however, broadcasting is a state monopoly and the country is serviced by a network of over 80 radio stations and 17 television stations. Unlike Barbados, however, media penetration is not very high due to a number of problems. The 1991 estimate of literacy was only 52 per cent,[75] and the daily newspaper circulation was 28 per 1000 people.[76] India has about 27 TV receivers (1989 estimate) and 100 radio receivers (1991 estimate) in use per thousand people.[77] With a GNP of US$297.5 billion, India is one of the world's poorest countries, a situation that is even more severe when one considers that the internal distribution of wealth is very uneven.[78] The most recent estimate available shows 50 per cent of total household income accounted for by the top 20 per cent of the population, with the bottom 40 per cent of households having only 16 per cent of total household income.[79] There is also the problem of a multiplicity of languages. In addition to English, 15 other languages are spoken by large proportions of the population.

Despite its restrictive press laws, India's image as the world's largest democracy was perhaps reinforced after the 20-month State of Emergency imposed by Prime Minister Indira Gandhi from June 1975 till she lost power at the polls in 1977. Mrs Gandhi imposed censorship, required publications to make security deposits that were arbitrarily set by the government and used various means to pressure the press, all under the guise of protecting national security. According to statistics released by the administration that succeeded Mrs Gandhi, during the Emergency 440 newspapers and periodicals were pre-censored, the government denied advertising to 98 publications, over 250 journalists were detained, seven foreign correspondents were expelled and 29 others were prevented from entering the country.[80]Through all this the press resisted by various means. For example, the managers of the *Statesman* blocked government attempts to assume control of the majority of the newspaper's stock; and the owner of the *Indian Express* was not afraid to petition the courts for protection from government pressure.[81]

India's mass media system is, unlike that of Barbados, very ideologically diverse. Whereas Barbados's politics are dominated by centre-right parties, India's political system supports two communist parties in addition to a variety of others. This diversity is also reflected in the media system, where there are communist publications as well as conservative publications, such as *The Times of India* and the *Statesman*. Indeed, the *Statesman's* chairman, Cushrow Irani, was given an award by the conservative Freedom House of the US and made chairman of the International Press Institute (IPI) after his successful resistance to Mrs Gandhi's intimidation during the Emergency. However, the fact that the IOJ chose New Delhi to be the venue for its 1984 Executive Committee Session is some testimony to the strength of the socialist dimension of the media system.

Although economic development is a high priority in India's foreign policy, it is also very concerned with its external security due to its territorial, political and religious differences with Pakistan to its north-west. Pakistan's alliance with the US makes India much more circumspect in its ties with the US than is the case with Barbados. Unlike Barbados, India is not in close geographic proximity to the US. It shares a border in the north-east with China, and is only separated from the former USSR by the Hindu Kush. India is also not as reliant on one partner for the bulk of its external trade or other sources of foreign exchange. In 1987 the US accounted for 15.3 per cent of its exports, the USSR 14.4 per cent, and Japan 9.6 per cent. The United States supplied 10.3 per cent of its imports, the United Kingdom 8.9 per cent and West Germany 7.8 per cent.[82]

Postures to the NWICO

Barbados and India have exhibited remarkably dissimilar attitudes to the NWICO. Not plagued with the severe problems of poverty, illiteracy, vast land area and the multiplicity of languages, Barbados has had relatively less need for aid for communications development from UNESCO. But its conservative foreign policy, predicated largely on its location in a zone of strategic significance to the US and its need to not aggravate its economic relations with Washington, has also meant that it steered clear of wholehearted adoption of the NWICO or even active participation in the Non-Aligned Movement.

As a founding member of the NAM, India has been in the vanguard of attempts to establish a NWICO. It was in recognition of India's attention to information and communication matters that it was one of the countries represented on the 16-member International (MacBride) Commission for the Study of Communication Problems. In 1979, when the 66-member UN

Information Committee was established to advise the General Assembly on the UN's Public Information policies and international communication in general, India also took a place on this body. Indeed, it was India that introduced a key resolution that year, on the behalf of the G77, that said, *inter alia*, that the new Committee on Information should promote the NWICO. From the General Assembly's passage of that resolution onwards into the 1980s, the NWICO never left the annual agenda of the Committee nor the General Assembly, and all resolutions sent to the General Assembly from the Committee said the UN should promote the NWICO, despite hostility towards the concept led by the USA. Following the establishment of the International Program for the Development of Communication (IPDC) at UNESCO, India was not only a member of the 35-member Intergovernmental Council that oversaw the programme, but also a significant contributor to its Special Account, donating US$500 000 by 1986.[83]

In stark contrast, Barbados was not even a full member of the NAM until the NAM's seventh summit (hosted by India) in 1983. Before 1983 and since 1970 Barbados had Observer status at NAM meetings.[84] It was only when Barbados was seeking to assume the Presidency of the UN General Assembly in 1987 that Barbados up-graded its representation at a NAM meeting to Ministerial level.[85] (In that race, Barbados's Dame Nita Barrow was defeated by Argentina's Dante Caputo who enjoyed the support of the United States.) Also, while India's Indira Gandhi was on record as an ardent supporter of the NWICO, Barbados's Prime Minister from 1976 to 1985, Tom Adams, opposed the NWICO on the grounds that it was an excuse for government control of the media.[86] Although Adams died of a heart attack in March 1985, the country's coolness towards the NWICO continued. At the fortieth session of the UN General Assembly in 1985 Barbados was the only Non-Aligned country to abstain on Resolution 40/164 A which said, *inter alia*, that the media and non-governmental organizations should disseminate information about the efforts of developing countries to achieve economic, social and cultural progress and about international initiatives to gain social justice and economic development. The resolution was approved by 121 nations, 19 voted against it, and seven others abstained with Barbados. (The Western countries said they did not vote for the resolution because it failed to note that the NWICO was – in the spirit of a compromise reached at UNESCO – 'seen as an evolving and continuous process'.)[87] An important factor in Barbados' posture towards the NWICO has been the fact that the maintenance of a viable organization to protect journalistic standards and maintain contact with journalists in other countries (as the Indian chapter of the IOJ does) has been a struggle, and as a result Barbadian journalists were generally not in an informed position to discuss the NWICO or even lobby their government to promote it.[88]

Theoretical Questions for Future Research

Scholarship on the NWICO (especially by members of the International Association for Mass Communication Research) has been generally favorably disposed to the concept. In much of the literature there is reference to the NWICO being a 'mass movement', or similar descriptions.[89] But a distinction has to be made between the postures of these scholars and non-governmental organizations that have championed the NWICO as a natural and obvious strategy for the South to pursue, and the foreign policy-makers in the South who very often make pragmatic choices based on consideration of the interplay of several factors.

Although India has long been a leader of the NAM and the Group of 77, its enthusiasm for the NWICO during the Gandhi years still did not guarantee similar compliance from other states in the Southern coalition. Indeed, in Singapore and Barbados we have two small states of considerable influence in their respective regions whose attitudes to the NWICO stood to seriously disrupt attempts at coalition-building. Therefore, the big question is: What is the interplay of forces that account for the cool postures of these states to the NWICO even though objective conditions would seem to indicate that they should logically support a proposal that would give states of their size more involvement in the global flow of news, images and other forms of information? In answering this question we get further along the way to understanding the shaky coalition dynamics that some scholars have already identified as a major problem accounting for why the attempts at broad global reform – in the shape of the NIEO and the NWICO – failed.[90] In other words, the study of the imperatives guiding foreign policy behaviour is a natural complement to theories of international cooperation.

The popular conceptual frameworks for analyzing the structure of communication in North–South relations have been basically of two types: (a) theories of imperialism and neo-colonialism; and (b) dependency theories. These theories are largely macro explanations, descriptive of the way international relations are or have been, and are of limited use in explaining why small states (or former colonies) make particular decisions in time and space about specific issues.

It is also taken for granted that, due to the legacy or fact of colonialism and dependency, the foreign policy orientations of 'Third World' states will be very similar, if not uniform on particular occasions. The most prolific scholar of foreign policy-making in the South, Bahgat Korany, notes that 'these countries are vulnerable, suffer from an acute sense of threat, face serious economic problems, and feel that the "system" is somehow rigged against them'.[91] However, he warns that

> Notwithstanding the presence of common characteristics and interests within the Third World, the analyst should avoid any overhomogeniza- tion (i.e., glossing over differences) among its different countries and clusters. Although Third Worldism is equated with [the] NAM, the groping toward expression of collective identity at the global level has had a multigroup involvement from the very beginning. These groups can be general (Bandung) or specific (G-77), ideological (radical versus moderates) or geographical (African, Latin American).[92]

What must be added to Korany's caveat is the tendency to assume specific of these countries will make certain decisions because of their shared her- itage. For example, the involvement of Eastern Caribbean states in the invasion of Grenada in 1983 served to legitimize the actions of the United States. However, in light of the history of frequent American interventions into the region, the behaviour of those states goes against the grain of what we might assume.

There has been a marked shortage of theoretical works on foreign policy-making in the South. What works there have been have tended to build on assumptions and assertions found in literature on North American and European foreign policy-making.

The framework that many theorists of foreign policy-making in both the North and South have built on is James Rosenau's 'pre-theory' of foreign policy. According to Rosenau, the actual policy is the product of the inter- relationship between five sets of variables: individual-level factors (values, beliefs, the personality of decision-makers), society, government, role (the roles the decision-makers believe they must play), and systemic factors (features in the external environment).[93]

Korany[94] has identified two approaches to the study of foreign policy: 'the decision-making [or "bureaucratic"] approach'; and the 'psychological- perceptual school'.

The psychological-perceptual school's main unit of analysis is the key decision-makers. It places emphasis on the decision-makers' social back- ground, psychological make-up, their responses to the stresses of the moment, and other factors that influence human behaviour, in an attempt to account for why they take particular courses of action on particular occasions. The main assumption is that 'decision-makers respond not to the real world but to their perceptions and images of this world, which may or may not be accurate representations of that world reality'.[95]

The main characteristics of that other school include: the assumption that foreign policy is an outcome not of the behaviour of one or a few individuals, but a set of political bargains that occur within a governmental bureaucracy; and the emphasis on a number of variables internal and external to the bureaucracy.

It is the psychological-perceptual school that dominates the analysis of foreign policy-making in the South. Two reasons account for the school's popularity as a set of conceptual frameworks for looking at the foreign policies of the South:

> First, it coincided with an important characteristic of the political systems of the Third World countries – their personalized political processes ...; and, second, competing models from the other school were, in the main, explicitly limited to industrialized countries ....[96]

It seems that the psychological-perceptual approach especially has been the preferred framework for examining foreign policy-making in the larger, more prominent states of the South, such as Egypt and India. These larger states have attracted the bulk of attention from foreign policy analysts in the scholarly journals and academic presses of the North, while the literature on smaller states (sometimes called 'micro-' or 'mini-states'), such as in the Commonwealth Caribbean, has been small.

Although, for the purposes of understanding foreign policy-making in the South, the decision-making approach pays too little attention to the significant roles individuals play in the formulation of the foreign policy of many states, the psychological-perceptual school can clearly be too reductionist, paying too little attention to the bureaucratic and other features that provide the context for the actions of individuals. Our comparison of Barbados, India and the NWICO suggests that the bureaucratic school is a more relevant approach for comparing foreign policy-making around a specific issue.

Interestingly, the decision-making approach has been attractive to scholars of the Caribbean.[97] The most recent comprehensive study of the Commonwealth Caribbean has been by Braveboy-Wagner who has proposed a 'Model of Caribbean Foreign Policy'.[98] The model identifies three major influences on the foreign policy-making processes of these small states:

(a) The *Operational Environment* refers to constraints (such as small size and economic dependence) and determinants (such as the history of the state and region, and the structure of the international system). The Operational Environment determines the political ideology and policy orientation of a state.

(b) The *Decision Situation* refers to the cluster of issues immediate to the taking of a particular course of action: for example, whether there is a crisis, and the personal preferences of the decision-makers.

(c) The *Organizational Factors* include the quality of communication and feedback, and the level of skill of foreign policy personnel.

Missing from Braveboy-Wagner's model is the role of interest groups, particularly professional bodies, in influencing foreign policy decisions on issues of particular concern to them. Our preliminary investigation of the cases of Barbados's and India's postures toward the NWICO does suggest two ideas. First, the absence of a strong professional association of journalists, with an agenda of specific concerns about the structure of international communication can mean indifference by policy-makers to such issues when they appear as foreign policy questions, or, at best, leave decisions vulnerable to the vagaries of personal preference, as was the case with the opposition of Barbados's Prime Minister to the NWICO. Second, a domestic environment where the media is very diverse ideologically, with a number of interest groups in the field of communication means that (as was the case with India) it is more difficult for foreign policy-makers to be indifferent to a particular issue when it appears on the international agenda. Indifference, or blatant censorship (as occurred in India under the State of Emergency), can produce embarrassing results for a government and the political party in power as happened when the IPI made Cushrow Irani its chairman and Freedom House gave him an award after his battle with censorship. The two organizations then became *de facto* forums for international exposure of the government's domestic policies in the particular issue-area. States without such professional groups are less likely to be exposed to such risks.

Another factor missing from Braveboy-Wagner's model is the history of legal and wider social framing of a particular issue in a country's domestic politics. The legal history and social scenario that fostered an active, diverse media in India by extension nourished professional organizations that lobbied the government and stood to embarrass rulers (through their international professional linkages) if their claims were not resolved satisfactorily. The obverse seems to be the case in a country like Barbados. Although the conservative Freedom House gave Barbados a high rating for freedom of the press, the laws governing the mass media date back to colonial times and were not changed after Independence for the obvious reason that they shielded government officials from public scrutiny and criticism. Such a situation is likely to foster cynicism and low professional esteem, factors that militate against the formation of journalists' associations with strong international links. We have already illustrated in Chapter 4 (with a quote from a journalist in Ghana) how such backward press laws mean that ruling élites in such former colonies have 'schizophrenic' attitudes to the press which in turn produce cynicism among journalists working among them.

CONCLUSION

This chapter has employed theories of international cooperation and foreign policy-making to further clarify the relationship between the structure of international power and international communication. As we have argued consistently throughout the book, the most profound question about the so-called communication and information revolutions is about its implications for the character of global political and economic power. But we have demonstrated in preceding chapters that configurations of political and economic power also shape the structure of international communication.

This chapter has concentrated on that superstructure of political and economic relations to explain why the regimes needed to change the nature of international communication could not be created nor the existing regimes reformed. We showed how the existing literature on international regimes do, and do not, explain what happened to the NWICO. We also argued that the NWICO fell victim to the fact that it has become more difficult to create new international regimes as the international system has expanded and the probability of achieving the degree of unanimity in the smaller international system of 100 years ago declines. This point makes it easier to understand why negotiating and bargaining strategies, to handle the plethora of competing actors and interests, are crucial factors determining the fate of any proposals for broad global reform.

The comparative analysis of foreign policy-making is a natural complement to theories of coalition-building and international cooperation. A comparison of the dynamic of foreign policy-making by two Southern countries towards a specific issue serves two main goals. First, it makes more rigorous our understanding of Southern coalitions seeking wholesale international reform. While objective conditions can dictate common international postures from a number of states of diverse size and geopolitical location, the expediencies and dynamics of foreign policy-making combine to make these coalitions unstable or even tear them apart. Second, the specific issue of international communication illustrates the role that domestic professional organizations and their international affiliations can play in the process of foreign policy-making. Foreign policy decisions are also the reflection of the history of legal and wider social framing of a particular issue in a country's domestic politics.

NOTES

1. Notions such as George Bush's 'New World Order' and 'globalization', were said to have replaced old-fashioned ways of conceiving international relations. Compared to the new system – where capitalism was becoming a world-wide ideology and new technologies were creating unified global systems of finance and production – the NWICO seemed to belong to another world where ideology was contested terrain and communications technologies were so primitive that national sovereignty could actually be preserved. For a critical analysis of the concept and rhetoric of 'globalization', see Marjorie Ferguson, 'The Mythology about Globalization', *European Journal of Communication*, Vol. 7, 1992, pp. 69–93.
2. To the technological determinist assumptions of Walter Wriston, who argues that the communications revolution allows wider political participation and hence promotes democracy, can be juxtaposed the criticisms of Raboy, Dagenais *et al.*, who question the concentrated ownership and control of the new technologies and mass media. See Walter B. Wriston, 'Technology and Sovereignty', *Foreign Affairs*, Winter, 1988/89, pp. 63–75; and Marc Raboy and Bernard Dagenais (eds) *Media, Crisis and Democracy: Mass Communication and the Disruption of Social Order* (London: SAGE, 1992).
3. See 'Resolution on the New International Information Order of the Fourth Meeting of the Intergovernmental Council for Co-ordination of Information among Non-Aligned Countries' (Baghdad, June 1980).
4. UNESCO Res. 4/19 – On the International Commission for the Study of Communication Problems (Belgrade, 21 October 1980), sec. VI, 14.
5. Academy For Educational Development (AED), *The United States and the Debate on the World 'Information Order'* (Washington, DC: USICA, 1979), Appendix I.
6. See Nordenstreng, *et al.*, pp. 111–254 and pp. 275–329. In addition to the practical step of the news agencies pool, the Movement established two standing bodies on information, both of which met for the first time in 1977. The Intergovernmental Council for the Coordination of Information among Non-Aligned Countries had its first session in Tunis in February; and in October in Sarajevo there was the First Conference of the Broadcasting Organizations of the Non-Aligned Countries (BONAC). While BONAC was not to hold its second conference until the eventful year of 1980, the Intergovernmental Council continued to hold annual meetings from 1977 onwards.

7.   While the NIEO has attracted its fair share of attention, scholars of International Relations have been content to only make passing reference to the NWICO. For example, although the NWICO was the most controversial area of North–South relations in the early 1980s at the time he was writing, Krasner devotes barely four paragraphs to the disputes over international communication. Questions about the electromagnetic frequency spectrum fall under the heading of the 'global commons', he explains, and after providing a cursory description of recent disputes at the ITU and the UN Committee on the Peaceful Uses of Outer Space (UNCOPUOS), Krasner quickly moves on to 'examine in greater detail the two other major issue areas treated as part of the global commons', oceans and Antarctica. See Stephen D. Krasner, *Structural Conflict: The Third World Against Global Liberalism* (Berkeley: University of California Press, 1985), pp. 228–30.

8.   See Colleen Roach, 'The US Position on the New World Information and Communication Order', *Journal of Communication*, Vol. 37, no. 4, Autumn 1987, pp. 36–51; and also her 'The Position of the Reagan Administration on the NWICO', *Media Development*, Vol. 34, no. 4, 1987, pp. 32–7.

9.   C. Anthony Giffard, *UNESCO and the Media* (New York: Longman, 1989).

10. Karl P. Sauvant, 'From Economic to Socio-Cultural Emancipation: The Historical Context of the New International Economic Order and the New International Socio-Cultural Order', *Third World Quarterly*, Vol. 3, no. 1, 1981, pp. 48–61.

11. Kaarle Nordenstreng, 'The Rise and Life of the Concept', in Kaarle Nordenstreng, Enrique Gonzales Manet and Wolfgang Kleinwachter, *New International Information Order Sourcebook*, (Prague: International Organization of Journalists, 1986), pp. 10–42.

12. Herbert Schiller, *Information and the Crisis Economy* (Oxford: Oxford University Press, 1986). See especially Chapter 4, 'The Developing Crisis in the Western Free Flow of Information Doctrine', pp. 47–76.

13. A. W. Singham and Shirley Hune, *Non-Alignment in an Age of Alignments* (Westport, Conn.: Lawrence Hill & Co., 1986).

14. Lawrence S. Finkelstein, 'The Struggle to Control UNESCO' in David P. Forsythe (ed.), *The United Nations in the World Political Economy* (New York: St. Martin's Press, 1989), pp. 144–64.

15. Clare Wells, *The UN, UNESCO and the Politics of Knowledge* (London: Macmillan, 1987).

16. Timothy Raison, Minister of Overseas Development, in a statement to the House of Commons on 5 December 1985, said Britain was withdrawing from UNESCO because of the degree to which UNESCO's work had been 'harmfully politicized'. The reason echoed similar criticisms of UNESCO by the United States. But one's understanding of this term varies according to one's sources. A favourable attitude to it can be found in Sauvant (see note 10), where he uses the term to refer to any situation in which an issue is moved away from the attention of specialists to being a priority of heads of state. He notes that during the 1960s economic development was an issue of 'low politics', handled by ministers of finance and planning, but in the 1970s

     this attitude changed and development questions became 'high politics': they were elevated from the level of heads of ministries to the level of heads of state or government. The development issues had been politicized. (p. 55).

In contrast, a negative view of politicization can be found in Robert Rothstein's article, 'Regime-Creation by a Coalition of the Weak: Lessons from the NIEO and the Integrated Program for Commodities', in *International Studies Quarterly*, Vol. 28, 1984. Rothstein criticized UNCTAD for politicizing negotiations over an Integrated Programme for Commodities, causing a 'clash of broad principles and a de-emphasis on the need to develop consensual knowledge as a foundation of the negotiations'. He defines politicization as the 'attempt to treat the negotiations as if they were primarily political encounters and as if only the absence of a mystical "political will" in the developed countries prevented immediate acceptance of Third World proposals.' p. 317.

17. Hamid Mowlana and Colleen Roach, 'New World Information and Communication Order: Overview of Recent Developments and Activities', in Michael Traber and Kaarle Nordenstreng (eds), *Few Voices, Many Worlds* (London: World Association for Christian Communication, 1992), p. 7.

18. Sewell's study of decision-making and influence at UNESCO found that the organization attempted to set standards through adopting conventions. At the beginning of the 1970s these included the Convention against Discrimination in Education, a convention on performers' rights, the International Convention for the Protection of Cultural Property in the Event of Armed Conflict, and the Universal Copyright Convention. However, UNESCO was extremely weak or totally ineffective in ensuring that states complied. As Sewell explained,

> Conventions (not to mention recommendations and resolutions) are more aptly described as ideals than rules. In UNESCO, contrary to the situation in some other organizations more heavily engrossed in standard setting and application, governments are most unlikely to be called to account when they fail to do what they had agreed to do. The effective veto comes not in setting standards, but in applying them through concerted action and in implementing them at home. No genuine regimen for review or surveillance in connection with standards has been authorized for UNESCO. Periodic reporting by governments is itself rudimentary when compared to that by ILO or Council of Europe members.

See James P. Sewell, 'UNESCO: Pluralism Rampant', in Robert W. Cox and Harold K. Jacobson (eds), *The Anatomy of Influence* (New Haven: Yale University Press, 1974), pp. 139–74, p. 151.

19. A very well-researched explanation of this can be found in Sewell, 'UNESCO'. A radical critique of the history of UNESCO can be found in William Preston Jr, Edward S. Herman and Herbert Schiller, *Hope & Folly: The United States and UNESCO 1945–1985*. (Minneapolis: University. of Minnesota Press, 1989). For a more recent analysis of the founding ideals of UNESCO in light of its troubles over the NWICO see Pierre de Senarclens, 'The Smashed Mirror of Past Illusions', *Society*, Vol. 22, no. 6 (Sept./Oct., 1985), pp. 6–14.

20. This characterization is borrowed from Cox and Jacobson's significant study of international organizations in which they characterized IOs as

being of two types: *forum* and *service*. Forum organizations provide forums for states to carry out various activities, such as exchanging views and negotiating legal instruments, while the actual programme of action is left to states or other IOs. Service organizations carry out programmes on their own for all states or some. The authors concede that many organizations are really a mixture of both service and forum orientations. See Robert W. Cox and Harold K. Jacobson (eds), *The Anatomy of Influence* (New Haven: Yale University Press, 1974), pp. 5–6.

21.   The two significant publications in this area are the *Statistical Yearbook*, published annually, and the *World Communication Report*, published at intervals every few years.

22.   Krasner's definition, as quoted earlier, in the Introduction, is

> sets of implicit or explicit principles, norms, rules, and decision-making procedures around which actors' expectations converge in a given area of international relations. Principles are beliefs of fact, causation, and rectitude. Norms are standards of behavior defined in terms of rights and obligations. Rules are specific prescriptions or proscriptions for action. Decision-making procedures are prevailing practices for making and implementing collective choice.

Stephen D. Krasner, *International Regimes* (Ithaca and London: Cornell University Press, 1983), p. 2.

23.   World Intellectual Property Organization, *WIPO: General Information* (Geneva: WIPO, 1990), p. 22.

24.   See Wallis and Malm's concerns about this problem in relation to the international music industry discussed below.

25.   See Binod C. Agrawal, 'Satellite Instructional Television: SITE in India', in George Gerbner & Marsha Siefert (eds), *World Communications: A Handbook* (New York: Longman, 1984), pp. 354–9. Only a handful of countries in the South had their own satellite systems by the late 1980s. They were Brazil, China, India, Indonesia and Mexico.

26.   The highlights of this struggle are as follows:

1973 – the Plenipotentiary Conference (Malaga–Torremolinos) – a new article was added to the ITU Convention, declaring the orbit/-spectrum a limited natural resource to which states should have equitable access.

1974 – the Maritime WARC – claiming the principle of equitable access, landlocked countries demanded access to maritime frequencies.

1976 – the 'Bogota Declaration' said equatorial nations had sovereignty over not only the atmosphere but the geostationary orbit, about 22 300 miles above the earth.

1977   at the Broadcasting WARC (that considered DBS) some states of Regions 1 and 3 advocated successfully that orbital/frequency slot assignments should be made *a priori* instead of FCFS. Region 2 could not follow a similar path because of strong opposition from its largest member, the US. It took six years before a compromise for Region 2 was found at the 1983 Regional Administrative Radio Conference. (For administrative purposes, the ITU divides the world into three regions: Region 1 is Europe, including the whole territory of the USSR, and Africa; Region 2 covers North, Central and South America, and the Caribbean; and Region 3 covers Asia and Australasia.)

27. In his seminal study of influence at the ITU Jacobson concluded that

> Influence goes to those states and private agencies that are technically prepared and that control the resources important in telecommunications, and extremely few meet these qualifications. Of course, these actors must be sensitive to the needs of others because they could always be voted down; but there is no substitute for technical knowledge and control of the physical resources involved.

Harold K. Jacobson, 'ITU: A Potpourri of Bureaucrats and Industrialists', in Robert W. Cox and Harold K. Jacobson (eds), *The Anatomy of Influence* (New Haven: Yale University Press, 1974), p. 74. To back up his point, Jacobson gave the examples of the 1963 Extraordinary Administrative Radio Conference on space telecommunications and the 1964 Study Group VII of the CCIR. The US had the resources and expertise to spend two years preparing for the former, with the help of the RAND Corporation, Lockheed and General Electric (which at one time had over 200 people working on its study). It was no surprise that the conference's results were more to the liking of the US. In the case of the latter, the US prepared 30 papers of the 53 before the Group, and the only other countries that offered papers were from the industrialized countries: the UK, West Germany, Czechoslovakia, Italy, Canada, Belgium and Japan. In the late 1960s more than 90 per cent of the vice-chairmen of the study groups of the international consultative committees were Western nationals. By the 1980s, although there had been some changes, the North, with its advantage in high technology still retained control of technical expertise for decision-making at the ITU.

28. For reports on the results of the two conferences and the view of ITU's Secretary-General on their achievements see the following sections of these two issues of *Telecommunication Journal* (the ITU's organ):
'Editorial – ORB(1): guaranteeing equitable access to the orbit', pp. 589–90, 'First Session of WARC ORB(1)', pp. 591–3, *Telecommunication Journal*, Vol. 52, no. 11, 1985.
'Editorial – The Geostationary-Satellite Orbit Conference', p. 789, 'ORB-88 adopts plans and regulatory provisions for geostationary satellites', pp. 790–4, *Telecommunication Journal*, Vol. 55, no. 12, 1988.
An outsider's critical perspective is supplied by Janis Doran, *Middle Powers and Technical Multilateralism: The International Telecommunication Union*, No. 4 In The Series Middle Powers in the International System (Ottawa: The North–South Institute, April 1989), pp. 36–41, 71–2.

29. Mustapha Masmoudi, 'The New World Information Order', *Journal of Communication*, Vol. 29, no. 2 (Spring, 1979). Masmoudi served as Tunisia's Permanent Delegate to UNESCO and as a member of the MacBride Commission.

30. US Dept of State, *United States Participation in the UN: Report by the President to Congress for the Year 1972* (Washington, DC: Government Printing Office, 1973), pp. 152–3.

31. See US Dept of State, *United States Participation in the UN: Report by the President to Congress for the Year 1979* (Washington, DC: Government Printing Office, 1980), p. 238; and the Report for 1980, p. 278.

32. US Dept of State, *United States Participation in the UN: Report by the President to Congress for the Year 1985* (Washington, DC: Government Printing Office, 1986).

33. Universal Postal Union, *The Postal Service in the World* (Berne: Universal Postal Union, c. 1989), p. 2.

34. At the 1984 Congress Adwaldo Cardoso Botto de Barros of Brazil was selected from a field of four to succeed Mohamed Sobhi of Egypt who had served his limit of two successive five-year terms as Director-General.

35. Universal Postal Union, *Documents of the 1984 Hamburg Congress* (Berne: International Bureau of the Universal Postal Union, 1985), p. 64.

36. Statistics for West Germany and the US serve to illustrate how the US dominated international postal traffic even among the industrialized countries. In 1979, 516.7 million items were posted from West Germany abroad, and that country received 666.7 million items from other countries. In contrast, the statistics for 1980 supplied by the US gave a figure of 963.7 million items posted abroad, in comparison to 700 million received. See Universal Postal Union, *Memorandum on the Role of the Post as a Factor in Economic, Social and Cultural Development* (Berne: UPU, 1982), pp. 22–3.

37. US Dept of State, *United States Participation in the UN: Report by the President to Congress for the Year 1974* (Washington, DC: Government Printing Office, 1975), p. 336.

38. US Dept of State, *United States Participation in the UN: Report by the President to Congress for the Year 1984* (Washington, DC: Government Printing Office, 1985), p. 269.

39. The Mass Media Declaration took six years to draft before it was adopted by the UNESCO General Conference in 1978. Western media interests preferred that there be no declaration on the media at all; and categorical opposition to it came from the International Press Institute, Freedom House, the World Press Freedom Committee, the Inter-American Association of Broadcasters, Reuters and *The Times*. In its final form the declaration was a slim document of only 11 articles called the *Declaration on Fundamental Principles Concerning the Contribution of the Mass Media to Strengthening Peace and International Understanding, to the Promotion of Human Rights and to Countering Racialism, Apartheid and Incitement to War*. These principles were meant to guide journalists the world over in the conduct of their profession. Although its passage can be regarded as a defeat for the West, Western opposition had still succeeded in moderating its content and so the Media Declaration was very descriptive in character instead of being a normative document.

40. Leonard S. Matthews, 'Designing a Muzzle for Media', *Business Week*, 15 June 1981, p. 20.

41. Letitia Baldwin and Christy Marshall, 'MacBride Report Gets UNESCO Hearing', *Advertising Age*, 26 July 1982, p. 59.

42. In a long article on the incident, Ken Boodhoo, of the Dept of International Relations at Florida International University, argued that the code

did not attempt to restrict sale of the actual product. The guidelines urged member countries to pass laws that would ban advertising of breast-milk substitutes; prohibit distribution of free samples; require wording on labels to acknowledge the superiority of breast-feeding and warn about health hazards posed by improper preparation; and prohibit companies from paying commissions and bonuses on sales of infant formula.

See Ken Boodhoo, 'The Great Health Robbery ... Third World Babies and Greed of the Multi-Nationals,' *Caribbean Contact*, Vol. 9, no. 7, November 1981, pp. 16 and 19.

43. The three were Bristol-Myers Co., Abbott Laboratories and American Home Products Corp. See 'The Breast Vs. The Bottle', *Newsweek*, 1 June 1981, p. 55. Boodhoo, 'Great Health Robbery'., notes that these companies were joined by the trade group Grocery Manufacturers of America 'which feared that the code might also be applied to other baby food products'.

44. Roger Wallis and Krister Malm, *Big Sounds from Small People: The music industry in small countries* (New York: Pendragon Press, 1984), p. 71.

45. Aggrey Brown, 'Mass Media In Jamaica', in *Mass Media and the Caribbean,* ed. Stuart Surlin and Walter Soderlund (Philadelphia: Gordon and Breach, 1990), p.19.

46. Damon Darlin, 'To Get US Films Shown In South Korea, It Takes More Than Friendly Persuasion', *Wall Street Journal*, 2 October 1989, p. B7.

47. See Robert Rothstein, 'Regime-Creation by a Coalition of the Weak: Lessons from the NIEO and the Integrated Program for Commodities', *International Studies Quarterly*, Vol. 28, 1984.

48. See Stephan Haggard and Beth A. Simmons, 'Theories of international regimes', *International Organization*, Vol. 41, no. 3 (Summer 1987), pp. 490–517.

49. For a short version of Susan Strange's critique of theories of regimes (including criticisms of American scholarship in international political economy) see her '*Cave! hic dragones*: a critique of regime analysis', in Stephen D. Krasner, *International Regimes.*, pp. 337–54. Strange makes her critique and lays out her alternative 'structural' theory of international political economy in her *States and Markets* (London: Pinter, 1988).

50. Stephen Krasner, *International Regimes*, pp. 18–20. (Also see n. 18, Chapter 2.)

(1) *Egoistic self-interest*. This is of two varieties. (a) States are willing to form regimes if they have no other choice – as is especially the case with the provision of public goods. (b) Regimes are formed to further self-interest because they facilitate the flow of information and this allows more precise calculations of other actors' behavior.

(2) *Political power. Regimes* are formed by the powerful to: (a) further the good of the system on the whole; or (b) to achieve the ends of one or more specific actors.

(3) *Norms and principles*. Based on the work of sociologists (e.g. Weber) and Marxists who conceive of a 'superstructure' that shapes human actions, Krasner notes that history, religion, and modes of production have provided certain norms and principles that make phenomena such as regimes natural courses of action.

(These two last factors do not account for regime formation on their own, but are supplemental to those factors mentioned above.)

(4) *Usage and custom.* 'A pattern of behavior initially established by economic coercion or force may come to be regarded as legitimate by those on whom it has been imposed. Usage leads to shared expectations, which become infused with principles and norms.' For example, much of Western commercial law and the English common law is based on usage and custom.

(5) *Knowledge.* This is not just any kind of knowledge, but the knowledge gained from social or 'pure' science that tell more about the human experience and foster a degree of prediction. 'For knowledge to have an independent impact in the international system, it must be widely accepted by policy makers.'

51.   Robert L. Rothstein, 'Regime-Creation by a Coalition of the Weak: Lessons from the NIEO and the Integrated Program for Commodities', *International Studies Quarterly* (1984), 28, pp. 307–28.
52.   Ibid., pp. 313–14.
53.   Ibid., p. 316.
54.   The concept of 'politicization' is problematical because it lacks a standard definition. One's understanding of the notion varies according to one's sources. (See note 16.)
55.   Robert Keohane and Joseph Nye, *Power and Interdependence*, Second Edition (Boston: Scott Foresman, 1989), Chapter 3, pp. 38–60.
56.   Masmoudi, 'New World Information Order'.
57.   R. Michael Gadbaw and Timothy J. Richards (eds), *Intellectual Property Rights: Global Consensus, Global Conflict?* (Boulder: Westview Press, 1988), pp. 3–5.
58.   Canadian Thomas McPhail, for example, has discussed his country's empathy for the position of many countries in the South because it has had to deal with similar questions with regard to maintaining its cultural sovereignty in the face of powerful American mass media next door. See Thomas McPhail, *Electronic Colonialism* (Revised Second Edition) (Beverly Hills: SAGE, 1987).
59.   Nordenstreng *et al.* (see note 11), pp. 18, 35.
60.   South Korea is not a member of the NAM, but North Korea is. Kang believes that this posture is the result of several features of South Korea's domestic and international situation:

   (1) It has pursued a dependent development strategy. In light of this, the NIEO and NWICO, products of the new thinking about development aimed at self-sufficiency, mean little to South Korea because it is reliant on the international communication structure, especially for economic news because its development is export-led.
   (2) South Korean media have a 'pro-business attitude' and the media system, as a result, is quite similar to that of the US where media enterprises have investments in areas as diverse as sports teams and electronics.
   (3) South Korea has no free press. Broadcast media are state-controlled while the print media are privately run. But all the media must operate

---

within perimeters defined by the government, and Kang suggests that there is no rebellion against this *status quo* because the people feel it understandable in light of the country's political status.

(4) South Korea is conscious of 'image imperialism' and has sought to rectify its bad image in the Western media through contracting Western PR agencies rather than lobbying for a NWICO.

Joon-Mann Kang, 'The New World Information Order: The South Korean Case', *Journal of Contemporary Asia*, Vol. 18, no. 1, 1988, pp. 77–88.

61. For example, the IOJ, representing journalists working for the government-controlled media in the Eastern bloc and other socialist countries around the world, lobbied in favour of the NWICO. It also published works documenting the history of the concept, such as Nordenstreng *et al.* (see note 11).

52. We need look no further than the example of the US, where large media organizations, such as *The Washington Post and The New York Times* were universally hostile to the NWICO and campaigned against it on their editorial pages over several years. See Chapter 5.

53. Dorcas White, *The Press and the Law in the Caribbean* (Bridgetown: CEDAR Press, 1977), p. 43.

54. 'Libel Laws', *Barbados Advocate*, 25 July 1989, p. 6.

55. For a complete analysis of Barbados's media system, see Mark Alleyne, 'Mass Media System in Barbados', in *Mass Media and the Caribbean,* ed. Stuart Surlin and Walter Soderlund (Philadelphia: Gordon and Breach, 1990).

56. See Mary Greaves-Venner, 'Keeping Track', *BAJ Bulletin* 1 (Aug./Sept./Oct., 1985), p. 7.

57. Economist Intelligence Unit, *Guyana, Barbados, Windward and Leeward Islands: Country Profile* 1991–1992 (London: Business International Limited, 1991), p. 27.

58. UNESCO, *Statistical Yearbook 1991* (Paris: UNESCO, 1991).

59. World Bank, *Caribbean Countries: Economic Situation, Regional Issues and Capital Flows* (Washington, DC: World Bank, 1988), p. 68.

70. Central Bank of Barbados, *Annual Report 1991* (Bridgetown, Barbados: Government Printing Department, 1991), p. 5.

1. Ibid., p. 10.

72. International Monetary Fund, *Direction of Trade Statistics* (September, 1992), p. 19.

3. The Ministry of Foreign Affairs, *Diplomacy and Development: A Review of the Foreign Policy of Barbados* (Bridgetown: Government Printing Department, 1987), p. 18.

4. Whitney R. Mundt, 'India', in George Kurian (ed.), *World Press Encyclopedia* (Vol.1) (New York: Facts On File, 1982), p. 481.

5. Economist Intelligence Unit, *India: Country Profile 1991–1992* (London: Business International Limited, 1991), p. 11.

6. UNESCO, *Statistical Yearbook 1991*.

7. Ibid.

8. World Bank, *Social Indicators of Development 1991–1992* (Baltimore: Johns Hopkins University Press, 1988), p. 143.

9. Economist Intelligence Unit, *India ...*, p. 9.

0. Mundt, 'India', pp. 482, 487, 492.

81. Ibid., p. 483.

82. International Monetary Fund, p. 65.

83. International Programme for the Development of Communication, *IPDC News*, no. 8, 1st semester, 1986, p. 24.

84. Barbados's Prime Minister from 1961 to 1976, Errol Barrow, is on record as saying: 'I always ask who are you non-aligned against? I don't see any advantages – long or short-term – in joining the non-aligned group.' See 'Barrow raps U.S. role in region', *Barbados Advocate-News*, 6 May 1976 quoted in Vaughan A. Lewis, 'The Commonwealth Caribbean', in Christopher Clapham (ed.), *Foreign Policy Making in Developing State.* (London: Saxon House, 1977), p. 124.

85. Confidential interview with a Barbados Foreign Service Officer Bridgetown, 24 and 25 May 1990.

86. See Anthony Irving, 'Time to Weep and Time to Laugh', *Sunday Advocate News*, 6 February 1983, p. 4.

87. Daphne Doran Lincoff (ed.), *Annual Review of United Nations Affairs 198.* (Dobbs Ferry, NY: Oceana Publications, 1987), pp. 317–24.

88. For a discussion of the history of journalistic organizations in Barbados, see Alleyne, 'Mass Media System'. I was President of the Barbados Association of Journalists in 1985.

89. See, for example, Robert A. White, 'NWICO has become a people's movement', *Media Development*, Vol. 35, January 1988, pp. 20–5.

90. See, for example, Robert L. Rothstein, 'Epitaph for a monument to a failed protest? A North-South retrospective', *International Organization*, Vol. 42 no. 4, (Autumn 1988), pp. 725–48.

91. Bahgat Korany, 'Coming of Age Against Global Odds: The Third World and Its Collective Decision-Making', in Bahgat Korany (ed.), *How Foreign Policy Decisions are Made in the Third World: A Comparative Analysi* (Boulder: Westview Press, 1986), p. 37.

92. Ibid.

93. James N. Rosenau, 'Pre-Theories and Theories of Foreign Policy', in R Barry Farrell (ed.), *Approaches to Comparative and International Politic* (Evanston, Ill.: Northwestern University Press, 1966), pp. 27–92.

94. Bahgat Korany, 'Foreign Policy Decision-Making Theory and the Third World: Payoffs and Pitfalls', in Bahgat Korany (ed.), *How Foreign Polic Decisions are Made in the Third World: A Comparative Analysis* (Boulder Westview Press, 1986).

95. Ibid., p. 51.

96. Ibid., p. 52.

97. In addition to Braveboy-Wagner (discussed below), see also Vaughan A Lewis, 'The Commonwealth Caribbean', in Christopher Clapham (ed.) *Foreign Policy Making in Developing States* (London: Saxon House, 1977) Lewis, in seeking to build on Rosenau's conceptual framework, has emphasized features in the domestic societies of Commonwealth Caribbean state as key variables in assessing the foreign policy-making in the region. For example, the significant percentage of Indians within their populations wa a major factor in the decisions of Trinidad and Tobago, and Guyana establishing ambassadorial representation in India. According to Lewis, 'specific

geopolitical locations and domestic structures have tended to suggest identifications of national interests which do not always coincide with each other [Commonwealth Caribbean state]' and 'for the Caribbean states, "domestic politics is international politics"'(pp. 123, 125).

98. Jacqueline Anne Braveboy-Wagner, *The Caribbean in World Affairs: The Foreign Policies of the English-Speaking States* (Boulder: Westview Press, 1989), pp. 226–9.

7 Communication and World Orders

The task left for the remainder of this book is to link our discourse on the relationship between international power and international communication to the fundamental questions in the study of international relations. Here we will make explicit observations that might have only been implicit in the preceding six chapters. However, as was the warning in the first chapter, the book will not necessarily provide definitive answers to questions about what implications inequality in the field of international communication has for the configuration of global political power.

What we should have by now, however, are signposts. We have shown so far that popular notions of 'cultural imperialism' or, in contrast, the 'global village', are simplistic labels for extremely complex processes. The first refinement that has been made is in the understanding of communication itself. We have separated the value of communication from the value of information, consequently arguing that they are basis of two kinds of power – the power of communication and the power of information. Although the power of communication is a means through which the power of information can be exercised, it does not always mean that valuable communication produces valuable information. High-quality communication technologies are of limited utility if they are used to relay low-quality, low-value information. For instance, even in the case of the Gulf War, with the live relays via CNN of news reporters speaking while bombs were going off behind them, did not tell a lot favourable about the capacity of the 'information revolution' to sustain peace. In the words of Raboy and Dagenais, 'we are allowed to see only that which we can no longer do more than absorb'[1] and 'media become not a forum for public discussion of policy issues, but a means of massaging the public with re-assurances that the authorities have the crisis well in hand'.[2] The logical conclusion from such an analysis is that the much-vaunted benefits of the 'information age' are only meaningful to the non-élites in the domestic and international political processes if the new communications systems and the information they provide assist all the actors in such systems in being proactive on issues.

Secondly, based on the premise that power is also the ability to define the rules, we have shown that the structure of international communication has been shaped not only by the power politics of states, but also by the

164

peculiarities of the various sectors of communication. Some areas, such as telecommunications and the mails, require high levels of international cooperation through multilateral institutions, while other areas, such as the trade in cultural products, do not. Also, in both the sectors covered by regimes and those that are not, there are definite consequences for the ecology of political power. For example, although states must surrender some national sovereignty to be part of international regimes, some states control these regimes by virtue of their technical expertise and their being underwriters of the international organizations needed to maintain the regimes. In the 'nonregime' areas national sovereignty is higher, but market conditions have still ensured the preponderance for those producers with comparative and competitive advantages.

Thirdly, we have sought to show that inertia in the *status quo* of global communication can be explained by a combination of factors on a number of fronts. In addition to the factors that account for the creation and evolution of international regimes, there is also the complex of conditions that shape the postures of various states to issues in international relations, as we have argued in Chapter 6.

Having made these refinements to the discourse on international power and international communication, in this chapter we now link our observations to the wider debate on international order. The discussion of order in international relations is fundamental to all enquiry in the field. Therefore, perspectives on all international phenomena implicitly are also views on the character of international order.

INTERNATIONAL ORDER

The definition of order that we use as our point of departure is that supplied by Hedley Bull who says it is the pattern of activity that sustains the primary goals of international society.[3] Such basic goals include: the preservation of the international system; the maintenance of independence or the external sovereignty of individual states; justice; and (the objective that accounts for the very origins of international relations as a field of study) peace.

In the twentieth century the end to parochialism, xenophobia and ethnocentrism – all to be achieved through enhanced international communication – have often been advanced as goals for a new world order, especially in the wake of major world conflicts.

The peace of 1919 was built on Woodrow Wilson's 'Fourteen Points' which were essentially the planks for a new world order. To solve the problem of nationalism that led to the war, a prominent one of Wilson's points was national self-determination. And, like President Bush 70 years later, Wilson called for free trade and arms reduction. International relations would also be conducted in the open without the secret treaties of previous times; and there was to be a general association of nations that would protect political independence, and the territorial integrity of large and small states. James Joll writes that the Fourteen Points 'seemed to be a real promise for a new order in Europe'.[4]

That new order failed due to a number of contradictions. Even though the idea of a League of Nations was that of an American President, the US never did join the League. And President Wilson and the European leaders applied the concept of national self-determination selectively. It did not apply to non-Europeans, many of whom would remain under the yoke of European colonialism for over 50 years after the postwar settlement. Indeed, Mussolini could invade Abyssinia in 1935 on the grounds that he did not have extensive colonies like his colleagues in Britain and France.

So the peace created by the new world order after the First World War was unstable not only because it was punitive (arousing as it did the resentment of the Germans), but also because it was based on hypocrisy and double standards (the goals were meant for some parts of the world and not others).

In the early 1990s there was the political rhetoric of the coming of a 'new world order', in the wake of communism's collapse in Eastern Europe and the Persian Gulf War. The 'new world order', as popularised by President George Bush, would be composed of: a complete end to the cold war; respect for international law; collective action by states to ensure their common security (collective security); increased effectiveness of the UN and other global and regional international organizations; democratic government worldwide; increased prosperity; arms reduction; and open minds to foster a community of mankind.[5] The President expanded on this last point in his address to the UN on 1 October 1990, saying,

> I see a world of open borders, open trade and, most importantly, open minds, a world that celebrates the common heritage that belongs to all the world's people, taking pride not just in hometown or homeland but in humanity itself. I see a world touched by a spirit like that of the Olympics, based not on competition that's driven by fear, but sought out of joy and exhilaration and a true quest for excellence.[6]

The rhetoric is very similar to that found in the preamble to the constitution of UNESCO in 1945 which said, *inter alia*, 'That since wars begin in the minds of men, it is in the minds of men that the defences of peace must be constructed ...'. As we have argued in Chapter 3, UN policy concerning international communication was based on this assumption about the power of ideas (the power of information). It was envisaged that international communication would be the conduit for disseminating the liberal, universalist ideas for the new world order succeeding the Second World War. Therefore, George Bush was merely repeating the rhetoric of a previous era.

Our analysis of the meaning of world order here serves to isolate the important point that rhetoric on order in the international system is always based on certain assumed objectives. Just what these goals are is obviously determined by political culture, ideology and other characteristics of the advocate of order.

Our concluding proposition in this book is that justice and national sovereignty – broadly defined and with allowances for diverse interpretations of the concepts – are two goals of international order most pertinent to the discourse on international power and international communication. Throughout the book our analysis of international power and international communication has taken us to questions about the prospects for justice and the maintenance of national sovereignty in world politics.

Communication, Power and Justice

We have argued throughout this book, implicitly and otherwise, that when communication and information are used as resources for the exercise of international power, justice – particularly 'distributive justice'[7] – is naturally threatened. However, it is arguable that order should be the locus of international relations because it is the foundation on which all primary goals are built. From this perspective, justice is an outgrowth of order, a value to be realised after order is achieved.

Bull argues that

> Order in social life is desirable because it is the condition of the realisation of other values. Unless there is a pattern of human activities that sustains elementary, primary and universal goals of social life, it will not be possible to achieve or preserve objectives that are advanced, secondary or the special goals of particular societies. International order, or order within the society of states, is the condition of justice or equality among states or nations; except in a context of international order there can be no such thing as the equal rights of states to independence or of nations to govern themselves.[8]

So although imbalances in the power of communication and power of information are threatening to justice, communication and information must also be seen as tools for the construction of world order. Inequality in international communication can be viewed as the price to be paid for achieving world order, but an equally valid argument is that injustice makes establishing order at best difficult. Theoretical schema that concentrate on communication and information as keys to understanding political processes illustrate this idea that communication can be used strategically to create order. 'Understanding the political process entails an appreciation of how information controls, initiates, regulates, harnesses, channels, and monitors the energies of a political community', Susser notes. 'It is about the kinds of messages that, if directed to the right receptors at a timely moment, can launch major campaigns and set masses of individuals into motion.'[9]

A counterpoint to the proposition that international communication can perform such a catalytic role is provided by Bull who, in explaining why the communications revolution has not produced a unity of outlook globally, quotes Brzezinski who noted that the 'paradox of our time is that humanity is becoming simultaneously more unified and more fragmented'. Bull argues:

> Not only does 'the shrinking of the globe' create new sources of tension between societies that are of different ideological persuasions, different sizes, different cultures or civilisations, and different stages of economic development; it is doubtful whether the growth of communications as such does anything to promote global rather than regional or national perspectives and institutions. Technological advances in the means of moving goods, persons and ideas around the earth's surface facilitate global integration, but they facilitate regional, national and local integration also.[10]

This position has been proved the more plausible by the course of history. The 'new world order' since the Second World War was not marked by the spread of universalist values to every corner of the globe, and indeed, at the time President Bush was espousing yet another 'new world order', even the United States had defected from membership of UNESCO. The President's rhetoric of a 'new world order' disappeared almost as suddenly as it appeared, buried perhaps in fires of ethnic conflicts in Bosnia, Somalia, Rwanda and other locations where the UN has had to be peace-keeper.

Therefore, communication and information do not have automatic value for building world order. And even when the power of communication and the power of information are marshalled by the politically powerful to promote world order, success is not assured. So even though communication and information are strategic resources, we must be careful not to exaggerate their impact on the international system as justifications for the inequality in the global communication structure. There is yet no evidence that they have been able to completely transform world order. The power of communication and the power of information can be harnessed and used, through cultural diplomacy and other means, to manage short-term crises (as we have shown in previous chapters). But there is no indication that they can completely change world order.

A promising development concerning the search for a more definitive explanation of the role of communication in relation to international order is the recent finding that democracies do not war with each other. This has profound implications for thinking on world order because it suggests that the pattern of activity needed to sustain one of the primary goals of international society – peace – must be one that is partial to the establishment and maintenance of democracies.

A striking fact, however, is that while communications scholars have been almost preoccupied with rights associated with communication being the primary gauges of democracies (such as 'freedom of information' or the 'right to communicate'), the relationship between communication and democracy is hardly ever discussed in a sophisticated way by the political scientists.[11] There is an extensive literature on communication in international relations, produced largely by communication scholars. But there has been little convergence between this scholarship and research published in the conventional international relations journals that have been the arena for the debates about democracy and war. In summarizing the thresholds set for democracy by most scholars in the discussion about democracy and war, Gleditsch[12] (for example) lists:'(a) free elections with opposition parties, (b) a minimum suffrage (10%) … (c) parliament either in control of the executive or at least enjoying parity with it … (d) "internally sovereign over military and foreign affairs" … (e) stable (in existence for at least three years) … (f) individual civil rights and – more controversially perhaps – (g) private property and a free enterprise economy.' We can compare this with the rhetoric of politicians at the United Nations, especially those from North America and Europe, and the assertions of communications scholars, that consistently refer to the 'right to hold and impart ideas' as a fundamental principle of any credible democracy. For example, in arguing that the promotion of a free press should be a priority in American foreign policy, Ungar has quoted Violeta Chamoro of Nicaragua as asserting (before she was elected president) 'freedom of the press is a basic criterion for determining if there is a democracy in a country'.[13] On his part, Ungar[14] declared that:(1) 'freedom of the media worldwide' was a vital precursor to the most basic goals of

US foreign policy, such as promoting liberty and free-market capitalism; (2) press freedom is a catalyst for other democratic reforms; (3) press freedom is the feature of American democracy that is the most transferable to other countries; and (4) a free press leads to transparent international relations that result in international peace – 'One need only look at the effects that Gorbachev's reforms in the Soviet Union engineered through a new openness and honesty in the Soviet media, have had on U.S.–Soviet relations and, as a result, on international peace and stability.'[15]

Another school of thought in communications, that is much more critical than that represented by Ungar and other 'mainstream' American writers on international communication, has tended to focus on the ideological role of systems of communication, such as the mass media, in shaping, structuring, or 'framing' domestic and international relations.[16] For this school of thought, any consideration of democracy and conflict must begin with an analysis of systems of communication. These systems not only assist in setting the agenda of political communication, but are key determinants in conditioning attitudes and actions towards the specific issues that comprise that agenda. This perspective is, therefore, not as enthusiastic about the 'information revolution' as are Ungar and others. It focuses on the role the media and other systems of communication play at key junctures in time and on key issues, such as times of war or the threat of conflict, or even in a situation labelled a 'crisis'.[17]

But this relationship between communication and democracy, and then, by extension, world order, is contingent upon the resolution of the hypothesis that democracies do not go to war against each other. Even though the proposition that democracies do not war with each other 'comes as close as anything we have to an empirical law in international relations',[18] the consideration of the relationship between democracy and the absence of war in the international system is not a closed case. There is the question of a possible 'third variable'. Is it the mere fact that these states are democracies that accounts for their reluctance to fight each other? Is there a feature external to their democratic political systems that is just as powerful a variable? Or, is there one characteristic of democracies that is the most determinant?

Communication, Power and Sovereignty

The coming of global communications technologies has spawned a number of concerns about the effect they can have on national sovereignty, including the debates about cultural imperialism and the more technologically deterministic reasoning about the spread of liberal democracy and civil society. Indeed, our argument is that trends of thought in the twentieth century about the impact of international communication on international politics have been largely influenced by developments in communications technologies and a key variable in these waves of thought is what they do and do not say about what international communication does to the nation-state and the principle of national sovereignty.

Beginning in the early years of the century and down to the 1990s, there have been four trends: (a) internationalist; (b) realist; (c) a 'free flow' inter-pretation; and (d) the approach of globalisation. Although the fortunes of national sovereignty have been a controlling factor, not all of this literature has been in the field of international relations. Therefore, writers on commu-nication and other fields have been concerned about national sovereignty for reasons other than the theoretical understanding of world order. For example, some arguments about violations of national sovereignty are raised in the wider context of the search for political freedom for individuals.

The internationalist approach is the view that international communica-tion is the glue that further unifies the international system. It accompanied the early technologies of telecommunications, such as the telegraph, that were in use at the dawn of the century. Writers such as Norman Angell[19] and Graham Wallas[20] (whom we discussed in Chapter 1) saw these new technologies bringing the world closer together by fostering interdepend-ence. However, this perspective did not regard the technologies of the day as threatening to the nation-state or the concept of national sovereignty. It was a view of a more interdependent world around the principle of national sovereignty.

In contrast, E.H. Carr's realist analysis[21] views the technologies and systems of communication of the 1930s as tools in power politics. True to the realist tradition, the viability and sovereignty of the nation-state are affirmed. But realists differed from the internationalists in their lack of emphasis on interdependence as a consequence of the new technologies.

The coming of international mass communications by satellite and the doctrine of 'free flow' in the post-Second World War period is what really sparked the wide interest in international communication as a field of study on its own and spawned the work of such scholars as Schiller, Nordenstreng and Mattelart.[22] This approach compares to that of the real-ists in its assumption that technologies of communication are strategic. However, emphasis is also put on the role of multinational corporations (non-state actors), especially those of a specific state, the United States. A thrust of their analyses is that the 'free flow' doctrine benefited those states with comparative and competitive advantages and reinforced the cycle dependency. The technologies, by being able to traverse territorial bound-aries, were seen as threats to national sovereignty.

The more recent discussion of globalisation regards the violation of national sovereignty and the encroachment upon the nation-state as done deals.[23] Also, no pejorative connotations are applied to such developments, as the critics of the 'free flow' doctrine are inclined to do. The violation of national sovereignty is viewed as precursor of a new, pacific, international civil society.

The perspectives on international communication and sovereignty surveyed above have dealt more with the power of communication than the power of information. This has been the case perhaps because (as we have discussed with regard to the cultural imperialism hypothesis in Chapter 3) it is rather difficult to prove trans-border media effects, and even when these effects are evident we must be cautious about generalization and assuming wholesale impacts. So it is easier to concentrate on the means of communication and what are really their *potential* for creating global interdependence or use as strategic tools in international relations.

As the technologies of international communication have got more efficient (now enabling live TV and radio programming and financial data and information to be transmitted globally by satellite), there has been more focus on the power of information. This has 'internationalised' discourses on the power of information that had hitherto taken place mainly at the domestic level. This attention to the power of information can be put into three categories: interest in the impact mass media have on violent behaviour; concern about the role of mass media in racial exclusion and stereotyping; and debates about the impact of media on various types of values (religious, moral, political, economic, and so on).[24]

In the quest to resolve these problems related to the power of information we must return to the power of communication (i.e. confronting questions about the control of the channels that produce and, or, distribute these kinds of information globally).

Our separate consideration of communication, power and justice, on the one hand, and communication, power and national sovereignty, on the other, both take us to one place: the position that the power of communication and the power of information seem to have their impact on world order from below, at the domestic level, within nation-states, rather than from above, at a universalist level. The impact on world order is really the result of an aggregation of effects at the domestic level. Communication is important to any definitions of democracies that are factors in the maintenance of world order. Also, domestic discourses on the power of information are merely 'internationalised' in the era of 'globalisation'.

Also see Harold A. Innis, *Empire and Communications* (Toronto: University of Toronto Press, 1972); and his *The Bias of Communication* (Toronto: University of Toronto Press, 1971). In *Empire and Communications* – now considered a seminal work – Innis introduced the notion that communications was not only a crucial element in the organisation of empires, but the nature of the means of communication used determined the character and very fate of the empire in question. Heavy media, such as stone tablets and parchment, were *biased* in favour of time – they stored information for long periods but were awkward to transport over long distances. In contrast, media biased in favour of space, such as papyrus and paper, were light and could be transported over vast distances, even though they were not as durable. After examining the ancient Egyptian, Babylonian, Greek and Roman empires, Innis came to the conclusion that the long survival of an empire depended on a delicate balance between its utilisation of both time and space biased media for communication. The dominance of one media tended to elicit an adverse reaction where there was an effort to assert the importance of a medium with an opposite bias. For example, empires dominated by time-biased media emphasised tradition and encouraged high status for priests who enjoyed monopolies of knowledge. Such empires are eventually displaced by new forms of organisation that use space-biased media which permit less centralisation and rule over wider land masses, as was the case with the Roman empire.

10. Bull, *The Anarchical Society*, pp. 273–4.
11. A notable exception has been the literature on communication and political development that mushroomed in the early 1960s, largely at the behest of UNESCO in the wake of decolonization. See, for example, Wilbur Schramm, *Mass Media and National Development* (Stanford, CA: UNESCO and Stanford University Press, 1964), and Lucian W. Pye (ed.), *Communications and Political Development* (Princeton: Princeton University Press, 1963). A more recent work is Brian Weinstein (ed.), *Language Policy and Political Development* (Norwood, NJ: Ablex, 1991).
12. Nils Petter Gleditsch, 'Democracy and Peace', *Journal of Peace Research*, Vol. 29, no. 4, pp. 369–70.
13. Violeta Chamoro, 'The Death of *La Prensa*', *Foreign Affairs*, Winter, 1986, p. 385, quoted in Sanford J. Ungar, 'The Role of a Free Press in Strengthening Democracy', in Judith Lichtenberg (ed.), *Democracy and the Media* (New York: Cambridge University Press, 1990), pp. 368–98.
14. Ungar, 'The Role of a Free Press', pp. 368–93.
15. Ibid., p. 393.
16. See, for example, Stuart Hall, 'Return of the Repressed in Media Studies,' in Michael Gurevitch, Tony Bennett, James Curran and Janet Woolacott (eds), *Culture, Society and the Media* (London: Methuen, 1982), pp. 56–90; and Raymond Williams, *Communications* (London: Penguin, 1962), *Television: Technology and Cultural Form* (New York: Schocken, 1974), *Raymond Williams on Television: Selected Writings* (London: Routledge, 1989).
17. See Marc Raboy and Bernard Dagenais, *Media, Crisis and Democracy* (London: SAGE, 1992).
18. Jack S. Levy, 'The Causes of War: A Review of Theories and Evidence', in Philip E. Tetlock, Jo L. Husbands, Robert Jervis, Paul C. Stern and Charles

Tilly (eds), *Behavior, Society and Nuclear War* (New York: New York University Press), pp. 209–313, quoted in Gleditsch, 'Democracy and Peace'.

19.   Norman Angell, *The Great Illusion* (New York: G.P. Putnam's Sons, 1913), pp. 54–5.

20.   Graham Wallas, *The Great Society: A Psychological Analysis* (New York: Macmillan, 1915), p. 3.

21.   E.H. Carr, *The Twenty Years' Crisis* (London: Macmillan, 1939).

22.   See, for example, Herbert I. Schiller, *Mass Communication and American Empire* (Boston: Beacon Press, 1971); Karle Nordenstreng and Tapio Varis, *Television Traffic: A One-Way Street?* Reports and Papers on Mass Communication, No. 70 (Paris: UNESCO, 1974); Armand Mattelart, *Multinational Corporations and the Control of Culture* (Atlantic Heights, NJ: Humanities Press, 1980); and Karle Nordenstreng and Herbert I. Schiller, *National Sovereignty and International Communication* (Norwood, NJ: Ablex, 1983).

23.   Two illustrations of this outlook are: Walter B. Wriston, *The Twilight of Sovereignty: How the Information Revolution is Transforming Our World* (New York: Scribners, 1992); and Michael O'Neill, *Roar of the Crowd: How Television and People Power are Changing the World* (New York: Random House, 1993). For more on globalisation see Marjorie Ferguson, 'The Mythology about Globalisation', *European Journal of Communication*, Vol. 7, 1992, pp. 69–93; and Yoshiko Kurisaki, 'Globalization or regionalization: An observation of current PTO activities', *Telecommunications Policy*, December 1993, pp. 699–706.

24.   A useful collection of articles on this plethora of issues is George Rodman (ed.), *Mass Media Issues* (Fourth Edition) (Dubuque, Iowa: Kendall/Hunt, 1993).

Index

Adams, Tom, 147
Advertising Age, 130
advertising: international regime for, 130–1
AFP (Agence France-Presse), 52, 72, 75–83
Allende, Salvador, 108
Alleyne, Mark D., 8 n.17,
Alliance Française, 97
American Association of Advertising Agencies, 130
American Federation of Television and Radio Artists, 51
American Film Marketing Association, 56
American University, The, 9 n.24,
Angell, Norman, 6, 10, 171
AP (Associated Press), 52, 72, 75–83
AP/Dow Jones, 71
ASCAP (American Society of Composers, Authors, and Publishers), 51
Association of American Publishers, 56
Attlee, Clement, 42
Australia, 56
Austria, 30

Babb, Eugene, 131
Babst, Dean V., 46 n.14
Barbados: media system in, 142–4; posture to the NWICO, 146–8
Barrow, Nita, 147
Bartholomew, Frank, 80
BBC (British Broadcasting Corporation): World Service TV, 47; as cultural diplomacy, 96; history of, 99–100; as British propaganda, 101; surrogate role of, 109–10
Bee Gees, the, 48
Belafonte, Harry, 51
Belgium, 31
Beltrán S., Luis Ramiro, 14–15
Benton, William, 46

Bern Treaty, 21–2,
Bertelsmann (publisher), 49
BMI (Broadcast Music Incorporated), 51
Bogsch, Arpad, 32 n.24
Boutros-Ghali, Boutros, 66
Boyd-Barrett, Oliver, 74
Braveboy-Wagner, Jacqueline, 150–1
British Council, 97, 99, 104–6
Brown, Aggrey, 34 n.29
Buchan, Alastair, 6
Bull, Hedley, 165, 167
Bush, George, 166–7

Canada: communication with the United States, 7–8; and ITU, 31
Caputo, Dante, 147
Caribbean Basin Initiative, 34, 133
Caribbean News Agency (CANA), 71
Carr, E. H., 6–7, 171
CBC (Canadian Broadcasting Corporation), 8
CBS Records, 48
CCIR (International Radio Consultative Committee), 28, 139
CCITT (International Telegraph and Telephone Consultative Committee), 28, 139
Chan, Steve, 46 n.14
Chile, 60, 108–9
CIA (Central Intelligence Agency): support for RFE and RL, 102
CNN (Cable News Network), 45, 47, 69, 73
Cohen, Benjamin, 30 n.18
Columbia Pictures, 47
Comer, Harry, 7
communication: defined, 2–3; in relation to information, 3–4; value of 3–4
Comor, Harry, 7
complex interdependence, 25
Computer and Business Equipment Manufacturers' Association, 56

177

NWICO (New World Information and Communication Order): scholarly support for, 9; as a challenge to the international *status quo*, 16–17, 84; contradictions in, 17; and functionalism, 24; cultural imperialism and, 57; defined, 119–23; attempt to create international regimes through, 133–41; significance of domestic media systems to, 142; postures of Barbados and India to, 146–8
Nye, Joseph, 4–5, 25, 61, 134, 138

Pan-African News Agencies (PANA), 71
Paramount, 47
Paris Treaty, 21–2, 24
perestroika, 79
Poland, 102
politicization: defined, 122 n.16
Polygram, 48, 55
power of communication: defined, 15–16; cultural industries and, 62; news and, 91; international cultural relations and, 106–12; information and, 164
power of information: defined, 15–16; cultural industries and, 62; news and, 91; international cultural relations and, 106–7
power: defined, 4
Preston, William, 85
propaganda: origins of, 7, 97–8; international law against, 85; definition of, 97 n.6; British, 99–101; American, 102; euphemisms for, 103; tactical, 107; strategic, 107
PRS (Performing Rights Society), 51
public diplomacy, 16
public relations firms: use by governments, 111–12

Radio Moscow, 96
Ramnarine, Deoraj, 29 n.16
RAND Corporation, 31
RCA, 48
Recording Industry Association of America, 56
Red Cross, 53

regimes: and the structure of international power, 16; defined, 25; compared to international organizations, 25; causal variables in, 30 n.18; theoretical shortcomings of, 134–41
Renaud, Jean-Luc, 81
Reston, James, 12
Reuters, 71, 72, 75–83, 90
RFE (Radio Free Europe): CIA support for, 102; surrogate role of, 109–10
Richards, Timothy J., 140
RL (Radio Liberty): CIA support for, 102; surrogate role of, 109–10
Roach, Colleen, 122
Rodgers, Everett M., 9
Rosenau, James, 149
Rothstein, Robert, 137
Rummel, Rudolph J., 46 n.14
Russia, 32, 100

Saatchi & Saatchi, 48, 111–12
Salwen, Michael, 61
satellites: value of, 125–6
Sauvant, Karl, 89, 122
Schiller, Herbert I.: approach to international communication, 9–10; support of South, 14; on Free Flow doctrine, 46, 171; materialist analysis, 57; approach to NWICO, 122
Screen Actors' Guild, 51
Scripps, E. W., 77
Singapore, 31
Singham, A. W., 58–60, 122
Somalia, 66
Souki Oliveira, Omar, 48 n.23
South Korea, 133
Soviet Union, 45, 102
Speier, Hans, 107
Sri Lanka, 141
stimulus/response, 9
Strange, Susan, 4 n.8, 134, 136
structure/superstructure, 60
Susser, Bernard, 168

TASS (Telegraph Agency of the Soviet Union)
Thorn-EMI, 48